Taking the Constitution Away
from the Courts

Taking the Constitution Away from the Courts

Mark Tushnet

PRINCETON UNIVERSITY PRESS

PRINCETON, NEW JERSEY

Third printing, and first paperback printing, 2000

Paperback ISBN 0-691-07035-0

The Library of Congress has cataloged the cloth edition
of this book as follows

Tushnet, Mark V., 1945–
Taking the constitution away from the courts / Mark Tushnet.
p. cm.
Includes bibliographical references and index.
ISBN 0-691-00415-3 (cloth : alk. paper)
1. Constitutional law—United States—Interpretation and construction.
2. Judicial review—United States. 3. Legislative power—United States.
4. Politics, Practical—United States.
I. Title.
KF4575.T874   1999
342. 73′02—dc21   98-27292

This book has been composed in Sabon

The paper used in this publication meets the minimum
requirements of ANSI/NISO Z39.48-1992 (R1997)
(*Permanence of Paper*)

www.pup.princeton.edu

Printed in the United States of America

3   5   7   9   10   8   6   4

In Memory of Martin Ira Slate,
1945–1997

Friend and public servant

CONTENTS

PREFACE

The people have the power
To redeem the work of fools
Upon the meek the graces shower
It's decreed
The people rule.

—Patti Smith

I HEARD Joan Osborne perform Patti Smith's song at a concert to benefit the political group Voters for Choice on the anniversary of *Roe v. Wade*, which I attend each year to remind myself of my small role in the Court's decision. (As a law clerk, I drafted a letter from Justice Thurgood Marshall to Justice Harry Blackmun, which some have thought influenced the structure of Justice Blackmun's final opinion.) The tension between celebrating a Supreme Court decision finding abortion laws unconstitutional and extolling popular political power is my theme here.

We can take the Constitution away from the courts in several ways. We could deny them the final word about the Constitution's meaning (the subject of chapter 1), or we could deny them any role in Constitutional interpretation whatever (the subject of chapter 7). Chapters 5 and 6 argue that taking the Constitution away from the courts in this sense need not occasion deep concern about the preservation of our liberties. We can also take the Constitution away from the courts and embed it in our own deliberations. Chapters 2, 3, and 4 describe how we can think about the Constitution without having the courts' decisions to guide us. The overall project is summarized in chapter 8's description of populist constitutional law.

Legislators and voters routinely face policy questions that also raise constitutional issues: Should they vote for a proposal that the Supreme Court might hold unconstitutional? What if the Court has already held a similar proposal unconstitutional? Less often, they have to consider whether to defy a Supreme Court ruling directly. How should we think about these questions? What implications does the Constitution have outside the courts? As we will see, questions about the Constitution outside the courts arise in many places. They are different, however, from the question, What does the First Amendment mean? My aim in this book is to clarify what we have to think about to answer questions of the first type responsibly.

Pioneering scholarship by law professors Paul Brest and Sanford Levinson has identified some of the issues raised by the Constitution outside the courts. (Brest, "Conscientious Legislator's Guide"; Brest and Levinson, *Processes of Constitutional Decisionmaking*.) Political scientist Louis Fisher and his law school collaborator Neal Devins have shown how members of Congress go about interpreting the Constitution. (Fisher, *Constitutional Dialogues*; Fisher and Devins, *Political Dynamics of Constitutional Law*. Two other political scientists examine some of the issues I address in a manner generally congenial to mine. Moore, *Constitutional Rights and Powers of the People*; Whittington, *Constitutional Construction*.) Legal historians Hendrik Hartog and William Forbath have shown how the American people have used constitutional language in their political debates. (Hartog, "The Constitution of Aspiration"; Forbath, "Why Is This Rights Talk Different from All Other Rights Talk?")

These important works have established that constitutional interpretation goes on outside the courts, and have sketched some ways in which the Supreme Court's constitutional interpretations interact with the Constitution as interpreted elsewhere. Constitutional theory must make sense of how people deal with the Constitution away from the courts if it is to provide an accurate account of our constitutional practice.

I attempt here to develop an approach to thinking about the Constitution away from the courts in the service of what I call a populist constitutional law. (Parker, "Here, the People Rule," uses the term in a slightly different way from mine, though our usages are related.) It is *populist* because it distributes responsibility for constitutional law broadly. In a populist theory of constitutional law, constitutional interpretation done by the courts has no special normative weight deriving from the fact that it is done by the courts. Judicial interpretations may have added weight because they come from experts who have thought seriously about the interpretive questions over a long period. Then, however, the normative weight comes from the expertise and the like, not from the office. It is *constitutional* because it deals with the fundamentals of our political order. I allude to practices in other constitutional democracies with some regularity, generally to highlight aspects of our practices that are not essential to having a vibrant constitutional system. The core of my argument turns on some distinctive features of the U.S. constitutional order, however, and I am aware of the dangers of unthinking appropriation of practices from other systems, even from systems that seem on the whole to be admirable.

The most problematic term here is *law*. How can constitutional decisions made away from the courts, particularly by ordinary citizens, be law? The reason for calling what I deal with in this book a populist constitutional law will emerge more clearly as the argument proceeds. For present purposes I can say that it is law because it is not in the first instance either the expression of pure preferences by officials and voters or the expression of unfiltered moral judgments. In short, it is not "mere" politics, nor is it "simply" philosophy. The distinctions drawn and technical arguments made rather prolifically in what follows justify calling it a work of legal rather than political or moral analysis. At the same time it accords a large place for politics, in two senses: Populist constitutional law gains its content from discussions among the people in ordinary political forums, and political leaders play a significant role in assisting the people as we conduct those discussions.

I emphasize that what follows is definitely *not* an argument that the populist interpretation is the only, or even the best, interpretation of the Constitution. Rather, my argument opens up issues that thoughtful voters and elected officials should think about, and that are obscured by the elitist constitutional law that dominates contemporary legal thought.

• • •

I have been thinking about the issues raised in this book for more than a decade, and snippets of its argument have appeared in other places. I presented most of chapter 1 as a lecture during the celebration of Princeton University's 250th anniversary by its Politics Department, and I thank Robert J. George for inviting me to do so. I received helpful comments on the lecture, and on other parts of the book, from Jeremy Waldron, Amy Guttman, George Kateb, and Mary Ann Case. A portion of the chapter appeared in "Two Versions of Judicial Supremacy," 39 William & Mary L.Rev. 945 (1998). A version of chapter 2 was presented as the William J. Lockhart Lecture at the University of Minnesota Law School in the spring of 1996, and I thank Daniel Farber for inviting me to present that lecture, which has been published as "The Hardest Question in Constitutional Law," 81 Minn. L.Rev. 1 (1996). A very early version of chapter 4, quite different from the one presented here, was published in James E. Wood, Jr. and Derek Davis, eds., *The Role of Religion in the Making of Public Policy* (1991); some portions also appeared in "Federalism and Liberalism," 4 Cardozo J.Int. & Comp. L. 329 (1996). A small portion of chapter 5 appeared in "Clarence Thomas: The Constitutional Problems," 63 Geo. Wash. L.Rev. 466 (1995). Parts of chapters 6 and 7 were presented at a seminar at Southern Methodist University Law School, and published as "The Critique of Rights," 47 SMU L.Rev. 23 (1993). A few paragraphs in chapter 6 are drawn from *Making Constitutional Law: Thurgood Marshall and the Supreme Court, 1961-1991* (1997). Part of chapter 8 was presented as a comment on a paper by Bruce Ackerman delivered at a symposium at Fordham University Law School, published as "Constituting We the People," 65 Fordham L.Rev. 1557 (1997). Some paragraphs in chapter 8 have been published in " 'What Then is the American?,' " 38 Ariz. L.Rev. 573 (1996) and "Living in a Constitutional Moment?: *Lopez* and Constitutional Theory," 46 Case Western Res. L.Rev. 845 (1996). Even those who read every word in these earlier publications—a universe that includes only me, I think—would find that the presentation here offers a more complete and complex view.

In addition to those already thanked, I want to acknowledge the assistance of the John Simon Guggenheim Memorial Foundation, which provided a fellowship that allowed me to complete the book, and Dean Judith Areen of the Georgetown University Law Center, who has been enormously supportive of my research. Stephen Heifetz, Jennifer Jaff, Timothy Lynch, and several anonymous reviewers made helpful comments on the entire manuscript. My reflections on conversations with Louis Michael Seidman and Vicki Jackson infuse every page of this book; I have learned something about the Constitution in every conversation I have had with them about constitutional law.

I cannot close this Introduction without noting the enormous intellectual contribution made to this project by the work of Sanford Levinson of the University of Texas Law School. Almost uniquely among constitutional scholars, Levinson has repeatedly raised the most fundamental issues about the status of the Constitution in our political order. I doubt that I would have thought seriously about the problems discussed here, which I now believe to be far more important than almost anything else in constitutional law, had I not been repeatedly provoked into thinking about them by Levinson's work.

Taking the Constitution Away
from the Courts

PROLOGUE

ADELL Sherbert, a Seventh Day Adventist, had a five-day workweek at a South Carolina textile mill. This schedule allowed her to avoid work on Saturday, her Sabbath. The mill changed its schedule in 1959, and started to require all workers to work six days a week. Mrs. Sherbert was fired when she refused to work on Saturday. She applied for unemployment compensation, but South Carolina's government refused to pay, saying that she had failed to accept suitable employment, without having good cause for the refusal. Mrs. Sherbert said the government's action violated her First Amendment right to free exercise of religion. Eventually the U.S. Supreme Court agreed.[1] According to the Court, denying the unemployment benefits did indeed "burden" her free exercise of religion: Forcing her to choose between working and receiving the benefits was no different from fining her for Saturday worship. Burdens of this sort might be justified, the Court said, but only if they were imposed to promote "some compelling state interest." The state asserted only one interest—avoiding fraudulent claims—and that, the Court said, was already protected by the individualized hearings provided in unemployment cases. So, the Court concluded, Mrs. Sherbert should get the benefits.

The Court applied the "compelling state interest" test over the next decades when people claimed that state laws applicable to everyone, as South Carolina's unemployment compensation law was, had the "incidental effect" of burdening their religious exercises. The Court actually did not find many constitutional violations. For example, it let the armed forces apply a general rule against wearing non-official headgear to an Orthodox Jew who wanted to wear his yarmulke.[2] But the constitutional standard, the Court repeatedly said, was the "compelling state interest" test.

In 1990 the Court revisited the question. Alfred Smith had struggled for years with his alcoholism. He eventually got control over his life, and became a substance abuse counselor. As part of his recovery process, Mr. Smith returned to his Native American traditions and became a member of the Native American Church. One of the Church's practices is the ritual consumption of peyote, a hallucinogenic substance. Mr. Smith's supervisor, a man of rather rigid views about substance abuse, fired Mr. Smith when he discovered Smith's use of peyote. Like Mrs. Sherbert, Mr. Smith applied for unemployment compensation. Mr. Smith acknowledged that peyote use was generally unlawful, but argued that barring its ritual use in religious practices violated the Free Exercise clause. This time, the Supreme Court rejected the constitutional claim.[3]

Justice Antonin Scalia's opinion for the Court abandoned the "compelling state interest" test. As Justice Scalia saw it, such a test forced the courts to engage in an inappropriate balancing of a ritual's importance to believers against the state's interest in controlling the use of illegal drugs. The Free Exercise clause, the Court said, protected people only against regulations targeted at religious practices, not from "the incidental effect[s] of a generally applicable and otherwise valid provision."

The Court's decision was immediately criticized by a wide range of religious organizations. Eventually a coalition that spanned the religious right and the secular left persuaded Congress to respond. Stating that Congress wanted to "restore the compelling interest test" established in Mrs. Sherbert's case, the Religious Freedom Restoration Act of 1993 (RFRA) directed the courts to apply that test whenever a government burdened a religious exercise.

New constitutional questions soon arose. The Roman Catholic parish in Boerne, Texas, a suburb of San Antonio, had outgrown its church as the area's Catholic population boomed. It planned to expand the existing church building. Learning of the plan, the city became concerned that the new construction would destroy the old church's appearance and would interfere with the city's economic development plan, which was to support efforts to promote tourism by preserving the area's historic character. It therefore designated the area around the existing church a historic preservation area, and refused the church's request for a permit to expand. The church sued, saying that the city's action violated its rights under RFRA: The denial burdened the church's religious exercise by making it much more difficult for the church to serve all its parishioners, and, the church said, it was not the least restrictive way of promoting a substantial state interest.

The Supreme Court held RFRA unconstitutional.[4] The Court invoked traditional ideas about congressional power: The Constitution lists the powers Congress has, and every statute Congress enacts is constitutional only if it falls under one of these enumerated powers. The only power Congress purported to invoke to justify RFRA was section 5 of the Fourteenth Amendment, which gives Congress the power to "enforce" Bill of Rights guarantees such as the protection of religious exercise. But, the Court said, RFRA could not reasonably be understood as "enforcing" free exercise rights. After all, the peyote case established that the only right people had was a right to be protected against laws targeted at their religious practices. Congress had taken evidence that lots of state laws *incidentally* burdened religious exercise, but, the Court said, there was precious little evidence that there was a serious problem of laws actually directed at religious exercise. So Congress was not remedying existing violations of free exercise rights. And Congress's response was out of proportion to any minor problem of laws targeted at religious exercise that somehow snuck through disguised as general laws.

This recent episode in constitutional history raises many of the questions addressed in this book. Can Congress "overrule" a Supreme Court decision by an ordinary statute? Should the Court's constitutional interpretations prevail over alternative interpretations offered by Congress? Does Congress do a decent job of thinking about the various constitutional issues—religious freedom, federalism, separation of powers—RFRA raises? What may Congress do when the Court decides a case in a way that large majorities think profoundly wrong-headed?

The controversy over RFRA raises these questions, but RFRA itself, and the Court's decisions, are not always the best vehicles for examining the most basic issues. In what follows I use a series of problems, some real and some hypothetical, to do so. The RFRA controversy occasionally emerges from the background, to remind us that the issues I discuss are indeed real and important ones that affect the ordinary process of government. By the book's conclusion, the problems RFRA raises will have been displaced by more profound ones.

Chapter One

AGAINST JUDICIAL SUPREMACY

PROPOSITION 187 IS UNCONSTITUTIONAL: DOES IT MATTER?

In 1982 the Supreme Court held unconstitutional a Texas statute denying a free public education to children of noncitizens illegally present in this country (*Plyler v. Doe*).[1] In 1994 California's voters approved Proposition 187, an amendment to the state's constitution that, among other things, would deny a free public education to that same class of children. A federal court promptly held this part of Proposition 187 unconstitutional and barred state officials from enforcing it.[2]

Consider the position of a state legislator after the voters approved Proposition 187. The legislature has to enact some new statutes to enforce Proposition 187. But the U.S. Constitution requires the legislator to take an oath to uphold the Constitution, and California law requires the legislator to uphold the state constitution and laws. Do those two oaths conflict? And if they do, would a legislator act in some way improperly if he or she voted to implement Proposition 187 notwithstanding the Supreme Court's decision in *Plyler*?

After the state legislature passes implementing legislation, someone actually has to enforce Proposition 187. School administrators, for example, may have to ask about the citizenship status of the parents of children who attempt to enroll in their schools. They are supposed to refuse to admit children affected by Proposition 187. Would a school principal do something wrong if she or he followed Proposition 187 and denied admission to a child even though *Plyler* says that doing so violates the U.S. Constitution?

The answer to these questions is, "Of course not. Legislators took an oath to support the Constitution—*the Constitution*, not the Supreme Court. What the Constitution means is not necessarily what the Supreme Court says it means. If legislators think the Court misinterpreted the Constitution, their oath allows them—indeed, it may *require* them—to disregard *Plyler*."

Explaining that answer, however, is more complicated than we might think. The first difficulty is that it seems to be in some tension with this country's strong tradition of judicial review. The Court established that tradition in the classic case of *Marbury v. Madison* (1803).[3] Rejecting the argument that the Court should not substitute its judgment about what the Constitution means for Congress's judgment, Chief Justice John Marshall wrote, "It is emphatically the province and duty of the judicial department to say what the law is."

Marshall's statement can be read in at least two ways. One has no implications for the Constitution outside the courts. He might have been saying, "Look, if you pass a statute asking us to do something—in *Marbury*, hear a particular class of cases—you can't keep us from saying what the law is. And the Constitution itself says that it is law—indeed, supreme law." On this reading, Marshall's statement simply refers to what courts do. It has nothing to say about the constitutional duties and powers of other departments, state officials, and ordinary citizens.

The second reading, however, does treat the courts and not just the Constitution as supreme: "It is emphatically the province and duty of *the judicial department*—and no one else—to say what the law is. Once we say what the law is, that's the end of it. After that, no one obliged to support the Constitution can fairly assert that the Constitution means something different from what we said it meant."

As we will see, that may be a slight overstatement of the judicial supremacy position. But the qualifications we will have to insert do not eliminate the problem Proposition 187 poses for state officials. And, unless we can figure out some answer to that position, the project of taking the Constitution away from the courts, of developing a populist constitutional law, cannot get off the ground: The Constitution outside the courts is identical to the Constitution inside the courts, with the modest exception that we do not know the answers to constitutional questions the courts have not gotten around to yet.

Two Episodes of Judicial Supremacy

Why would anyone think that judicial supremacy was the right way to understand our Constitution? It would not be surprising to find judges supporting judicial supremacy; it makes their job more important and interesting. But there is more to the position than self-interest.

In 1958 the Supreme Court faced a challenge to its authority (*Cooper v. Aaron*).[4] Four years earlier *Brown v. Board of Education* held school segregation unconstitutional. The Court then held that states had to desegregate their schools "with all deliberate speed." Responding to a lawsuit and orders from lower federal courts, the school board in Little Rock, Arkansas, developed a plan to desegregate the city's schools gradually. The state's governor, Orval Faubus, opposed desegregation, and generated a big public controversy over Little Rock's plan. As the school board put it in its brief to the Supreme Court, the "legislative, executive, and

judicial departments of the state government opposed . . . desegregation
. . . by enacting laws, calling out troops, making statements vilifying federal law and federal courts, and failing to utilize state law enforcement
agencies and judicial processes to maintain public peace."

The lower federal courts found that the public disorder was a reason
to delay desegregation. The Supreme Court disagreed. More important
here, it rejected Governor Faubus's claim that he was not required to
follow *Brown*'s directives. Relying on Marshall's statement, the Court
asserted that *Marbury* "declared the basic principle that the federal
judiciary is supreme in the exposition of the law of the Constitution."
Calling that principle "a permanent and indispensable feature of our
constitutional system," the Court said that "it follows that the interpretation of [the Constitution] enunciated by this Court in the *Brown* case is
the supreme law of the land." The oath to support the Constitution that
Governor Faubus and state legislators took gave that interpretation
"binding effect."

The Little Rock case presented a particularly appealing setting for asserting judicial supremacy. *Brown* was unquestionably right, or so the
justices and a large part of the country thought. Governor Faubus's resistance had provoked a real crisis of law and order, with white opponents
of desegregation credibly threatening to inflict violence on anyone—including African-American children—who tried to desegregate the
schools. And the Court correctly asserted that a century and a half of
judicial review had led many Americans to believe that the Court's constitutional interpretations were indeed supreme.

But there are other cases where strong assertions of judicial supremacy
are less appealing. The notorious Dred Scott case makes the point.[5] The
case arose when Dred Scott, held as a slave in 1836, was taken by his
owner to the free territory of Minnesota for several years. After Scott and
his owner returned to Missouri, a slave state, Scott sued for his freedom,
claiming that he had become free because of his residence in Minnesota.
Hoping to take contention over slavery off the national political agenda
in the 1850s, the Supreme Court held unconstitutional congressional efforts to restrict the expansion of slavery into the nation's territories. According to the Court, Congress lacked affirmative power to do so, and
denying slave owners the right to take their slaves into the territories deprived the slave owners of their property without due process of law.

After the Court's decision Abraham Lincoln offered an alternative to
judicial supremacy. Debating Democrat Stephen Douglas during their
1858 campaign for Senate, Lincoln replied to Douglas's effort to defuse
the slavery controversy by relying on the Court's decision. Douglas said
that the courts were created "so that when you cannot agree among your-
selves on a disputed point you appeal to the judicial tribunal which steps

in and decides for you, and that decision is binding on every good citizen." Using language not that much different from the Court's in *Cooper v. Aaron*, Douglas said that when the courts resolved the questions, that was the end of it: "[W]hen such decisions have been made, they become the law of the land."[6]

Lincoln would have none of it. He agreed that the Court's decision resolved the precise controversy before it; Dred Scott would remain a slave. But he rejected the decision "as a political rule which shall be binding on the voter . . . [or] binding on the members of Congress or the President to favor no measure that does not actually concur with the principles of that decision."[7]

In his First Inaugural Address, delivered even as the South prepared for war over slavery, Lincoln again made his position clear. *Dred Scott* was "binding . . . upon the parties." In addition, the Court's decisions were "entitled to a very high respect and consideration in all parallel cases by all other departments." Even an "erroneous" decision could be followed when "the evil effect of following it, being limited to that particular case, with the chance that it may be overruled and never become a precedent for other cases, can better be borne than could the evils of a different practice." But, Lincoln continued, "the people will have ceased to be their own rulers" if "the policy of the government, upon vital questions affecting the whole people, is to be irrevocably fixed by decisions of the Supreme Court, the instant they are made, in ordinary litigation between parties in personal actions."[8]

Lincoln was an incredibly subtle constitutionalist, and his statements contain nearly everything we need to work out a theory that would explain the result in *Cooper v. Aaron* without committing us to a theory of judicial supremacy that would be inconsistent with populist constitutional law.[9]

THE CONSTITUTION, THICK AND THIN

Developing the argument against judicial supremacy and for a populist constitutional law requires me to introduce a distinction that will pervade this book—between the *thick* Constitution and the *thin* Constitution. The thick Constitution contains a lot of detailed provisions describing how the government is to be organized—for example, a provision stipulating that the president "may require the Opinion, in writing, of the principal Officer in each of the Executive Departments, upon any Subject relating to the Duties of their respective Offices."[10] We should note several characteristics of the provisions that thicken the Constitution.

Importance. Taken as a whole they are important. Without them there would not even be a government regulated by the Constitution's other provisions. And even in detail they identify important principles that undergird our constitutional system. The "opinions in writing" clause, for example, is a way of ensuring that executive officials will be responsible to the president for their actions, and that the people can hold the president responsible for what happens throughout the government.

Judicial silence. The courts rarely have anything important to say about them. Sometimes that is because their terms are so clear that no one would think of departing from their obvious requirements. Sometimes it is because the people we elect have political incentives to comply with their requirements.[11] Sometimes it is because the provisions are so pointless today that people ignore or evade them in ways that no one cares enough about to bring a lawsuit.[12] And sometimes it is because we can accomplish what we want by working around the provisions without obviously violating them.

Judicial errors. The courts have not done an obviously admirable job when they *have* dealt with these provisions. Consider an important case involving the legislative veto. Responding to the need it saw for administering the modern era's large national government, Congress has increasingly given executive agencies authority to implement laws Congress stated in quite general terms. But Congress reasonably enough wanted to retain some control over the law the agencies actually developed. It invented the legislative veto to offset the power it had delegated to executive officials. The legislative veto comes in several variants, but its basic idea is this: Congress gives broad authority to an executive official to act; it then sees what the official has done, and if Congress does not like the action, it "vetoes" the official's action. The Supreme Court held that legislative vetoes were unconstitutional because they did not satisfy the thick Constitution's requirement that all "Laws" be submitted to the president for signature.[13] Chief Justice Warren Burger's opinion appeared to acknowledge that this result produced a government that was "clumsy, inefficient, [and] even unworkable," but found the result required by the "hard choices . . . consciously made" by the framers.

We do not have to examine the merits of the Court's holding here in detail. The Court's decision is easily evaded: Instead of seeing what the executive official actually does, Congress can require the official to report on his or her *proposed* action, and can pass a law barring the proposal. True, *that* law has to be signed by the president, which means that the Court's decision changes the political dynamics somewhat. But the effect is not obviously large, because the president has to expend some political capital in opposing Congress, and it is not obviously a good thing, in light of the expansion of presidential power in the twentieth century.

Public indifference. The thick constitution's provisions do not thrill the heart. They do not generate impassioned declarations—except perhaps among constitutional scholars—about how the Constitution provides essential protections for human liberty. As Justice John Paul Stevens wrote in a different context, "few of us would march our sons and daughters off to war to preserve" the president's right to require opinions in writing from cabinet members.[14]

The thin Constitution is different in this regard. We can think of the thin Constitution as its fundamental guarantees of equality, freedom of expression, and liberty. Note: Not "the First Amendment" or "the equal protection clause." The reason for referring only to fundamental guarantees and not specific constitutional provisions is to avoid the suggestion that the thin Constitution consists of, or is the same as, what the Supreme Court has said about those provisions. As law professor Robert Nagel has explained in a classic analysis, much of what the Court has said is as desiccated as the thick Constitution's provisions.[15] The Court has told us that to think about free speech, we have to worry about distinctions between content-based and content-neutral regulations, and between subject-matter and viewpoint-based restrictions. Even good lawyers get confused about these distinctions. Similarly, the Court has told us that to think about equality, we have to decide whether a race-based classification can satisfy "strict scrutiny," which Justice Sandra Day O'Connor assures us is not "fatal in fact," by promoting a "compelling state interest" in a "narrowly tailored" way.[16] These formulas are ways the Court uses to get at important considerations, but they are not what ordinary citizens need to recite when we try to figure out what free expression or equality requires.

What, then, is the thin Constitution? Political scientist Gary Jacobsohn has helpfully retrieved an obscure note written by Abraham Lincoln, describing "[t]he Union and the Constitution" as "the picture of silver," the "frame[]," around the "apple of gold," the principles of the Declaration of Independence: "The picture was made for the apple—not the apple for the picture."[17] The project the Constitution established for the people of the United States, Lincoln believed, was the vindication of the Declaration's principles: the principle that all people were created equal, the principle that all had inalienable rights. This is the thin Constitution.

I use the formulations I have—replacing "men" with "people," omitting the Declaration's statement that people were "endowed by their Creator" with inalienable rights—to emphasize that the project is vindicating *principles*. Those principles may differ from the interpretation Thomas Jefferson had: The principle of equality encompasses all people even though Jefferson referred only to men and owned slaves.[18] They may be justified on grounds other than the ones Jefferson had: The principle of rights can rest on secular grounds even though Jefferson offered a deistic justification.[19]

Frederick Douglass's comment on the Dred Scott decision restated these points helpfully. He focused on the Constitution's first words—"We the People." Douglass said, " 'We, the people'—not we, the white people—not we, the citizens, or the legal voters—not we, the privileged class, and excluding all other classes but we, the people; not we, the horses and cattle, but we the people—the men and women, the human inhabitants of the United States, do ordain and establish this Constitution."[20] As Douglass understood, the national project includes vindicating the parts of the Constitution's preamble that resonate with the Declaration: the nation's commitment to "establish Justice, ensure domestic Tranquility, provide for the common defense, promote the general Welfare, and secure the Blessings of Liberty to . . . our posterity."

Populist constitutional law vindicates the thin Constitution. As Douglass and Lincoln knew, ordinary people could be committed to the thin Constitution in ways they could never be committed to the thick Constitution. And the thin Constitution is indeed admirable in ways the thick Constitution is not. The thin Constitution protects rights that it has taken centuries of struggle for people to appreciate as truly fundamental. Perhaps more important, the nation's commitment to the thin Constitution constitutes us as the people of the United States, and constituting a people is a morally worthy project.

My claims about the thin Constitution blend a description of the people of the United States with an argument about why the thin Constitution, as I describe it, is an element in a good society. As I argue in more detail in chapter 8, the thin Constitution gives us the opportunity to construct an attractive narrative of American aspiration, and constructing such a narrative is an important constituent of the human good. As a matter of description, of course the people are unconcerned about the thick Constitution. But the thin Constitution is the material out of which Fourth of July speeches are fashioned. Politicians believe, probably correctly, that their constituents care about the thin Constitution, at least in the sense that constituents are troubled by politicians' positions that seem to them incompatible with the thin Constitution's principles. Perhaps not every constituent is concerned, and perhaps many are not troubled enough to throw the politician out of office solely because the politician favors one program some constituents think inconsistent with the thin Constitution, but politicians become cautious when they worry that enough constituents care enough.

We can give some more substance to the idea of the thin Constitution by considering Lincoln's role in the Civil War.[21] As Lincoln saw it, the Constitution should be interpreted to advance the Declaration's project, when its terms were fairly open to such an interpretation. Public officials should take advancing the project as a "political rule." The Constitution should be amended as quickly as political circumstances made possible, if its provisions impeded the project. And a political leader can provoke a constitutional crisis when political circumstances make it impossible to advance the nation's project. Challenged during the Civil War that his suspension of the writ of habeas corpus was unconstitutional, Lincoln noted that the secessionist South was resisting "the whole of the laws," and said, "Are all the laws but one to go unexecuted, and the Government itself go to pieces, lest that one be violated?"[22]

The Declaration and the Preamble provide the substantive criteria for identifying the people's vital interests. They show why we are dealing with a populist *constitutional* law rather than simple disagreements about the everyday stuff of political life. And the thinness of the populist Constitution is essential if the position I am developing is to be at all defensible.[23]

But of course the Declaration's principles are not self-interpreting. People will inevitably disagree over the question of what policy actually advances the Declaration's project in particular circumstances. The fact that surveys show public ignorance of abstractly stated provisions in the Bill of Rights, sharp disputes about what "the Constitution" requires, and disagreement with what the Supreme Court has said particular provisions mean, says nothing about whether the American people are in fact constituted by our attachment to the thin Constitution. Justice Clarence Thomas believes that the Declaration's principle of equality invalidates race-based affirmative action programs, for example, while his adversaries believe that the same principle justifies such programs.[24] The people may indeed divide over whether restricting access via the Internet to sexually explicit material is consistent with the nation's free speech ideals. That does not mean that proponents of restrictions are "against free speech." It means that people disagree about what free speech requires. This analysis leaves open a wide range in which public officials—with sufficient leadership ability—can reject the general theory of judicial supremacy without undermining the nation's most fundamental commitments even if they thereby do provoke a constitutional crisis.

The range is not infinite, however. Law professor Geoffrey Miller suggests that a president or legislator can provoke a constitutional crisis by defying the courts when doing so is necessary to preserve an energetic government with sufficient effective power to address the nation's pressing problems.[25] Perhaps defiance may be appropriate only when the Declaration's human rights principles are at stake—or, more narrowly, when the president's or legislator's position does not contradict those principles.

A remark by President Andrew Jackson provides a good example of the limits. In the 1820s and 1830s Jackson supported the state of Georgia's efforts to force the Cherokee Indians from the state. Among other moves, Georgia made it a crime for a non-Indian to live on Cherokee land. It prosecuted Samuel Worcester, a missionary, for doing so. Eventually the case got to the Supreme Court, which held the Georgia statute unconstitutional.[26] An unconfirmed story has President Jackson saying, "John Marshall has made his decision; now let him enforce it."[27] Had Jackson actually defied a Supreme Court judgment against him, he would have been wrong. A defender of Georgia's position might have maintained that removal was necessary to ensure domestic tranquility. The problems of law and order Georgia faced, however, were of its own making, not the Cherokees'. And, although the precise legal issue in Worcester's case was the relation between a national treaty and state law, individual rights were at stake because defiance in support of Georgia's racist Indian removal policy would contradict the Declaration's principles.

Even more strongly, Governor Faubus could not plausibly have claimed that his actions advanced the Declaration's project. The most he could establish was that he was acting on behalf of states' rights, which he might connect to the Preamble by citing its first purpose, "to form a more perfect union." I omitted that purpose from my earlier quotation of the Preamble precisely because it does not resonate with the Declaration's principles as the other purposes recited in the Preamble do. The Constitution's detailed arrangements regarding federalism, states' rights, and the separation of powers are the frame of silver that was made for the apple of gold.

The role the Declaration's principles plays in the analysis shows why someone who rejects judicial supremacy does not thereby defend an anarchic system in which the law is whatever anyone thinks it ought to be.[28] The Declaration's principles define our fundamental law. Vigorous disagreement over what those principles mean for any specific problem of public policy does not mean that we as a society have no fundamental law in common. I argue throughout this book that disagreements over the thin Constitution's meaning are best conducted *by the people*, in the ordinary venues for political discussion. Discussions *among* the people are not discussions by the people *alone*, however. Politics does not occur without politicians, and political leaders play an important role in the account of populist constitutional law I develop here. Most generally, the politicians we ought to admire most are those who help us conduct our discussions with reference to the Declaration's principles, and not simply as political contests over what different groups of people happen to want.[29]

COMPLEXITIES IN SOME SEEMINGLY EASY CASES:
PARDONS AND VETOES

With the idea of the thin Constitution in hand, we can begin by noting a peculiar feature of *Cooper v. Aaron*. There was no judicial order directing Governor Faubus to desegregate the Little Rock schools. So, in the narrowest sense, Faubus's position was entirely consistent with Lincoln's: At least in a purely legal sense Governor Faubus was not refusing to comply with a judicial order in a case already resolved against him.

Of course Governor Faubus *could* be brought into a lawsuit. If he continued his resistance after that, he would directly present the question of judicial supremacy. But it is worth pausing to think about situations in which it might seem that an official could reject the Supreme Court's constitutional interpretations without running the risk of becoming the defendant in a lawsuit.

The classic examples involve Presidents Thomas Jefferson and Andrew Jackson.[30] As political controversy intensified in the 1790s, Jefferson's opponents, the Federalist party, controlled Congress and the presidency. They enacted a law making it a crime to criticize the president (but not the vice president, who happened to be Jefferson). Several of Jefferson's political allies were convicted under this anti-sedition statute. Jefferson pardoned them after he took office in 1801, asserting that the statute violated the First Amendment's protection of free speech.

A few years later Jefferson explained his position to Abigail Adams, the wife of his Federalist adversary John Adams.[31] "You think it devolved on the judges to decide on the validity of the sedition law. But nothing in the Constitution has given them a right to decide for the Executive, any more than to the Executive to decide for them. . . . The judges, believing the law constitutional, had a right to pass a sentence . . . because that power was placed in their hands by the Constitution. But the Executive, believing the law to be unconstitutional, was bound to remit the execution of it; because that power has been confided to him by the Constitution." If the judges could "decide what laws are constitutional . . . for the Legislature and Executive also, would make the judiciary a despotic branch." As Jefferson saw it, his constitutional power to pardon authorized him—indeed, he said, *required* him—to act on his judgment that the anti-sedition law was unconstitutional even though the courts had upheld it.[32]

Andrew Jackson had a similar view. In 1819 the Supreme Court held that the Constitution gave Congress the power to create a national bank. Jackson disagreed with that decision. When his political opponents tried to make renewing the bank's charter a political issue, Jackson happily vetoed the proposal. He told Congress that the "opinion of the judges has no more authority over Congress than the opinion of Congress has over the judges, and on that point the President is independent of both."[33]

These cases differ from our *Plyler* problem in several ways. There is no obvious way to get judicial review of a veto or a pardon even if the president's decision is made entirely on constitutional grounds. In addition, we might think that presidents can veto laws and pardon people for policy as well as constitutional reasons. Even if we somehow devised ways of

reviewing vetoes and pardons, we would not be able to distinguish between decisions based on the president's constitutional interpretations
and those based on merely policy grounds. Jackson's veto of the bank
recharter, for example, prefaced its constitutional argument with several
arguments that the bank was a bad idea because, among other things, it
gave too much power to its private owners. And finally, Jefferson and
Jackson acted on their views that certain laws were *un*constitutional in
the face of judicial determinations that the laws were constitutionally permissible. In contrast, the *Plyler* problem involves an official who believes
that a statute is constitutional in the face of a decision that it is not.

These differences, while real, may not be important in developing an
argument against judicial supremacy. Students of the U.S. Constitution
are comfortable with the idea that some decisions, even constitutional
decisions, may not be subject to judicial review. The Supreme Court itself
has devised an important rule, the political questions doctrine, that leaves
some constitutional decisions to Congress and the president with no possibility of judicial review.[34]

The fact that some decisions are not open to judicial review under the
present U.S. constitutional system does not in itself fatally undermine the
theory of judicial supremacy.[35] The limits on judicial review show at most
that, as we understand our system today, the domain of judicial supremacy might not be as extensive as we can imagine it to be. As law professor
Michael Stokes Paulsen puts it, "If it is illegitimate for the President to
defy 'the law' (as declared by the courts) where his actions *can* be reviewed, it is no less illegitimate for the President to defy the law where
his actions *cannot* be reviewed."[36] And conversely, if it is legitimate to defy
the courts when an official's actions *cannot* be reviewed, it is legitimate to
do so when they *can*.

With this in the background, the difference between officials like Presidents Jefferson and Jackson, who reject a prior judicial determination that
a statute is constitutional, and those like Governor Faubus, who reject a
determination that a statute is *un*constitutional, dissolves. The courts said
to the presidents, "You can do this if you think it appropriate on policy
grounds, but you don't have to." Now supplement their statement: "You
can do this if you think it appropriate on policy grounds, and you *must*
do it if your only objections are constitutional, because *we* think it is
constitutional." In the face of such a statement, an official who refuses to
act on constitutional grounds—who vetoes a bill rather than signs it, who
refuses to prosecute for violating the anti-sedition act—is defying the
courts just as much as a person who acts pursuant to a statute the courts
have held unconstitutional.[37]

In short, the fact that our constitutional system does not have a way to
get the courts to review some official decisions that conflict with the

courts' constitutional interpretations does not really counter the theory of judicial supremacy. It identifies an awkward procedural "defect" in our constitutional system without rejecting the theory directly.

IGNORING THE COURTS

When may a legislator disregard the courts' constitutional interpretations?[38] As Lincoln's analysis indicates, sometimes legislative action apparently inconsistent with a prior judicial constitutional interpretation is not inconsistent with a general theory of judicial supremacy. As his analysis also indicates, sometimes it is. But in *those* situations the case for judicial supremacy is weak and the case for a populist constitutional law implementing the thin Constitution is strong.

Start with the first set of situations, where a legislator's apparent rejection of a court's constitutional interpretation actually is not inconsistent with judicial supremacy.

Distinguishable Legislation. A legislator could certainly support proposals that "actually concur[red] with the principles" the courts laid down. Supporting a proposal does not challenge judicial supremacy if the proposal is different from the one the courts held unconstitutional. Of course the legislator cannot know whether the courts will actually distinguish the proposal. For example, after *Dred Scott*, an abolitionist senator might have wanted to exercise Congress's power to "exercise exclusive Legislation" over the seat of government by abolishing slavery in the District of Columbia. That power is different from the power to "make all needful Rules and Regulations respecting" the territories, at issue in *Dred Scott*. A lawyer could credibly argue that an "exclusive" power is broader than a power to make "needful" rules, and therefore that the District of Columbia proposal did not conflict with *Dred Scott*. What about *Dred Scott*'s due process holding? Perhaps a lawyer could treat that as a legal analysis unnecessary to dispose of *Dred Scott* and therefore not controlling in later cases. The Supreme Court might not agree with either of these efforts to distinguish *Dred Scott*. Enacting the District of Columbia statute does not reject the Court's constitutional interpretation even so, if the legislator can make a legally credible argument that the cases are different.

Governor Faubus, however, could not make a legally credible argument that the situation in Little Rock was distinguishable from the situation anywhere else affected by the Court's desegregation decisions. There was public tension in many places, for example, and white opposition to desegregation was no more intense in Little Rock than it was in southern Virginia or South Carolina, where two of the Court's desegregation cases arose.

Finally, what of Proposition 187? It contains a provision barring aliens
not lawfully present in the country from receiving publicly funded nonemergency medical services. That provision is clearly distinguishable—in
the appropriate sense—from the one held unconstitutional in *Plyler*.
There the Court thought it important to its constitutional analysis that
the children denied a free public education were likely to remain in the
country for many years, and would be more productive contributors to
the nation if they had an education. Nonemergency medical services
might be different, because they might be more easily available from private charitable sources, and because the social consequences of denying
them might be less substantial. Of course, a court might disagree and find
nonemergency medical services indistinguishable from education.[39] But
the legal argument that the cases are different has enough credibility to
make legislative support of *this* provision of Proposition 187 consistent
with judicial supremacy.

What about the denial of a free public education? In *Plyler* the Court
found no indication in the record that the burdens the children placed on
the Texas economy were significant, and suggested that the outcome
might differ if there had been such evidence. Proponents of Proposition
187 may reasonably hope to place appropriate evidence of such burdens
in the record. The *Plyler* opinion itself indicates that this might be enough
to distinguish the cases.

Legislation Relevant to the Court's Constitutional Decisions. A legislator need not take the controlling precedent as a "political rule," according
to Lincoln. Lincoln meant that legislators could support laws that were
distinguishable from the one the Court held unconstitutional, but we can
give the term a somewhat broader meaning.

Sometimes the Court's doctrine makes what legislatures have actually
done relevant to its constitutional interpretations. The Court's death penalty cases, for example, make "evolving standards of decency" the bench-
mark for deciding whether a practice violates the Eighth Amendment's
ban on "cruel and unusual punishments." The Court looks to the statutes
enacted by state legislatures in determining what those standards are. In
holding unconstitutional the imposition of capital punishment for what
it described as a simple rape, the Court emphasized that only a single
state's legislature authorized the death penalty in such cases.[40] In contrast,
when it refused to find it unconstitutional to execute people who were
sixteen or seventeen when they murdered their victims, the Court found
that many of the states with capital punishment allowed the execution of
those who murdered as youths.[41]

The Court in *Plyler* took Congress's inaction into account in finding
that there was no national policy that supported denying education to the
affected children. The Court stressed that Congress had primary responsi-

bility over immigration and naturalization, and that Congress had done nothing to indicate its belief that those children should be denied a free public education. Congress has considered amending the immigration laws to authorize states to deny free public education to such children. In light of the Court's analysis in *Plyler*, there is certainly no impropriety when a senator supports such an amendment: The "principle" of *Plyler* is not obviously inconsistent with a national law restricting education in that way.

But when Proposition 187 was adopted, and even through 1998, Congress has not enacted such a law, and for many of the reasons the Court itself gave: Congress was apparently still troubled by the social consequences of denying free public education. So, although parts of Proposition 187 are readily distinguishable from *Plyler*, the one dealing with education is not.

A change in national policy—perhaps even one not expressly about education for those children—would be relevant to assessing the constitutionality of Proposition 187. Again, when Proposition 187 was adopted, there had not been such a change in national policy, so a legislator could not rely on this interpretation of the "political rule" exception to justify supporting Proposition 187. Enactment of immigration reform statutes in 1996 might, however, justify a legislator who invoked the exception in 1997.

Ordinary Litigation. A legislator might disregard an apparently controlling precedent, Lincoln suggested, when it was reached in "ordinary litigation between parties in personal actions." Lincoln's meaning here is not entirely clear because he does not spell out the distinction he has in mind between "ordinary litigation" and "extraordinary litigation." We can make sense of the distinction, however. The problem with a precedent set out in ordinary litigation is that the litigation may not have attracted enough public attention for the courts to have been fully informed of the case's significance. At the most basic level, the lawyers for the losing party may not have been very good even though there were many extremely good lawyers who would have leaped at the chance to represent that side—had they known the case was pending.

Even *Dred Scott* was not "ordinary litigation" in this sense. Every politically alert lawyer knew that the case was important, and the lawyers who represented Scott in the Supreme Court were among the nation's most distinguished. The same could be said about *Brown v. Board of Education* and *Plyler*. Neither Governor Faubus nor a California legislator could reasonably dismiss the applicable precedents on the ground that they had been rendered in ordinary litigation.

The Chance of Overruling. According to Lincoln, a legislator may support a law indistinguishable from one held unconstitutional when there is a "chance that [the earlier decision] might be overruled." The easiest way to give the Court a chance to overrule a precedent is to enact a statute indistinguishable from the one it held unconstitutional.[42]

For example, in 1996 a federal court of appeals held unconstitutional a Texas university affirmative action policy. The policy set up two admission tracks to the state's main public law school. By the time the appeals court decided the case, the law school had changed its policy, but the new one still took race into account in weighing applicants' credentials. The court of appeals held the original policy unconstitutional because, it said, the Constitution barred states from taking race into account in any way in admissions. The Supreme Court refused to hear the law school's appeal. Two justices noted that the case was not a good one to consider the court of appeals' broad constitutional holding because everyone agreed that the old policy used to deny the plaintiffs' applications was unconstitutional.[43]

The court of appeals decision applies to public law schools in Texas, Louisiana, and Mississippi. Can the dean of Mississippi's law school direct its admissions committee to continue to take race into account? In some sense, that directive would amount to defiance of the court of appeals' legal ruling. But it seems unduly harsh to chastise the dean for defying the courts when the obvious purpose behind the directive is to set up a new test case, one that the Supreme Court *would* find suitable for review.[44]

What evidence does a legislator need to have to think there is a chance of overruling? Sometimes the Court itself indicates its discomfort with its precedent. Strong dissents may show that the justices find the scope of the precedent troublesome. Or the Court may limit the precedent, distinguishing it in new cases in ways that are legally credible but not terribly persuasive. The fact that the justices find it necessary to limit the reach of a precedent may suggest that they would overrule it given the chance.

There is another way for the Court to show there is a "chance" that a decision will be overruled. In 1940 the Supreme Court upheld a state law requiring all students to salute the national flag, even if they had religious objections to doing so, as Jehovah's Witnesses did.[45] There was only one dissent. Following a spate of terrorism directed at Jehovah's Witnesses, four justices indicated in a case involving a different legal issue raised by Jehovah's Witnesses that they now thought the 1940 decision was wrong. By counting heads, lawyers could see that the 1940 decision was ripe for overruling. A lower court held a flag salute statute unconstitutional even though it was indistinguishable from the one upheld in 1940. The Supreme Court promptly affirmed the lower court's decision and overruled the 1940 precedent.[46]

Some lawyers express discomfort at this sort of head-counting.[47] We are, it is said, a government of laws and not of men and women. Counting heads to see what the Court will say the Constitution means makes it dramatically apparent that at least to some degree we are indeed a government of men and women. Whatever the theoretical merits of that concern, I doubt that a legislator is somehow required to ignore what he or she knows to be a fact, that the Court's composition affects its constitutional rulings.

Again, however, Governor Faubus could not reasonably think in 1957 that the Supreme Court was likely to repudiate its desegregation decisions, handed down only a few years earlier. There had indeed been some changes in the Court's composition, but the new appointees were likely to support the desegregation decisions. In fact, when the Court announced *Cooper v. Aaron*, it took an unprecedented course: The Court's opinion was announced under the name not of the Court or of any individual justice, but under the names of them all. And the opinion expressly said, "Since the first [desegregation decision] three new Justices have come to the Court. They are at one with the Justices still on the Court who participated in that basic decision as to its correctness." Governor Faubus should have known that from the beginning.

The *Plyler* case, however, is quite different. The Court's composition has changed dramatically since *Plyler*. Only one justice in the Court's liberal majority remained on the Court when Proposition 187 was adopted, whereas Justices William Rehnquist and Sandra Day O'Connor, who dissented in *Plyler*, had been joined by two other justices, Antonin Scalia and Clarence Thomas, whose constitutional theories make it clear that they would vote to overrule *Plyler*. That head-count makes four, so a legislator could not be as sure about overruling as in the flag salute cases. And there is an additional complication. In reaffirming what they called the "core holding" of the Court's 1973 abortion decision, three justices—O'Connor, Anthony Kennedy, and David Souter—coauthored a joint opinion that stressed the importance of stability in constitutional law and said that, although they might not agree with the basic abortion decisions, they would not overrule them.[48] A legislator therefore could not confidently count even Justice O'Connor among those likely to vote to overrule *Plyler*.

But, as we have seen, the legislator does not need a guarantee. All the legislator needs is some reasonable ground for believing that the Court would overrule *Plyler* if given the chance. The head-count is enough to make it constitutionally responsible for a legislator to support Proposition 187 on the ground that there is sufficient chance that the Court would overrule *Plyler*.

Constitutional Crises and the Rule of Law

We have now "solved" the *Plyler* problem with which we began, but we have done so in a way fully compatible with a general theory of judicial supremacy. To make further progress, we have to confine our attention to Governor Faubus.

Lincoln thought there were some "evils" associated with disregarding clearly controlling Supreme Court precedents. To understand what those evils are, consider first a different case. In 1989 and again in 1990 the Supreme Court held unconstitutional state and national laws making it a crime to burn the American flag in political protests.[49] A clear majority of the nation's people continues to think that those decisions were deeply wrong.[50] Suppose a prosecutor discovers an anti-flag-burning statute that has not yet been held unconstitutional by her or his state's courts, and decides to prosecute a political protestor for burning a flag. The prosecutor accomplishes relatively little other than making political points by bringing the criminal case: A court is sure to dismiss the prosecution because the statute violates the Constitution, and the prosecutor will have imposed on the defendant some costs in money, time spent on the defense, and emotional distress.[51]

Now consider what Governor Faubus might reasonably have thought he could accomplish by his actions, and again put aside the obvious observation that he thought he would win political points among Arkansas's whites by the stance he took. Here too the answer is, "Not much." His actions were highly likely to generate and exacerbate social tensions, as they did. And, any injunctions courts issued directing him to stop would be much less likely to repair the disruption than dismissing a frivolous prosecution would.

There is another "evil" associated with disregarding Supreme Court precedents. Doing so is inconsistent with a powerful national tradition of deference to the Supreme Court, a tradition that in its strongest version takes the form of a general theory of judicial supremacy. That theory might be wrong, or at least inconsistent with the alternative account of populist constitutional law I am developing, but it certainly is relevant to someone deciding whether to disregard a controlling precedent. As Governor Faubus's actions did, disregarding precedents may provoke a constitutional crisis as the public sees a legislator or executive official "defying" the Supreme Court. Senator Daniel Patrick Moynihan suggested a more moderate version of this approach.[52] He thought that Congress could pass a law inconsistent with a Supreme Court decision to alert the Court to the deep disagreement its decision provoked.

There is nothing wrong in principle with constitutional disagreements, or even with constitutional crises as such. Or, to adapt Lincoln's phrase, a constitutional crisis may be a good thing when "vital questions affecting the whole people" are involved.

It will be helpful to develop a distinction between two forms a constitutional crisis can take, although in the end the two forms turn out to be identical. Take the flag-burning prosecution first. A court dismissing the prosecution, it would seem, need not be relying on a general theory of judicial supremacy. As in the limited reading of *Marbury*, a judge dismissing the prosecution could say, "Look, when you bring a criminal prosecution you are asking *me* to do something. And when you do that, you have to live with the fact that among the things I do is interpret the Constitution. You can't get me to go along with you unless I agree with you about what the Constitution means. And I don't."

Governor Faubus seems to be in a different position. He was not asking the courts to do anything. *Cooper v. Aaron* thus seems to raise the question of judicial supremacy in a way that the flag-burning prosecution does not. If the courts issued an injunction against Governor Faubus, his disregard of their constitutional interpretations would be open defiance in a way that the prosecutor's filing charges is not.

But it really is not different. After the injunction is issued, Governor Faubus might say, "I don't care what you say, I'm going to continue to oppose desegregation. Put me in jail for contempt of court if you have the troops to do so." After the flag-burning prosecution is dismissed, the prosecutor might say, "I don't care what you say. I've sent the police to throw the protestor in jail. Send troops to get her out."

Once again Abraham Lincoln provides our best example. Shortly after his inauguration Lincoln faced serious military opposition in Maryland. He directed his military commander to arrest suspected secessionists and imprison them in military jails. The commander arrested John Merryman, a lieutenant in a secessionist unit that had burned some bridges to obstruct the movement of troops and supplies. Merryman's lawyers asked Supreme Court Chief Justice Roger Taney, who had written the leading opinion in *Dred Scott*, for a writ of habeas corpus to release Merryman. Taney issued the writ, which directed the military commander to bring Merryman to court. But Lincoln had issued his own order suspending the writ, so the commander refused. Taney then stated that Lincoln's suspension was unconstitutional and directed Merryman's release. Taney knew, however, that his orders were futile. "I have exercised all the power which the constitution and laws confer upon me, but that power has been resisted by a force too strong for me to overcome."[53] Lincoln's position in *Merryman* shows that even the apparently modest interpretation of *Marbury*, that is, ultimately raises questions of judicial supremacy: Everything a legislator or executive official can try to do using the courts, he or she can do without using them.

Yet, as we have seen, it really does look like we might have a constitutional crisis when a public official does those things. Are there any criteria for identifying when a constitutional crisis is a good thing? Here it will help to tone down the rhetoric a bit. Conflicts between the courts and the president or Congress have two dimensions. They implicate the substance of the constitutional provision at issue, and they also implicate the general question of judicial supremacy. Conflicts provoke one type of constitutional crisis when the conflict between the constitutional provision and the policy at stake is a "big" or important one like habeas corpus during the Civil War or the First Amendment during the McCarthy era—between the thin Constitution as interpreted by the courts and what policy-makers outside the courts want to do. They provoke a different kind when they involve a provision of the thick Constitution.

Lincoln's formulation—when the "vital interests of the people as a whole" are affected— points in the right direction. Who is going to specify what those interests are? Certainly people will disagree about what they are, and we would not have a good constitutional system if anyone who wanted to reject a court's interpretation of the Constitution could get up and say, "Well, this is a vital interest of the people as a whole, so it's time for a constitutional crisis."

Instead, only those who speak for "the people as a whole" can fairly identify their vital interests. It would have to be, that is, a political leader.

But not just any political leader, either. A political leader will have to forge substantial agreement on the proposition that the position he or she is asserting really does involve the vital interests of the people, often in the face of significant opposition. When an important constitutional provision is involved, we will face the "evils" of a constitutional crisis that cannot be resolved except at high cost, a cost we ought to bear in extraordinary situations but not routinely. Political leaders may provoke a major constitutional crisis and attempt to persuade the public that their view should prevail, when they are faced with an issue crucial to their political program. We have rarely faced these problems precisely because political leaders have regularly calculated that they ought not provoke a crisis either because the issue was not of such great importance or because they believed they could not prevail in a crisis, in the face of opposition from other political leaders motivated both to preserve the Constitution and to advance other policy goals.

The political leader's task differs when the thick Constitution is involved. Here we should bring into the discussion the most recent prominent opponent of a general theory of judicial supremacy—Reagan administration attorney-general Edwin Meese III. Meese made a widely noted and highly criticized speech in 1986, asserting that Supreme Court decisions "do not establish a 'Supreme Law of the Land' that is binding on all persons and parts of government, henceforth and forevermore."[54] Although this sounds a lot like Lincoln, whom Meese explicitly invoked, liberals who admire Lincoln nonetheless found Meese's position a threat to the constitutional order. Why did people think that Meese's position raised the specter of a constitutional crisis, but do not see such a crisis looming when the courts disregard congressional and executive interpretations *they* think wrong—when, that is, the courts exercise the power of judicial review?

Meese did not articulate his position with anything like Lincoln's subtlety. And he was asserting it on behalf of an administration that sought to reject judicial supremacy primarily with respect to the presidency's prerogatives. Those prerogatives are important in our constitutional system, but neither Meese nor President Reagan proved able to make the case to the public that a vital interest of the people was affected when the courts directed executive officials to follow judicial interpretations of the Constitution and federal statutes.

The problems Meese and President Reagan faced were serious ones, in their eyes. But the public did not initially—or, as it turned out, eventually—think that they were great enough to justify acting against our tradition of judicial supremacy. President Reagan should have understood that his difficulty arose from public willingness to accept a general theory of judicial supremacy, whatever they might say about particular court interpretations in public opinion surveys. Leadership in those circumstances meant attempting to undermine that public belief gradually, by selecting a highly technical issue on which to "defy" the courts and then persuading the public that the courts' constitutional interpretations come at too high a cost to public policy. If political leaders succeed once, they will have reduced public belief in judicial supremacy, and may be able to make a bolder move next time.

The basic idea here is that a constitutional crisis or efforts to bring about a gradual transformation in public views about judicial supremacy may be acceptable when able political leaders lead the public to understand that the people's vital interests are at stake. Success matters because failure imposes costs of disruption without accomplishing anything. Of course, success and failure come in degrees, and sometimes a partial success will be enough to justify the associated costs. But actions in conflict with our tradition of judicial supremacy have to accomplish *something* to offset the "evils" associated with such actions. Despite the fact that he was admired by a segment of the public, Governor Faubus was unable to persuade the people of the United States that their vital interests were at stake in Little Rock, in the face of opposition from President Dwight Eisenhower, who saw the Little Rock crisis as a threat to presidential authority and an embarrassment in foreign affairs. Neither was President

Reagan able to do so in the 1980s, despite the latter's manifest ability as a communicator of core ideas to the public.

And, strikingly, neither was Lincoln. He understood that slavery was one of those extraordinary cases in which the nation had to accept extraordinary costs to resolve a constitutional crisis. As he put it in a chilling passage in his Second Inaugural Address, "Yet, if God wills that [the war] continue until all the wealth piled by the bond-man's two hundred and fifty years of unrequited toil shall be sunk, and until every drop of blood drawn with the lash shall be paid by another drawn with the sword, as it was said three thousand years ago, so still it must be said, 'the judgments of the Lord, are true and righteous altogether.' "[55]

"INTERPRETIVE ANARCHY" VERSUS THE RULE OF LAW?

The RFRA experience provided the occasion for important discussions of judicial supremacy. According to Justice Anthony Kennedy's opinion for the Court, "[w]hen Congress acts within its sphere of power and responsibilities, it has not just the right but the duty to make its own informed judgment on the meaning and force of the Constitution."[56] The exercise of that right and duty, he continued, explains "the presumption of validity" the Court gives to congressional statutes. The Court's action invalidating RFRA shows, however, that Congress's decisions *about* the limits of "its sphere of power and responsibilities" receive no deference.

One obvious justification for the Court's approach is that Congress is self-interested when it defines the scope of its own power. Members of Congress have an interest in maximizing their own power by expanding their sphere of power and responsibilities. *Any* decision they make, no matter how fully deliberated, will be shaped, and perhaps distorted, by this self-interest. A rule giving their decisions some deference would endorse this self-interested behavior, while a rule denying deference has at least the potential to offset it.

Note, however, that this is an objection equally available to those who would question the Court's version of judicial supremacy. If members of Congress have an incentive to maximize the sphere of their power and responsibilities, so do Supreme Court justices with respect to *their* sphere. And *Boerne* shows the Court fully exercising its power-maximizing capacity.[57] If the Court is properly skeptical about Congress's decisions defining the scope of its sphere of power and responsibilities, so should Congress and the citizenry be skeptical about the Court's decisions defining—and maximizing—the scope of *its* sphere of power and responsibilities.[58]

But surely this cannot be right, a critic of this claim might reply. Someone has to decide what the scope of each institution's sphere of power and responsibilities is. The skeptical position is that the only two candidates—

Congress and the courts—are self-interested: Each has an incentive to maximize its own sphere. Then, however, we appear to have no ground for choosing who should prevail in circumstances where, by hypothesis, neither decision-maker is disinterested.

Law professors Larry Alexander and Frederick Schauer have offered the most sophisticated recent defense of judicial supremacy, but they fail to recognize that the problem is one of choice between self-interested institutions.[59] They argue that the rule of law requires that people refrain from making independent judgments about what the Constitution requires, accepting without examination the interpretations provided by what Alexander and Schauer call a "single authoritative decisionmaker." Otherwise, they argue, a regime of "interpretive anarchy" will leave people unable to coordinate their actions in matters on which they disagree. And coordination is important so that people can go about their lives without continually reopening matters that are settled in ways they can live with, though they might prefer them to be settled with some other result. Alexander and Schauer suggest that the courts, and particularly the Supreme Court, serve this "settlement function" of law. Allowing public officials to act on a constitutional interpretation different from the one provided by the Supreme Court would introduce an undesirable degree of instability into law: The settlement function can be performed well only if there is "a single authoritative interpreter to which others must defer." Alexander and Schauer thus defend judicial supremacy.

Or so it might seem. On closer examination, however, Alexander and Schauer actually defend a much weaker proposition, one entirely compatible with the analysis I have developed.

Alexander and Schauer appear to argue that the rule of law entails their version of judicial supremacy to ensure the stability necessary to guarantee that the law's settlement function will be performed acceptably. But their argument actually supports a rather different conclusion. What they establish is that the rule of law entails that a legal system have a set of institutional arrangements sufficient to ensure the degree of stability necessary to guarantee that the law's settlement function will be performed acceptably.

Perhaps, as Alexander and Schauer put it in their conclusion, "at times good institutional design requires norms that compel decision-makers to defer to the judgments of others with which they disagree." The question regarding judicial supremacy is, "Who are the decision-makers and who are the others?" One might think that questions about institutional design are fundamentally empirical.[60]

Nothing in Alexander and Schauer's formal argument precludes the conclusion that "at times good institutional design requires norms that compel [Supreme Court justices] to defer to the judgments of [Congress] with which they disagree." Rather, everything would seem to turn on the question of what a good institutional design is.

Alexander and Schauer concede that the single authoritative interpreter *could* be Congress. They offer several reasons why the Supreme Court is preferable to Congress as the single authoritative interpreter.[61] One is that the settlement function requires stability "over time as well as across institutions," and that courts respect the principle of *stare decisis* while legislatures do not. And yet, as Alexander and Schauer realize, the Supreme Court acknowledges its power to overrule its precedents, more readily in constitutional law than elsewhere. In 1991 the Supreme Court overruled an important death penalty precedent it had announced only four years earlier; in 1997 it overruled an important establishment clause precedent decided twelve years before.[62] And, of course, decisions regularly modify or undermine precedents in ways that open up new vistas for constitutional transformation.

This weakens the claim that the Supreme Court is a uniquely stable source of authoritative decisions. So does the reason officials sometimes "count heads" in attempting to predict what the Court will do: Randomly timed appointments to the Supreme Court introduce a new set of instabilities. In addition, Alexander and Schauer assert that legislatures and executives are less bound by principles of precedent. That may be true, although it probably underestimates the possibility that legislatures are regulated by norms prescribing that it is generally a good idea to do things the way they have been done before.

In any event, the question for institutional design is not what *principles* govern the institutions, but what *practices* they engage in. Here Alexander and Schauer's inattention to empirical questions seems particularly damaging to their argument. Legislative inertia is a powerful force in general, which means that a legislative solution once arrived at is likely to persist for a reasonably long time. Of course there are examples of short-term oscillations in legislative policy, but then, so too are there examples of short-term oscillations in judicial doctrine. Only an empirical investigation could tell us whether such oscillations, particularly on fundamental questions, are more common in courts or legislatures. We have relatively few examples of statutes addressing fundamental constitutional questions, partly because of Congress's deference to the Supreme Court. But my guess is that any such statutes would have at least as long a shelf-life as the Supreme Court's constitutional decisions; I think it quite unlikely, for example, that Congress would have revisited the core principles of RFRA within four or twelve years after its enactment.[63]

What, then, does "good institutional design" require in the way of institutions to ensure the degree of stability sufficient to guarantee that law's settlement function will be performed acceptably across institutions and over time? It almost certainly does not *require* judicial supremacy in any strong form. As Jeremy Waldron has put it, what reason could we have to think that a rule requiring deference to the judgments of five people, who are replaced at random intervals, produces more stability than a rule requiring deference to the judgments of a majority of the House of Representatives and the Senate, ordinarily concurred in by the President? Or, if one is bothered by the unrealistic prospect of dramatic short-term shifts in a purely majoritarian system in which power is divided among several institutions whose members are elected by majorities or, sometimes, pluralities, and serve varying terms of office, consider the following rule of institutional design: The Supreme Court's interpretations of the Constitution's requirements prevail in general, unless they are rejected by wide majorities in both houses of Congress in legislation that expresses a reasonable interpretation of the thin Constitution's requirements. This rule does reject judicial supremacy to some extent, but there is no reason to think that it fails to satisfy the entailments of the rule of law that Alexander and Schauer identify.[64]

We can deepen our understanding of Alexander and Schauer's argument by considering another possibility, more in the domain of political science than law. The argument here begins by noting the inaccuracy in saying, as Alexander and Schauer do, that the Supreme Court is the "single authoritative decisionmaker" their account of the rule of law requires. "The Supreme Court" is actually an institution, whose decision-making rule is, "Majority vote among nine individual members." In Alexander and Schauer's usage, a "single" authoritative decision-maker cannot possibly be one person. It is an institution, located in their view in one building in Washington, D.C. But if a "single" decision-maker can be a group of people who work in one building, why can't a "single" decision-maker be a group of people who work in two buildings—the Supreme Court building and the national Congress across the street?

Alexander and Schauer's conceptual analysis establishes the need for an institution of authoritative decision-making. But institutions are complex patterns of regular behavior, not single individuals—as their example of the Supreme Court demonstrates—or even aggregates of individuals who happen to work in the same building. Whether the Court actually is supreme will be determined by a complex and extended process of interbranch interaction, and that interaction constitutes the institution that is the single authoritative decision-maker that the rule of law requires, according to Alexander and Schauer. All that is needed is enough stability to allow the law's settlement function to be performed. And, I believe, it would be impossible to establish that the complex system of interbranch interaction, in which members in each branch make their own decisions about what the Constitution requires, would be any more unstable than the system of judicial supremacy.[65]

VOTERS AND THE THIN CONSTITUTION

So far we have considered the limits, if any, on a public official's disregard of controlling Supreme Court opinions. What of ordinary citizens?[66]

The first point to note is that native-born citizens do not typically have to take an oath to uphold the Constitution, as public officials and naturalized citizens do. An ordinary citizen does not break faith with any duty he or she has undertaken if the citizen ignores what the Supreme Court has said, even if the Supreme Court's interpretations of the Constitution are the supreme law of the land. A public official asked to enforce Proposition 187 faces a problem: "I swore to uphold the Constitution, and the Supreme Court has said that its constitutional interpretations are the supreme law of the land and that a key part of Proposition 187 is unconstitutional. How can I reconcile enforcing that part with the oath I took?" In contrast, a California voter entering the booth to vote on Proposition 187 could say, "I'm going to vote for it even though I know the Supreme Court has said that a key part of it is unconstitutional. What's that to me?"[67]

We might call this a mild form of civil disobedience. The term is slightly out of place. The citizen is disobeying the Supreme Court, but in the service of the law as the citizen sees it. Most constitutional theorists believe that even stronger forms of civil disobedience are sometimes justified, again in the service of law even though the person may be disobeying a specific statute or disregarding a specific Supreme Court decision. Civil disobedience has its costs, which a prudent citizen would take into account before deciding to engage in it. We saw, however, that the case for legislative and executive actions inconsistent with a general theory of judicial supremacy could take such costs into account without difficulty.

At this point in the argument, liberals might raise the specter of the Second Amendment. The relevant judicial opinions uniformly hold that the Second Amendment does not protect an individual's right to own guns. The cases say that the amendment's explanatory preface—"A well-regulated Militia, being necessary to the security of a free State"—shows that the right to bear arms implicates only the right of state governments to organize collective measures of social protection. Academic opinion is divided, but recently something close to a consensus has emerged that the judicial understanding is wrong, and that the amendment really does create an individual right.[68]

The "individual right" view is widely held by the American people as well. Does the argument that ordinary citizens can generally ignore the courts' constitutional interpretations mean that there is nothing problematic about that fact? In the end, it does. But here is some work to do before the end.

Once again we must turn to the Declaration and the Preamble. Unlike Governor Faubus, proponents of the "individual right" interpretation of the Second Amendment can plausibly connect their position to the Preamble: Individual ownership of guns helps ensure domestic tranquility, and it might provide an additional guarantee that our representatives remain under our control. Proponents of gun control of course think otherwise. In their view private ownership of guns enhances the risk of crime and civil disorder.

This is no different from the disagreement between Justice Thomas and his adversaries about the Declaration's meaning. If that disagreement raises no fundamental questions about our constitutional order, neither should this one.

There is a deeper point. A populist constitutional law rests on a commitment to democracy, a commitment itself embodied in the Declaration's principles. No one can guarantee that democratic processes will always yield results I agree with. Reasonable people can disagree with the judgments I make about what the Declaration's principles require. Democracy is a way of resolving such disagreements without routinely risking severe social disorder. Of course if democracy regularly produced disagreeable results, or occasionally produced truly vile ones, I would rethink my commitment to democracy. But the simple fact that on some issues people would adopt policies—or constitutional interpretations—I disagree with is hardly bothersome. It establishes instead that if I care enough I ought to try to persuade people that a different policy would better advance the Declaration's project.

A PRELIMINARY CONCLUSION, AND AN INTRODUCTION

Does this mean that an ordinary citizen can disregard not just Supreme Court decisions but the Constitution itself? Chapter 8 expands on the reasons for answering "No." For now, repeating the hints of the argument I have already provided must suffice. Ordinary citizens ought to continue the Declaration's project—and therefore ought to take the Constitution into account when it advances that project—in part because the Declaration's principles state unassailable moral truths and because the Declaration's project is what constitutes us as a people.

This chapter has not established that populist constitutional law is a good idea. Nor has it fleshed out the idea of populist constitutional law except for the modest proposition that populist constitutional law embodies democratic commitments to carry out the Declaration of Independence's project. Instead, I have argued only that there are good reasons to reject a general theory of judicial supremacy. With that ground cleared, we can explore what a populist constitutional law would be, and evaluate its merits later.

Chapter Two

DOING CONSTITUTIONAL LAW
OUTSIDE THE COURTS

THE "NOMINATION" OF GEORGE MITCHELL

Chapter 1 argued that people acting outside the courts can ignore what the courts say about the Constitution, as long as they are pursuing reasonable interpretations of the thin Constitution. This chapter takes up seemingly more difficult questions: In implementing the thin Constitution, can people acting outside the courts ignore the thick one? How much of the Constitution can we safely take away from the courts? Developing the answers to these questions requires us to examine the reasons we might have for directing public officials to refrain from acting on their best judgments about what they ought to do. Those reasons are quite complex, and support such directions only under restrictive conditions. The arguments that establish that result, I believe, should help reduce fears people might have about populist constitutionalism's implications, although they will not eliminate those fears.

Suppose you were a Democratic senator during the spring of 1994, when Justice Byron White announced his retirement from the Supreme Court. Suppose also that President Clinton announced his intention to nominate Senator George Mitchell, your majority leader, to fill the vacancy. A problem would arise in connection with the nomination. Congress had passed a law increasing the salaries of Supreme Court justices in 1989. Senator Mitchell was serving a term that began in 1988. Article I, section 6, provides, "No Senator . . . shall, during the Time for which he was elected, be appointed to any civil Office under the Authority of the United States, . . . the Emoluments whereof shall have been increased during such time. . . ." The Emoluments Clause is part of the thick Constitution.

Its text seems clear enough. If the president appointed Senator Mitchell to the Supreme Court, it would be "during the Time for which he was elected," and Congress would have increased the "Emoluments" of the position during that time. Recently, however, a convention appears to have arisen that might avoid the difficulty.[1] Insiders know it as the "Saxbe fix," because it was used to allow Senator William Saxbe to serve as President Richard Nixon's last Attorney General after the Watergate investigation led him to fire Attorney General Elliott Richardson. Under the Saxbe fix, Congress enacts a statute reducing a cabinet member's salary to the point it was at when the senator's term began, allowing the senator to take a position as a cabinet officer. The thought is that the senator can accept an appointment to the position because the salary is no longer greater.

The Saxbe fix is in some tension with the Constitution's text and its apparent purpose.[2] Textually, the salary "shall have been increased" during Senator Mitchell's term, and rescinding the increase does not mean that the salary "shall not have been increased"; it simply means that the salary shall have been both increased and reduced during the term.

The provision's purpose is to avoid the corrupting influence that hope of an appointment might have on a Congress-member's actions. Corruption can take a narrow or a broad form. The Emoluments Clause might be aimed at preventing members from voting in a manner that benefits one of them monetarily. Or it might be aimed at barring Congress from passing laws specifically to benefit one of its own members. Because these types of corruption are unlikely to occur in open daylight, they can be controlled only by a prophylactic rule barring appointment even if there is no direct evidence of a corrupt bargain.

Reducing a cabinet officer's salary may alleviate the problem of corruption, although it does not eliminate it. It is unlikely to alleviate the problem to any substantial degree when a Supreme Court position is involved. A cabinet member's term of service is likely to be limited by political reality, although not by constitutional command. Congress could reasonably return the salary to the level it was at prior to the Congress-member's appointment for the entire period of the cabinet member's service without serious impact on the member's economic well-being. That solution is unavailable for judges with lifetime appointments. The alternative is to allow Congress to reduce the salary for a brief period and then give the appointee a "catch up" increase when "the Time for which [the appointee] was elected" ends.[3] That, however, would substantially reduce the constitutional provision's anticorruption effect: In exchange for a relatively short-term loss the Congress-member can get a lifetime appointment and a permanent salary increase.

The Emoluments Clause might make it impermissible to rescind the salary increase for a prospective Supreme Court justice even if its anticorruption purpose is the narrow one of avoiding appointment of corrupt individuals. The Clause probably ought to be taken as having a broader purpose, however. The Framers were concerned about creating a self-perpetuating national government, in which members of Congress and the executive branch would collaborate to separate the governing elite from the people. Even the appearance of self-dealing undermines the relation between representatives and the people. The narrow reading of the

Clause's purposes focuses on the temptations an individual member faces; the broader reading focuses on the systemic impact of making it possible for Congress as an institution to reward some of its members with special legislation. The best understanding of the Emoluments Clause, then, is entirely consistent with its plain language: Congress-members cannot pass laws whose sole purpose appears to be to provide a benefit to one of them. As a witness testifying against the constitutionality of rescinding a salary increase to allow Senator William Saxbe to serve as Attorney-General put it, the Saxbe fix "smacks of clever manipulation" and makes a constitutional provision "the subject of deft maneuver."[4]

Suppose your colleagues in the House and Senate disagree, and have enacted a salary-reduction statute. The time has come to vote on Senator Mitchell's confirmation. You are convinced that the Saxbe fix cannot overcome the textual difficulties. You also realize that the sequence of events is precisely what the Framers worried about. But you also think that the constitutional provision makes no sense today.

The rise of a party system has made implicit trades quite common, so our sense of what a corrupt bargain is no longer tracks the Framers' understanding. The danger against which the provision guards is no longer a serious one, at least compared to similar dangers against which the Constitution does not protect us. Further, the rise of an aggressive investigative press has made explicit trades impossible. To the extent that the constitutional provision guards against a real danger, there are now better ways to avoid the danger than the provision's broad prophylactic ban. Finally, you appreciate that your judgment about the costs and benefits of the constitutional provision may be distorted. You know Senator Mitchell, for example, and you are aware that you might be overestimating the distinctive contribution he can make to the Supreme Court. And you are also aware that the Framers were concerned about subtle, imperceptible distortions of judgment that might occur as senators saw one of their number receiving an appointment and thought to themselves about the possibility that they too would receive an appointment.

Still, after the most careful consideration of the merits and the factors that may have distorted your assessment of the merits, you have concluded that the constitutional provision, applied according to its terms and the Framers' intentions, would deprive the nation of the valuable service Senator Mitchell could provide as a Supreme Court justice.[5] In short, you have conscientiously decided that the constitutional provision serves no useful purpose.

When you were sworn in, you took the constitutionally prescribed oath "to support this Constitution." Your investigation leads you to conclude that Senator Mitchell's appointment would contravene the Constitution's text and the provision's purposes, and that his appointment would be a very good thing for the nation. Is it consistent with the entire Constitution for you to vote to confirm Senator Mitchell's appointment, despite your best understanding of the most directly applicable constitutional provision? Put more catchily, though somewhat inaccurately, will you violate your oath of office if you vote to confirm the nomination?[6]

TRYING TO MAKE THE PROBLEM GO AWAY

There are a number of dodges designed to make the problem go away. The first one plays a subliminal role in much of what follows. Some of the rest make the problem go away by relieving the senator of responsibility for disregarding his or her best understanding of the most directly applicable constitutional provision. The others make it go away by stipulating that the senator must follow that understanding.

Triviality. I use the Emoluments Clause question to try to get leverage on a deep constitutional problem, but I cannot do so because the Emoluments Clause problem is fundamentally trivial, in the sense that no one could care much how it was resolved. The problem really cannot be used to explore deep questions about the extent to which a representative, executive official, or citizen can properly disregard a constitutional provision that he or she conscientiously regards as important. This dodge fails for two reasons.

We can devise analogous problems that really would be serious. Consider the peculiar tie-breaking provisions of the Twelfth Amendment.[7] Suppose that one of our major political parties splinters and the spin-off party runs a candidate for president but not for any congressional seats. The presidential election produces a popular plurality of 45 percent for party A, 40 percent for party B, and 15 percent for the splinter party C. The electoral college is divided in the same way, thereby throwing the election to the House of Representatives. Party A wins majorities in enough districts to give it control of the House. Party B, however, wins majorities of the state delegations in a majority of the states (imagine Party A winning large majorities of the delegations in the nation's largest states while Party B wins majorities in the nation's smallest). The Twelfth Amendment directs that "in choosing the President, the votes shall be taken by states, the representation from each state having one vote." Under these circumstances one can imagine the presidential candidate of Party B becoming President even though three obvious measures of support (popular and electoral vote pluralities, and even geography as measured by a majority of the districts in the House of Representatives) favor selecting Party A's candidate. This scenario can be spun out in many ways, and I do not want to place too much weight on it, except to suggest that it raises the possibility that the person charged with certifying the House's vote might decide that, all things considered, she should certify the election of Party A's candidate. That would clearly be a nontrivial instance of the problem we are considering here.

More important, the triviality dodge fails because it requires its proponent to distinguish between fundamental constitutional provisions and less fundamental ones, which is precisely to engage in the practice of disregarding some constitutional provisions because they seem silly. Saying that it is all right to disregard the Emoluments Clause because it is a trivial clause is to say that we are not troubled by legislators who ignore the Constitution in the service of the public good as they see it—at least when trivial clauses, which might include all the clauses in the thick Constitution, are involved.

Judicial Review. If Senator Mitchell is placed on the Supreme Court, the Court itself will eventually face the constitutional question.[8] One variant of the judicial review dodge says that, because the Court will eventually consider the question, you do not have to. You can argue that you took an oath to support the entire Constitution, which includes the institution of judicial review. As we saw in chapter 1, you support the Constitution when your actions leave open the possibility of judicial review of the constitutionality of your actions.

A second variant of the judicial review dodge says that when the Court considers the question, it will apply normal interpretive techniques. Assume that these techniques would allow the Court to consider text and purposes, but not whether the provision makes sense today.[9] What harm has been done if the Court concludes that the appointment was invalid because it is inconsistent with text and purposes? Perhaps only— "only"—the harm occurring because you will appear not to have followed your oath to support the Constitution. After all, you agreed with the Court on the issues it considered.

Suppose, however, that the judicial review dodge is unavailable because you are convinced that no litigant will ever have standing to challenge the constitutionality of Senator Mitchell's appointment.[10]

Constitutional Amendment. The Constitution itself provides a mechanism, the amendment process, for getting rid of provisions that seem silly today. It has been so used in the past,[11] and could be so used again. Given the possibility of constitutional amendment, it is inconsistent with the oath of office for a legislator simply to disregard the conclusions of his or her conscientious examination of the existing Constitution.

You think, however, that the amendment process is too cumbersome to deploy in the service of an important but highly technical "correction" of the Constitution. It would take too long to ensure Senator Mitchell's appointment. Further, you may be concerned that the public may not fully appreciate how silly the constitutional provision has become. You may think that the focus on investigative journalism, for example, is something only people deeply embedded in Washington's political culture could appreciate. The amendment dodge may lead you regularly, perhaps permanently, to vote against what you believe would be truly valuable appointments. And, from your point of view, to no good end.[12]

And, finally, you may reasonably believe that the Constitution's cumbersome amendment procedures, which allow slight majorities in thirteen states to block a change desired by large numbers of people elsewhere, simply do not make much sense. Here the difficulties of the amending process actually provide a reason for ignoring the Emoluments Clause as you understand it. In short, just as the framers made a mistake, as you see things, in including a permanent Emoluments Clause in the Constitution, so they made a mistake in designing the amendment procedure: It is too complicated to be invoked for the kind of problem you are facing. The existence of a flawed amendment process gives you no reason to avoid dealing with your concerns about the Emoluments Clause.[13]

Prudentialism. A conscientious constitutional decision-maker properly takes practical consequences and realities into account in interpreting the Constitution. This dissolves the problem by showing that the Constitution itself, considered as a whole, licenses a decision-maker to ignore one of the Constitution's specific provisions. Sometimes practical consequences and realities can overcome the otherwise controlling words and purposes of the constitutional text. The prudentialist's central example is *Home Building and Loan Ass'n v. Blaisdell.*[14] In the midst of the Depression, Minnesota enacted a mortgage moratorium law that suspended foreclosures on defaulted mortgages. The statute was a classic debtor-relief law, apparently just what the Framers were concerned to preclude through the Constitution's ban on state laws impairing the obligation of contracts. Yet, a sharply divided Supreme Court upheld the statute in the face of the apparent difficulties caused by text and purposes.

After an introduction explaining why the statute was in tension with the Contracts Cause, Chief Justice Hughes relied on "a growing appreciation of public needs and of the necessity of finding ground for a rational compromise between individual rights and public welfare" to explain the Court's result. This comes close to a pure prudentialist position. On the one hand there are the individual rights protected by the Constitution; on the other there are the considerations of public welfare. The two must be compromised, which means that sometimes the Constitution gives way to concerns about real-world consequences and realities. Or, putting it more positively, the Constitution properly interpreted sometimes allows those consequences and realities to override the implications drawn from a more limited examination of text and purposes.

Finally, because conscientious decision-makers can honestly disagree about the strength of practical consequences and realities, you should not be concerned that the Supreme Court might invalidate Senator Mitchell's appointment based on a different prudentialist assessment. You will have honored your oath by a fair-minded consideration of relevant matters, including text, purposes, consequences, and realities.

Blaisdell is surely a strong case for prudentialists. It may not be enough to carry the day, however. Chief Justice Hughes's opinion went to some lengths to explain that Minnesota's mortgage moratorium law did not "impair" the obligation of contracts in a constitutional sense.[15] Other cases suggest the Court's discomfort with openly prudentialist arguments. As we saw in chapter 1, Chief Justice Burger's opinion in the legislative veto case rejected a prudentialist argument: "The choices we discern as having been made in the Constitutional Convention impose burdens on governmental processes that often seem clumsy, inefficient, even unworkable, but those hard choices were consciously made. . . . There is no support in the Constitution or decisions of this Court for the proposition that the cumbersomeness and delays often encountered in complying with explicit Constitutional standards may be avoided. . . ."[16]

Probably most important, prudentialism may conflict with constitutionalism understood as a system of restraints on decision-makers. Consider what a conscientious decision-maker would do in a system without constitutional restraints on power. She or he would examine the situation carefully, locate all the relevant considerations, and decide what course of action best promoted the people's welfare. How do constitutional restraints change the decision-maker's calculus? All they can do is withdraw some otherwise relevant considerations from the decision-maker's ken. Why do that? Perhaps on the ground that the decision-maker's all-things-considered judgments are less likely actually to promote the people's welfare than would decisions based on less than all the relevant considerations. And why might that be? Perhaps because the decision-maker, driven by particular interests or incentives, may be particularly prone to misestimate the significance of the consideration the constitution withdraws from her or his ken.

This is a fairly standard argument. I invoke it here only to point out the tension between a full-fledged prudentialism and constitutionalism. Of course, you might respond, you are not advocating a full-fledged prudentialism that would completely displace text and purposes. Rather, you would take text and purposes into account in coming to your all-things-considered judgment.

"James Madison Was a Smart Guy." The Framers thought long and hard about how to design a well-functioning government. The very fact

that they thought a provision important enough to include in the Constitution counsels against your conclusion that the provision is silly today.

True enough, but insufficient to displace your all-things-considered judgment, because you have already built your appreciation of the Framers' wisdom into that judgment. Based on your understanding of the Framers' worries, you too worried, for example, that your own lurking hopes for an appointment by the president might have led you to overestimate the importance of investigative journalism today. But, having thought the problem through as thoroughly as you can, and having duly taken into account the Framers' wisdom, you have concluded that on this point they failed to appreciate how the political and economic life of the country would change in ways that now make the constitutional provision silly.

Thomas Jefferson made a similar point in an 1816 letter, "Some men look at constitutions with sanctimonious reverence. . . . They ascribe to the men of the preceding age a wisdom more than human. . . . I knew that age well; I belonged to it, and labored with it. It deserved well of its country. It was very like the present, but without the experience of the present, and forty years of experience in government is worth a century of book-reading; and this they would say themselves, were they to rise from the dead."[17] James Madison, in short, was a smart guy, but he wasn't infallible.[18]

Conservation of Political Energy. Recent writing dealing with the purposes of having a constitution appears to have converged on an answer to the question, Why let judgments made in the past constrain today's all-things-considered judgments?

Imagine two people working out a deal they believe will benefit them both. They know that reaching their goal will take some time. And they realize to their chagrin that partway into the project one or the other will be in a position to walk away with more than his or her share, leaving behind a forlorn partner and an uncompleted project. This possibility leads each to discount any promises the other makes, and so makes it harder to reach agreement—even though the potential cheater would gain more from making and honoring the agreement than he or she would gain by making the agreement and then walking away in the middle.

The solution is simple: The partners should design something that will make it more expensive for them to walk away opportunistically in the middle of the project. They can write a contract promising not to walk away, for example, and rely on the courts to enforce the promise.

Constitutions might be thought of similarly—as ways of guaranteeing that we can carry out beneficial long-term arrangements without worrying that someone will take advantage of us in the middle of the process. Constitutions allow us to take some perhaps contentious issues off the table, and thereby allow us to get on with the task of governing. As political scientist Stephen Holmes puts it, "If we can take for granted certain procedures and institutions fixed in the past, we can achieve our present political goals more effectively than we could if we were constantly being side-tracked by the recurrent need to establish a basic framework for political life." A constitution's drafters "emancipate[] the present generation" by "disencumber[ing]" it of the necessity repeatedly to revisit fundamental questions of constitutional order.[19] Or in political theorist Russell Hardin's words, "[T]he power to make a decision and then to get on with life rather than to keep the issue permanently open is beneficial. . . . [T]he point of establishing a constitution . . . is to put obstacles in our way in order to force us the more readily to organize ourselves for progress, rather than to dissipate our energies in random directions."[20]

I believe there are several difficulties with this argument. First, it is unclear that *constitutions*—written to govern a wide range of political projects—are a good way of tying our hands. It seems more likely that the right restrictions are going to be specifically designed for particular projects, rather than general restrictions applicable across the board. Nor does it seem likely that the specific arrangements that those who wrote the Constitution thought necessary to ensure agreement on *their* project remain suitable for us to secure agreement on *ours*. The Constitution's framers barred "direct" taxes except in proportion to a state's population as part of their fundamental compromises over slavery; with slavery abolished, it may not make sense to prohibit today's legislators from imposing direct taxes.[21]

Second, the argument overlooks the problem created by interpretive ambiguity—even invented interpretive ambiguity. Once the possibility of the Saxbe fix is on the table, for example, political decision-makers have no choice but to spend some time considering what to do. Of course asking them to rethink the constitutional provision's wisdom calls on them to engage in a somewhat more substantial process than asking them simply to determine what the provision's words and purposes imply for the rescission question. But it seems unlikely that the marginal dissipation of political energy will be large. In this sense, the search for new solutions is not random, as Hardin suggests.

Finally, and perhaps most important, the standard argument may well offer good reasons for taking *some* constitutional fundamentals to be provisionally settled.[22] Consider political theorist Jon Elster's version of the argument: "[I]f all institutions are up for grabs at all times, individuals in power will be tempted to milk their positions for private purposes, and those outside power will hesitate to form projects which take time to bear fruit. Moreover, if nothing could ever be taken for granted, there would be large deadweight losses arising from bargaining and factionalism."[23]

This could well be true, but note how much turns on the scope Elster gives the problem: "all institutions up for grabs at all times." Elster's argument, which is only a specific version of the conservation-of-political-energy argument, does not explain why any particular provision must be taken as settled at any particular time. We can gain nearly all the benefits of the conservation of political energy by allowing people to reconsider one constitutional fundamental at a time—perhaps one a year.[24]

Nearly all, but not all: Some constitutional provisions are so interconnected that it would be unwise to consider changing only one. It would not be sensible, for example, to consider reducing the terms of senators to four years without considering whether it made sense to change the terms of members of the House of Representatives, or to have all senators elected in years in which there is no presidential election.[25] The Emoluments Clause, however, seems an unlikely candidate as a provision so closely connected to other provisions that altering or disregarding it would introduce broad instability in the constitutional system's daily operations.

We might note as well that in an important sense, all constitutional provisions *are* up for grabs at all times. Your position as a senator may lead you to think that we ought to have a rule, "The Constitution means what 50% plus one of Congress says it means." At present, of course, the rule is, "The Constitution means what 50% plus one of the Supreme Court says it means." The Supreme Court operates with a "Rule of Four": The Court hears a case when four justices vote to do so. In 1963 Justice Arthur Goldberg tried to persuade his colleagues to hear a case questioning the constitutionality of capital punishment. Only two other justices agreed with him at the time.[26] Do the Supreme Court's decision procedures introduce instability into our constitutional system? Or, more precisely, would we get more instability than we have if we allowed Congress, using its own rather complex decision procedures, to place constitutional issues on the table?[27]

INTERPRETING THE CONSTITUTION IN LIGHT OF THE DECLARATION

Is there a *direct* defense of interpreting the Constitution only on the basis of text and purposes, or in any way other than by making all-things-considered judgments?[28] Refraining from making such judgments, and relying on some criteria that—necessarily—are less comprehensive, is formalism. In this sense, reliance on text and purposes, and refraining from making prudentialist judgments, is formalism. Frederick Schauer has provided our generation with the standard defense of formalism, a defense that resonates with his defense of judicial supremacy examined in chapter 1.[29] But, as we will see, the defense of formalism, if successful, is suitable for *judicial* practices. I suspect that the nearly automatic assumption that other actors in the constitutional system ought to interpret the Constitution in the way courts do results from a failure to understand why the courts can justifiably be formalist, and why other actors need not be, and perhaps cannot coherently be, formalist.[30]

Schauer's defense of formalism begins by observing that judges stand in a supervisory relation to other actors—lower court judges, executive officials, and legislators. The judges have to articulate rules, standards, or guidelines that will lead those other actors to comply to the greatest degree achievable with the Constitution as understood by the judges. Consider a judge who arrives at an all-things-considered judgment about how a good government should be designed, and an account of how the Constitution is consistent with that judgment. That judge might nonetheless refrain from articulating that judgment as an interpretation of the Constitution. The reason is that in articulating the judgment, the judge is setting out a rule, standard, or guideline that the other actors will follow when similar questions come before them.

The judge may think, however, that those other actors will be less adept at applying the rule, standard, or guideline than the judge herself is. The judge would articulate the rule if she were confident that she, or people just like her, would be applying it. But, telling the other actors to follow the rule the judge herself would follow may lead to lower levels of compliance with the Constitution as the judge understands it because the other actors are not just like her—they are less talented, we might say. Better, the judge might think, to give the other actors a less subtle rule, standard, or guideline, which they will find easy to apply. In the present context, the formalist directive is, "Consider only text and purposes, but not consequences or practical realities."

Suppose the judge can identify a specific reason that leads other actors into constitutional error, a consideration that when injected into their all-things-considered judgments induces more errors than correct decisions. The consideration is relevant to an accurate all-things-considered judgment, and the judge herself takes it into account in making such judgments. The other actors, however, do badly when they try to use it. The judge might be able to achieve a higher level of compliance with the Constitution by directing those officials to refrain from taking that consideration into account.

The judge can eliminate some constitutional errors by telling the other actors to follow a formalist rule, standard, or guideline. The formalist approach may induce some new errors, however. Consider, for example, *Palmore v. Sidoti*.[31] There a family court judge, applying the standard of "the best interests of the child"—a classic all-things-considered standard—concluded that, all things considered, the child involved would be better off if placed with her white father than if placed with her white mother and an African-American stepfather. Reversing, a unanimous Supreme Court acknowledged that "[t]here is a risk that a child living with a parent of a different race may be subject to a variety of pressures and stresses not present if the child were living with parents of the same racial or ethnic origin." The particular child in *Palmore*, that is, may be worse off under the Court's formalist rule barring consideration of the effects of "private biases" on the child's well-being because such biases are in fact relevant to the child's well-being. But, taking all child-custody decisions into account, and in particular being aware that family court judges themselves may be infected by biases that lead them to make distorted all-things-considered judgments, the Court concluded that the formalist rule barring consideration of private racial biases would lead to more accurate determinations of what was in the child's best interest than a rule allowing family court judges to take everything into account.[32]

We reach some point on the scale of constitutional goodness with a nonformalist set of rules, standards, and guidelines. If we direct lower-level officials to follow a well-designed set of rules, standards, and guidelines, which includes some formalist elements directing them to ignore some considerations relevant to an accurate all-things-considered judgment, they will make a total of more correct decisions even when we subtract the new mistakes the formalist rule produces.[33]

FORMALISM AWAY FROM THE COURTS

The defense of formalism turns crucially on the fact that the person devising the set of rules, standards, and guidelines stands in a supervisory relation to other actors. Otherwise formalism could induce more errors than it eliminates. Perhaps judges will improve the system's overall performance when they tell other actors to follow the formalist approach, "Consider only text and purposes, but not consequences and practical reality." This defense of formalism is unavailable when the decision-maker is not articulating a set of rules, standards, and guidelines for other decision-makers to follow.

Consider in this connection the proposition that the Framers stand in the appropriate relation to contemporary decision-makers. That is, they specified a set of formalist rules for today's decision-makers to follow because they concluded that the public good would be maximized if decision-makers were barred from making all-things-considered judgments. One difficulty should immediately be apparent: How can the Framers guarantee that today's decision-makers will in fact comply with their formalist directives? Judges supervising police officers may ensure compliance by reviewing their actions, but the Framers cannot act similarly.

More important, the formalist defense actually assumes its conclusion. Recall that a formalist judge decides that she would maximize the public good, *as she understands it*, by issuing and enforcing formalist directives. Return to the question you face as a senator. You have decided that the public good, *as you understand it*, will be maximized by your making an all-things-considered judgment. You have no reason, other than the "James Madison was a smart guy" dodge, to accept the (asserted) Framers' judgment.

You understand the value of directives to follow only text and purposes. The very fact that the Supreme Court has articulated such directives in other contexts reflects the justices' determination that you, among other lower-level officials, are less adept at making all-things-considered judgments than the justices are. Two things naturally occur to you, however. First, on the assumption that there will be no judicial review, no one else is ever going to make an all-things-considered judgment. Your all-things-considered judgment may in fact be worse than the justices', but you are the only one who is in a position to make any such judgment at all. Because formalist approaches can induce errors, you have to worry that, if you rely only on text and purposes to override your all-things-considered judgment, you will be making one of those induced errors.

Second, and more important, you do not have to share the justices' evaluation of your abilities relative to theirs, as we saw in chapter 1's discussion of the Religious Freedom Restoration Act. They may think that they are more adept than you are; that is hardly surprising. You may think, in contrast, that their evaluations of relative abilities are shaped by their own self-interest and, more generously, by their isolation from problems of making a wide range of decisions about public policy with constitutional overtones in a pluralist society. The fact that they think they are more adept than you are is of course a datum for you to take into account, but it is hardly conclusive for you—and, I should add, for anyone else in the polity—on the question.

Now shift attention from your problem as a senator to the problems faced by police officers daily. Suppose a police officer believes that the Supreme Court's decision in *Arizona v. Hicks*[34] is as silly as they come. Lawfully present in a suspect's apartment, the officer shifts a television set around to see its registration number. *Hicks* says that this violates the Fourth Amendment. Are the arguments I have made available to the officer as well?[35]

The first point to note is that I have insisted that the decision-maker act conscientiously.[36] That includes serious deliberation on the Constitution's purposes and, particularly, on the possibility that the decision-maker's judgment may be distorted by the pressures of the moment.[37] The officer *may* engage in such deliberation. Like the senator skeptical about the justices' ability to appreciate how contemporary politics actually operates, the officer may be skeptical about the ability of Supreme Court justices removed from the day-to-day exigencies of law enforcement to assess accurately what the Fourth Amendment's requirements are. Even so, I suspect that many people would themselves be skeptical about the proposition that police officers would in fact act conscientiously. They might cite Justice Robert Jackson's comments on the "often competitive enterprise of ferreting out crime," for example.[38]

Second, all decisions by police officers are ultimately subject to judicial supervision, at least as a matter of constitutional form. An officer who disregards *Hicks* runs the risk that no prosecution will be brought, or that courts will exclude the evidence or reverse any subsequent conviction. The officer will have imposed the costs of being arrested and perhaps prosecuted on someone who ultimately will be released. Surely we can fairly conclude that so acting, with these consequences, is quite imprudent even if the officer has acted in what might abstractly be considered a constitutionally permissible manner in conscientiously concluding that *Hicks* was wrongly decided.

So much for form. What of reality? Suppose the police officer, again acting conscientiously, calculates that the risk of losing a conviction is quite low: Most defendants plead guilty, and many judges—less conscientious than the officer, perhaps—will distort rather than disregard *Hicks* in an effort to save a conviction. As a practical matter, the officer is the final and unreviewable decision-maker. Does the officer act in a constitutionally inappropriate manner if she disregards *Hicks*?

One answer is yes, on the ground that form matters far more than practical reality. I am puzzled about why. One possibility would emphasize that the form at issue here is an aspect of the hierarchical structure of our constitutional system. It would distinguish between the Constitution's structural provisions, which establish the framework for determining what the rules of the game are, and its substantive ones, some of which specify those rules. One might be willing to let decision-makers whose primary charge is setting the rules of the game to decide for themselves what the Constitution's structural provisions mean, while denying similar authority to those charged with administering the rules. That distinction seems to me defensible only on the supposition that the incentive to engage in conscientious deliberation about all the relevant considerations is greater for the rule-designers than for the rule-administrators. For myself, I doubt that that is true.

The other answer is no. Like the senator, the conscientious police officer acts appropriately in disregarding a constitutional provision that, in his or her all-things-considered judgment, obstructs the achievement of the public good. The risk here is twofold. Police officers may too often erroneously think they are conscientious, and so they should be forcefully told by higher authorities that they are to refrain from making such judgments. Or, even if they are conscientious, the independent and effectively unreviewable judgments made by thousands of police officers daily may introduce too much instability into the constitutional system to be tolerable. My personal view is that these risks are great enough to justify rejecting the argument that low-level bureaucrats like police officers should be allowed to make all-things-considered judgments, although I find the question to be quite close.

Finally, we might develop a thought offered by Charles Black a generation ago. Black argued that judges ought not give the same deference to decisions by investigators and prosecutors that they might give to decisions by legislators.[39] The reason goes beyond the question of the scope of judicial review. Decisions by elected legislators have greater democratic justification than decisions by even the most conscientious police officer. A legislator might therefore have a broader authority to make all-things-considered judgments.

FORMALISM AND CHARACTER BUILDING

I suspect that nearly everyone will be uncomfortable with the conclusions I have reached, even though I have sometimes only described competing considerations and suggested how I would resolve the questions without suggesting as well that my resolution is the only sensible one. The senator's problem may seem less bothersome than the one posed by the conscientious police officer, both because the Emoluments Clause seems like a hypertechnical constitutional provision, and because we may think senators more likely to deliberate seriously about the public good than police officers will.[40]

The underlying concerns are serious. To show why, it will help to return to the earlier discussion of constitutions as a way of conserving political energy.

Perhaps we might agree that political energy would be conserved enough if only one constitutional fundamental could be placed on the table during any particular year. But, we might also believe, that would open a can of worms, to use Holmes's phrase. For, after all, why should the Emoluments Clause be this year's candidate for reconsideration rather than, for example, the Constitution's ban on term limits for members of Congress?[41]

This is a slippery slope argument, which comes in several variants.[42] The basic form is of course familiar: You run the risk that you and your colleagues will follow your example in the future if you allow your conscientiously arrived at all-things-considered judgment to override the Constitution's text and purposes today. Although you are convinced that your judgment today is correct, you may worry that next time around your judgment, or your colleagues', might not be as good.[43]

The first variant of the slippery slope dodge focuses on your colleagues. Here the problem you face, on the first level, is simple. You are thinking about forgoing your own best judgment about what should be done because you fear that your colleagues will later use your behavior as to the Mitchell nomination as a precedent for overriding the Constitution's text and purposes when, as a matter of fact, an all-things-considered judgment ought to lead them to follow the text and purposes. The difficulty is that you are going to give something up today with no guarantees that your colleagues will reciprocate when they are again faced with the question of whether to allow their all-things-considered judgments to displace text and purposes.[44] When the time comes and you complain that you voted against Senator Mitchell's confirmation because you thought that such judgments could never displace text and purposes, they can sensibly respond, "But you were wrong." As Michael Stokes Paulsen puts it, "Why play fair and lose when everybody else plays unfairly?"[45]

The second variant of the slippery slope argument focuses on your own actions. You are convinced that you have conscientiously arrived at the best all-things-considered judgment as to Senator Mitchell, but you may fear that next time around, your judgment may not be as reliable as you think it is now. Here too the problem is obvious. When the time comes, you may realize that your judgment is not as reliable, in which case you will not follow it. How are you in a better position *then* to recognize its unreliability if you refrain from acting on what you *today* believe to be a reliable judgment? Or, more likely perhaps, when the time comes you will not realize that your judgment is unreliable. Facing a new issue about which you feel deeply, you may unconsciously overvalue the benefits of disregarding the Constitution's text and purposes in the new context, explaining to yourself that your prior behavior makes such overriding permissible and failing to recognize the distortions of judgment in the present case even though your judgment in the prior one was undistorted. How will the fact that you voted against Senator Mitchell's confirmation today improve your assessment of your judgment next year?

I suspect that if you vote against Senator Mitchell today, and a similar question comes up in the future, you are likely to regard your vote against

Senator Mitchell as a mistake not to be repeated, rather than a precedent to be followed: You may ask yourself, "Why deprive the nation of a valuable public servant twice instead of only once?"

The difficulties with these slippery slope arguments are not conclusive. In one sense, both variants confront the difficulty that action today is designed to induce action tomorrow, with no enforcement mechanism. The slippery slope arguments might explain why you should refrain from voting to confirm Senator Mitchell if you could insert some sort of enforcement into the scheme.

Consider, then, the actions you hope to induce. With respect to your colleagues, you want them to exercise some forbearance, so that they refrain from acting on *their*—to your mind erroneous—all-things-considered judgments. With respect to yourself, you want to enhance your ability to recognize the unreliability of your all-things-considered judgments.

One strategy for inducing those actions is to generate character traits associated with deliberation and forbearance. If your colleagues have such traits, when the time comes they will forbear from acting on their all-things-considered judgments, and if you have such traits, you will have a keen appreciation of the limits of your own judgment. The question then is how can you build such character traits. Perhaps you can do so by modeling them today. That is, you can demonstrate the importance of forbearance to your colleagues by forbearing yourself. They might come to emulate your exemplary behavior. Similarly, you can teach yourself to be cautious about the reliability of your own judgments by refraining from acting on your all-things-considered judgment about Senator Mitchell and the Emoluments Clause—even though you firmly believe today that you have arrived at the right all-things-considered judgment.

I find the character-building account of why you might vote against Senator Mitchell's confirmation despite your best all-things-considered judgment to be the strongest argument available. Jon Elster has identified a serious difficulty with that account. According to Elster, "[s]ome mental . . . states . . . have the property that they can only come about as the by-product of actions undertaken for other ends. They can never, that is, be brought about intelligently or intentionally, because the very attempt to do so precludes the state one is trying to bring about."[46] The character trait of constitutional forbearance might be such a state. You cannot acquire it by trying to acquire it, or by knowingly forbearing. Elster suggests that what he calls "technologies for self-management" can produce these states.[47] Procedural rules that keep you from considering whether to vote for a nominee whose appointment might violate the Emoluments Clause are perhaps an example of such a technology. The question has been put to you nonetheless. If forbearance is a by-product state, you do no good by forbearing in order to build character.

The National Character

We can generalize the character-building argument. Some political scientists who study the Constitution have observed that the people of the United States are in some fundamental sense constituted by our commitment to the thin Constitution.[48] The normative argument for the thin Constitution holds that at the level of national self-definition, not race, not religion, not ethnicity, but a commitment to constitutional principles defines the people of the United States.

Allowing public officials to disregard the Constitution in favor of their conscientious all-things-considered judgments might compromise the people's self-understanding as a people. The slippery slope, that is, is not one in which decision-makers get more and more comfortable with trampling on constitutional rights. Rather, it is one in which the people of the United States lose the only thing that constitutes us as a people: adherence to constitutional principles. If they paid attention, as they should, the people would doubt that you voted for Senator Mitchell's confirmation on the ground that, all things considered, the Emoluments Clause was silly. Rather, they would see you as having acted anti-constitutionally. And acting anti-constitutionally, it might be said, rejects our national identity.[49]

Does acting anti-constitutionally reject the American national identity, constituted as it is by adherence to constitutional principles? Perhaps not. My argument is that we are constituted as a people by the thin Constitution, not the thick one. Rejecting silly constitutional provisions piecemeal[50] does *change* two elements in the people's national identity. Narrowly, it changes the particular constitutional provision at issue. Surely, however, a people constituted by a Constitution without the Emoluments Clause would not be so different from the one constituted by the existing Constitution that they would be denied the fundamental human good of having a connection to a historically embedded political community.

More broadly, rejecting silly constitutional provisions changes our understanding of how constitutional change can permissibly occur. I doubt that even this change implies that the people are no longer constituted by commitment to the Constitution's principles. Rather than seeing the Constitution as embracing a fixed set of principles, we can see it, in terms suggested by law professor Bruce Ackerman, as an "aspiration-creating machine" that allows us to transform ourselves, adopting new principles while preserving those most fundamental to our constitutional identity, the principles of the Declaration and the Preamble. The "we" who exist after the transformation are "the same" as the "we" who existed before, because we will have used the Constitution's forms as the machine for our self-transformation and will have maintained our core commitments nonetheless.

By this point, if not earlier, the argument has taken on a decidedly odd cast. It is too fancy and academic. Imagine a senator who asked what the Emoluments Clause meant, and was told that it meant that rescinding a salary increase could not solve the Mitchell problem. I am reasonably confident that for nearly all senators that would be the end of the matter. How could they vote for Senator Mitchell's confirmation after being told that the Emoluments Clause meant that he could not take a seat on the Supreme Court? They and some of their constituents might feel that they would be breaking the faith that was embodied in their oath of office. Other constituents might not even pay attention, of course, or think that getting Senator Mitchell confirmed was more important than any constitutional technicality. Those constituents have already decided that legislators need not follow the thick Constitution as long as they advance the public good.

But which senators and constituents are being constitutionally conscientious? Suppose the ones who worry even about the thick Constitution are the conscientious ones. Consider a senator who is conscientious in this sense. As my discussion of Abraham Lincoln and Ronald Reagan in chapter 1 suggested, not every political actor has the talent and capacity to lead the American people to transform our constitutional self-understanding. A senator with the ability to lead such a transformation might appropriately use the vote on Senator Mitchell's confirmation as part of the transformative process. A lesser senator would act inappropriately in pursuing a course for which he or she was not well suited.[51]

THE THIN CONSTITUTION AND THE NATIONAL CHARACTER

In this light one might re-construe the entire argument in constitutionalist terms. As a senator you occupy the position you do because of the Constitution considered as a document creating a frame of government. That document licenses you to act as you do, even to the point of disregarding other constitutional provisions. At least, one might think, it does so when you act conscientiously. Here we can give a precise, and constitutional, definition of acting conscientiously: You do so when your all-things-considered judgments are guided by constitutional principles as articulated in the Preamble and the Declaration of Independence. In short, it is consistent with the entire Constitution for you to vote to confirm Senator Mitchell's appointment, despite your best understanding of the most directly applicable constitutional provision if you conclude that confirming Senator Mitchell's nomination would "establish Justice[,] . . . promote the general Welfare, and secure the Blessings of Liberty to . . . posterity," within a framework committed to the principles of equality and inalienable rights embodied in the Declaration of Independence.

The role of the thin Constitution in this argument shows why a Senator who disregards the Emoluments Clause is not acting in a way inconsistent with the rule of law. According to one formulation, an "official's . . . decision to do something other than what the law requires because he believes that action would be more just, is tantamount to abandoning the very idea of law— namely, the very idea of the community taking a position on an issue on which its members disagree."[52] The Senator, however, would be doing *what the law requires*—what is consistent with the thin Constitution even though it is inconsistent with the Emoluments Clause.

Would this introduce an undesirable instability into our fundamental law? As things now stand, the Constitution is what a majority of the Supreme Court says it is—for the moment. This too can introduce instability as the Court's composition changes. The position I have developed would make the Constitution what a majority of Congress says it is. But congressional processes are complex. As a practical matter, for example, nearly all national laws today pass by huge margins, because forty senators can block enactment, and thirty-four can sustain a presidential veto. The difficulty of getting laws passed unless they have really strong support means that making our fundamental law depend on what Congress enacts would almost certainly be no more unstable than making it depend on what five justices say.

Perhaps, however, this is simply the ultimate dodge. The senator's problem has been dissolved by reducing the entire Constitution to the Preamble and the Declaration. This raises two questions. The less difficult is this: What is the point of having specific constitutional provisions if the Constitution, when properly interpreted, consists simply of the command to promote the general welfare? Perhaps the specific provisions function as default rules written by particularly intelligent people, and so ought to be followed unless it seems worth expending the political energy to displace those rules, in circumstances where, on reflection, the default rules appear to obstruct the promotion of the general welfare.

The more serious difficulty is this: This view of the Constitution may deprive it of any important connection to the people of the United States who are constituted by it. That is, a conscientious decision-maker in *any* constitutional system would take promoting the general welfare to be his or her aim. Conscientiousness in a legislator might be defined in part precisely by the legislator's orientation to the general welfare. If being conscientious just means promoting the general welfare, the U.S. Constitution is not at all distinctive, and so cannot provide the important human good of membership in a particular political community.

Here too the Declaration may play an important role. Although historically it is the origin of our nation's constitutional commitments, those
commitments themselves are universal in aspiration. "All men," after all,
were "created equal" and were "endowed by their Creator with certain
inalienable rights." If we see the Constitution and the Declaration working together, we would conclude that the people of the United States are
constituted by our commitment to the realization of universal human
rights, which when realized would render the community defined as "the
people of the United States" politically unimportant. It is not an entirely
unattractive self-understanding.

Chapter Three

THE QUESTION OF CAPABILITY

An Insider's View of Congressional Constitutional Interpretation

Chapter 2 concluded that populist constitutionalism could be defended when talented public officials conscientiously considered the thin Constitution's implications for the policies they sought to advance. But will public officials be conscientious? If we take the Constitution away from the courts, will it be lodged in people whose judgments are trustworthy? We can divide those questions into two parts: Do the officials have the information, training, and talent to take the thin Constitution seriously? Do they have incentives to do so? As the discussion of police officers in chapter 2 suggests, we will get different answers when we ask about different public officials: Members of the executive branch and Congress may have resources available to them that members of local city councils do not, for example. This chapter focuses primarily on Congress, and the arguments I make would have to be modified, and perhaps abandoned, were we to focus on city councils or even state legislatures. After examining why evidence from contemporary congressional behavior might not fairly illuminate the question of Congress's ability to enforce the thin Constitution, I consider whether Congress members have the incentives to protect the rights in the thin Constitution that the courts *do* protect, and whether the courts and Congress really differ so much in their ability to think seriously about the thin Constitution.

Abner Mikva is one of the twentieth century's foremost public servants. Beginning his political career challenging the dominant Democratic machine in Chicago, Judge Mikva served in the Illinois legislature before being elected to the House of Representatives, where he served five terms. President Jimmy Carter appointed Judge Mikva to the United States Court of Appeals in Washington, D.C., the nation's second most important federal court, in 1979. In 1994 Judge Mikva resigned to take up a post in the executive branch as Counsel to the President.

Having seen all three branches from the inside, Judge Mikva is in a position to know how well legislators actually do the job of interpreting the Constitution. He is skeptical, to say the least.[1] At his most generous, he says that Congress treats some constitutional issues as important, but does not give them "top priority." The reasons, according to Judge

Mikva, are institutional and political; in the terms I have introduced, the reasons involve capacity and incentives. Congress is large, "making the process of engaging in complex arguments during a floor debate difficult." Speeches "are designed to get a member's position on the record rather than to initiate a dialogue." Time pressures lead members to pay little attention to statutory details, even though many constitutional issues, some quite technical, lurk in those details. As a result, members rely heavily on others—directions from their party's leadership, what the member's staff says, what lobbyists say. Although many members are lawyers, "they have not kept up-to-date on recent legal developments." The Constitution is designed to limit what the people can accomplish through their representatives, which means that constitutional principles are "generally abstract [and] unpopular." Constitutional principles are not easily reduced to a sound bite that gets a member on television. Finally, Judge Mikva points out, legislators rely on the courts to bail them out if they make a constitutional mistake.

I will suggest later that parts of Judge Mikva's picture are overdrawn, but for now we can use it to explore the question of capacity. It is obviously a pretty depressing picture for someone who would like to think that we can take the Constitution away from the courts. Judge Mikva can paint part of the picture, however, *because* legislators act in the court's shadow. We really cannot know how Congress would perform if the courts exited, if Congress does badly because the courts are on the scene. One who would take the Constitution away from the courts must also deal with the other part of Judge Mikva's picture—the fact that legislators run for election and respond more directly to the immediate political concerns of the moment than to longer term constitutional considerations.

THE JOE McCARTHY PROBLEM

We need to put aside one common observation about legislative capability before we take up a more detailed analysis. Defenders of constitutional interpretation outside the courts always have to respond to the question, "But what about Joe McCarthy?" That question stands for a broader skepticism.

We know that some, perhaps many, legislators not only lack interest in constitutional principles but may even hold them in contempt. How could anyone rely on a Senate with Joseph McCarthy in it to uphold constitutional principles?

Of course some legislators are constitutional fools. It would not be hard, however, to compile a list of Supreme Court justices about whom much the same could be said: James McReynolds, so anti-Semitic that

he broke with the Court's custom in which each justice shakes the hand
of the others, because he could not bring himself to shake Louis Brandeis's
hand; James Byrnes, a devoted segregationist; Charles Whittaker, so
paralyzed by his inability to make decisions that he resigned from the
Court to avoid a serious nervous breakdown. And, because there have
been so many fewer justices than members of Congress, it does not take
a long list to get to the point where the proportion of constitutional fools
on the Supreme Court approaches that in Congress. Supreme Court justices also may serve longer than members of Congress, and because there
are fewer of them at any time, a single justice may be more influential
in the smaller group than a single senator or member of the House of
Representatives.

The Supreme Court at its best is clearly a lot better than Congress at
its worst. But Congress at its best is better than the Court at its worst.
The McCarthy era makes the point. The Supreme Court's response to
McCarthyism was weak, to put it generously. It upheld convictions of
Communist party members for violating federal laws barring advocacy
of revolution, and it upheld the broad outlines of the federal government's
efforts to screen out "security risks" from government employment. True,
in 1957 the Court issued a series of decisions restricting the government's
power to investigate and prosecute subversion. Prominent members of
Congress denounced these "Red Monday" decisions, and the Court soon
beat a dramatic retreat. And this, remember, was the Court presided over
by Earl Warren. McCarthyite excesses were subdued not by judicial chas-
tisement, but by the mobilization of a political elite that found itself under
attack. The Senate itself censured McCarthy when he overreached.

There is a more difficult issue lurking here, however. The Court's illib-
eral decisions during the McCarthy era obviously did not *say* they were
repudiating basic constitutional principles. They said instead that the
challenged practices were consistent with those principles. Indeed, so did
Senator McCarthy. As he saw it, subversion might lead to revolutionary
turmoil and the creation of a Soviet-style totalitarianism; aggressive inves-
tigations of subversion in government and elsewhere were therefore essential to "insure domestic Tranquility . . . and secure the Blessings of Liberty
to . . . our Posterity," just as the Preamble says.

How can we say he was wrong unless we have a vigorous theory of
constitutional interpretation outside the courts? After all, Supreme Court
decisions certainly did not make it clear that Senator McCarthy's constitutional position was indefensible while Senator McCarthy held sway. The
ones that did, came much later—rather too late, we might note, to help
those most directly victimized by McCarthyism. Consider the position of
Senator McCarthy's opponents. They might say, "What you are doing is
unconstitutional, and the Supreme Court will tell you so." When the

Court rejects their constitutional challenges, what can they say?[2] They would be better off to say, "What you are doing is unconstitutional, because here is how we all ought to understand the Constitution." Senator McCarthy's constitutional position is wrong, as they see it; the Supreme Court's constitutional interpretation can be wrong too.

From anyone's point of view, legislatures and the courts are bound to make constitutional mistakes. The real question is whether in general legislatures or courts make more, and more important, constitutional mistakes. And we *must* have a decent theory of constitutional interpretation outside the courts even to be able to pose that as a question.

THE INFLUENCE OF THE JUDICIAL OVERHANG

The judicial overhang distorts what legislators say about the Constitution in several ways.

Promoting Irresponsibility. The National Industrial Recovery Administration was one of the centerpieces of President Franklin Roosevelt's New Deal. It allowed companies in a single industry to get together and develop "codes of fair competition." The theory was that the companies would restrict production and stabilize employment. Economists today think that this is a silly way to deal with the severe unemployment problems the Depression created, but Roosevelt and his advisers liked the idea a lot. In 1935 the Supreme Court held the NIRA act unconstitutional.[3] The Roosevelt administration had proposed a similar act to cover the coal mining industry, which was under consideration by Congress when the Court's decision was announced. Roosevelt wrote a leading member of Congress that Congress should go ahead and pass the law. "Manifestly," Roosevelt wrote, "no one is in a position to give assurance that the proposed act will withstand constitutional tests. . . . But the situation is so urgent and the benefits of the legislation so evident that all doubts should be resolved in favor of the bill, leaving to the courts, in an orderly fashion, the ultimate question of constitutionality."[4] Congress passed the act, and the Court promptly held it unconstitutional.[5]

Over a hundred years ago legal scholar James Bradley Thayer gave a talk at Chicago's World's Fair celebrating Columbus's arrival in the Americas. His talk became what is probably the most influential article about constitutional law ever written.[6] Thayer advocated what we now would call a theory of judicial restraint. He made several arguments. One anticipated what President Roosevelt did. As Thayer understood our constitutional system, legislatures had a duty to consider constitutional questions: "They cannot act" without making a decision about constitutionality. Legislatures actually "felt little responsibility" to consider constitutional questions because they relied on the courts to bail them out of any diffi-

culties they got into. Judicial review tends "to drive out questions of justice and right, and to fill the mind[s] of legislators with thoughts of mere
legality. . . . And moreover, they have felt little responsibility; if we are
wrong, they say, the courts will correct it." But, Thayer believed, courts
actually did not do that very often; they were, in his terms, "but a broken
reed." The result was a system of constitutional irresponsibility, in which
legislators deferred constitutional questions to the courts, which did not
decide them.

Thayer may have been wrong about the last point in 1893, and his
observation about the courts as a weak reed may not hold true today.[7]
But Roosevelt's letter shows how the judicial overhang can deflect legislators from considering constitutional questions.

These concerns make it particularly difficult to use examples from today's legislatures to show that they ignore important constitutional concerns as they go about their jobs.[8] Legislators may define their jobs as
excluding consideration of the Constitution precisely because the courts
are there. The judicial overhang may make the Constitution outside the
courts worse than it might be.

Distorting Legislation. If legislators do pay attention to the Constitution *inside* the courts, they may produce unsatisfactory laws—and not
merely because legislators are not conversant with recent constitutional
developments.[9] Los Angeles's airport commission had the courts in mind
when it adopted a regulation barring all "First Amendment activities"
from the airport. Properly observing that this would stop people from
selling newspapers or even talking to friends, the courts held the regulation unconstitutional.[10] This is a silly regulation, but it resulted from concern about the courts, not from thinking about policy: The commission
simply wanted to stop people from aggressively soliciting travelers for
contributions. The airport commission would have done a better job if
its lawyer had told it, "Just figure out the most sensible policy you can,
and don't worry about what the courts will do."

A more instructive example comes from Congress's response to the Supreme Court's decision striking down a Texas law banning flag-burning
as a method of protest.[11] According to the Court's free speech doctrine,
governments cannot ban speech because of the speech's "communicative
impact" or because they seek to promote some social goal by the very act
of suppressing speech. Texas's anti-flag-burning statute made it illegal to
burn a flag if doing so would cause "serious offense," which is a communicative impact. And, the Court said, Texas was attempting to promote
the social goal of preserving the flag as a symbol of national unity in the
only way it could, by banning speech that impaired the value of flags as
such a symbol.

The Court's opinion suggested, however, that a different statute might be constitutional. If a legislature banned flag-burning to preserve "the physical integrity of the flag," it would not be responding to a flag-burning's communicative impact, nor would it be suppressing speech because the speech interfered with the message the legislature thought the flag should send.

The Court's decision provoked a national outpouring of sentiment to do something. President George Bush proposed a constitutional amendment to authorize anti-flag-burning laws. To defuse the political issue the president's proposal created, Democratic members of Congress proposed a new federal law that, they asserted, would fit within the Court's decision. It would protect the flag's physical integrity by making it an offense to mutilate, deface, physically defile, or burn a United States flag.[12] They obtained opinions from prominent liberal constitutional scholars that, to put the best face on them, asserted that the claim that the new statute might survive judicial review was not frivolous.[13]

When a challenge to this statute reached the Court, Justice William Brennan again wrote for a majority finding the statute unconstitutional.[14] The act protected the flag's physical integrity, but the reason it did so, according to the Court, was not because there was something special about maintaining the flag as a piece of cloth, but because the government still wanted to preserve the flag as a symbol of the Nation: "[T]he mere destruction or disfigurement of a particular physical manifestation of the symbol . . . does not diminish or otherwise affect the symbol itself in any way. . . . Rather, the Government's desire to preserve the flag as a symbol for certain national ideals is implicated 'only when a person's treatment of the flag communicates [a] message' to others that is inconsistent with those ideals." The government's *interest*, that is, remained related to speech.

The federal Flag Protection Act was a bad law, but not (simply) because the Supreme Court held it unconstitutional, or because it was inconsistent with free speech principles—a distinction, note, that only someone who rejects judicial supremacy can make. The Flag Protection Act was a bad law as well because it had to be written in a way that its sponsors could credibly claim would satisfy the Supreme Court, but writing it that way meant that the statute had almost nothing to do with what its supporters thought a flag protection law ought to do.[15] As the Court understood all along, people who dislike flag-burning do so because they disagree with the message that flag-burning sends. It does nobody any good to pretend that people care about the flag's "physical integrity" divorced from the flag's meaning.

In dealing with flag-burning, the issue we as a people have to confront is whether the flag's symbolic value is so great that we should protect it

even at some cost to the protection of free expression. The Court's decisions made it nearly impossible for Congress to face that issue. In this
sense, President Bush's proposal of a constitutional amendment was more
consistent with a populist constitutional law than Congress's response.[16]
The judicial overhang made the amendment process the only way we
could discuss the issue that really mattered.

The flag-burning episode shows how hard it is to spell out exactly how
the judicial overhang *distorts* legislation. After all, the episode may show
only that Congress wanted to pass an unconstitutional statute, which it
is not supposed to do. The distortion, however, is that the judicial overhang led Congress to pursue a course that could not accomplish what its
members, and the American people, apparently wanted—an effective law
against flag-burning.[17]

Distorting Legislative Discussion (even if it does not distort the laws
that result). Courts may design some doctrines to reflect their sense of
their own limited abilities, not to reflect directly substantive constitutional
values.[18] A key term here is *scrutiny*. When you see it, you should know
that the courts are talking about themselves, and that it would be a mistake for legislators to think about the constitutional implications of what
they were about to do in the same terms.

The Court gives some laws what it calls *strict scrutiny*. These laws,
according to the Court, have to be "narrowly tailored" to serve "important" or "compelling" government purposes. The Court will uphold
other laws, however, if they satisfy a lower level of scrutiny, which the
Court calls *minimal rationality* review. Social welfare laws are a good
example of laws that get low-level scrutiny. When a legislature designs
public assistance schemes, it has to draw lines between different possible
beneficiaries, if only to ensure that the public assistance budget does not
spiral out of control. In the late 1960s some states tried to limit their
welfare budgets by placing caps on what any family would receive. For
example, Maryland set a "standard of need" for every recipient of public
assistance. It also set a cap on what any single family could receive, no
matter how large was its need as calculated by adding up the "standard
of need" for all the family members. Recipients challenged this as an unconstitutional discrimination between small and large families. The Court
rejected the challenge.[19] "In the area of economics and social welfare,"
the Court wrote, "a State does not violate the Equal Protection Clause
merely because the classifications made by its laws are imperfect. If the
classification has some 'reasonable basis,' it does not offend the . . .
Constitution."

The Court's reason for giving low-level scrutiny to social and economic
laws is that anything more would convert the Court into a general supervisor of the wisdom of everything a legislature enacts. No classifications are

perfect enough to avoid the challenge that some more "narrowly tailored" rule could have done almost all the state wanted. The Court could force legislatures to enact only those laws the courts thought good enough by insisting on "narrow tailoring."

The reason the word *scrutiny* matters is that it signals that we are concerned with something special about courts. It says, "Here's how *we*—the courts—are going to look at what *you*—the legislature—do." It would not make much sense for a legislator to think in those terms.

Suppose Congress is considering a health care reform proposal to finance cancer treatments. Lots of effective cancer treatments are covered. But, out of concern to keep the program's cost within budget limits, the proposal does not cover a certain type of bone marrow transplant to treat leukemia, even though that is the only effective treatment for a particular form of leukemia. A member offers an amendment to include these treatments in the plan, arguing that it is unfair—inconsistent with our ideas of equal treatment, as expressed in the Equal Protection Clause and so part of the thin Constitution—to exclude this treatment when so many others are included.

There is no question about what would happen if the case ever came to court. The courts, applying low-level scrutiny to this social-economic legislation, would find no constitutional violation. And yet it seems quite senseless for a member of Congress to respond to the proposed amendment by saying, "Excluding the treatment is minimally rational, so we are going to exclude it." The minimal-rationality standard is one the courts have devised for themselves. The question for Congress cannot be whether the exclusion is "merely rational." It must be whether the exclusion in fact satisfies our sense of fairness.[20]

This example illustrates a broader point. As we saw in chapter 2, some defenses of judicial review rely on formalist doctrines so that courts can control officials who, the judges believe, are less capable than the judges themselves. That approach makes sense to the judges, but it should not make sense to the officials. A legislator should be able to say, "Who are they to tell me that I'm no good at my job?" Where the court's constitutional interpretation is shaped by a formalist judgment that legislators are not as good as judges at determining what the Constitution means, a legislator would only reinforce that judgment by thinking that the Constitution itself required the doctrines the judges develop.

Judge Mikva thinks that the judges are right. Congress does not have enough expertise to do a decent job of interpreting the thin Constitution. We could work out ways to improve the legislature. Judge Frank Easterbrook has noted that few people could credibly say that the executive branch did not do a technically competent job of interpreting the Constitution.[21] The reason is simple: The executive branch has several important

institutions devoted to constitutional interpretation, most notably the So-
licitor General's office and the Office of Legal Counsel in the Department
of Justice. We could easily improve legislative performance by creating
similar institutions. State governments in Australia typically have a parliamentary committee to examine the constitutionality of proposed legislation; in Belgium the legislative section of the Council of State advises parliament on the constitutionality of proposed laws. Similar institutions
in the United States might help legislators understand constitutional
doctrine.[22]

Some of the things Judge Mikva criticizes Congress for—that members
take direction from others, for example—might be understood as ways
in which members become expert enough to interpret the thin Constitution.[23] Even today, Congress regularly holds hearings at which experts
testify on the constitutionality of proposed legislation. Having testified at
such hearings, I confess to some puzzlement at their point, but staff members tell me that the testimony matters to their employers. Of course,
sometimes the testimony is cast in ultimately unhelpful terms drawn from
Supreme Court opinions. The lawyers testify that the proposal is or is not
narrowly tailored, does or does not involve a viewpoint-based restriction
on speech, and the like. But liberated from the judicial overhang, testimony might make Congress as able as the courts to interpret the thin
Constitution.[24] Congressional hearings on the Religious Freedom Restoration Act exposed members of Congress to substantial constitutional arguments supporting the statute, made by leading constitutional scholars.
The Supreme Court disagreed with the constitutional interpretation advanced by those scholars and accepted by Congress, but that in itself does
not establish the Court's superior capacity, only its supremacy in the constitutional world we presently inhabit.

We might also challenge the claim that judges are better at interpreting
the thin Constitution than others because of their technical training and
expertise. According to law professor Charles Black, "Human-rights
claims are made *in the name of the law,* as the outcome of *reasoning from
commitment*; judges are practiced in this kind of reasoning, and some of
them are expert at it." But, Black says, members of Congress and the
president are neither practiced nor expert in it.[25] Perhaps it is true that
judges reason from commitment all of the time, although not always
about human rights, but it would be silly to claim that members of Congress never do. The question, once again, is whether members of Congress
do so often enough, and whether they do so well enough when they do.
And, again, people reasoning from commitment about the thin Constitution may disagree about its meaning without demonstrating their lack of
attachment to its principles: That the Supreme Court held RFRA unconstitutional establishes absolutely nothing about Congress's ability to de-

velop constitutional interpretations that adherents of the thin Constitution ought to accept.

Misleading Legislators. Legislators may think that they ought to reproduce in the halls of Congress the discussions that go on at the Supreme Court. They are likely to do that badly: As Judge Mikva points out, not enough are lawyers, and they do not have time to keep up with the Court. Two examples from the modern Supreme Court nomination process illustrate the problem, but also suggest a different perspective on what legislators should do when they talk about the Constitution.

Members of the Senate Judiciary Committee routinely press nominees for their views on controversial issues, and the nominees now routinely resist providing much in response. Sometimes the exchanges do have content, but the content is different from a replication of judicial doctrine. Discussing the constitutional limits on government regulation of speech, for example, nominee Judge Robert Bork and Senator Arlen Specter referred to two Supreme Court tests for determining when a speech restriction violates the Constitution: the *Brandenburg* test and the clear-and-present-danger test.[26] Senator Specter found a speech in which Judge Bork treated the tests as the same, and when Judge Bork tried to explain why he thought the tests were different, Senator Specter jumped on him for changing his position.

Specialists in free speech law would say that Bork was right at the hearings and wrong in his earlier speech. Justice Oliver Wendell Holmes created the clear-and-present-danger test in upholding convictions for interfering with the draft during World War I; the defendants had circulated a leaflet denouncing the draft and the War as serving "Wall Street's chosen few."[27] The question, Holmes said, was "whether the words used are used in such circumstances and are of such a nature as to create a clear and present danger that they will bring about the substantive evils that Congress has a right to prevent. It is a question of proximity and degree." Later applications of the clear-and-present-danger test suggested that it was not a terribly stringent one, at least when the "substantive evils" were grave. Upholding the convictions of leaders of the Communist party in 1951, for example, Chief Justice Fred Vinson said that the test was: "whether the gravity of the 'evil,' discounted by its improbability, justifies such invasion of free speech as is necessary to avoid the danger."[28]

Free speech scholars came to think over the next few decades that the clear-and-present-danger test, at least as the Court understood it, did not provide enough protection to speech: Prosecutors, juries, and judges were likely to succumb to the pressures of their immediate circumstances to exaggerate the gravity of the evils a speech posed, or to overestimate the likelihood that the speech would bring about those evils. When the Court decided *Brandenburg v. Ohio* in 1969, those scholars thought the Court had tightened the standard. According to *Brandenburg*, the free speech test was that the state could not prohibit advocacy of the use of law violation "except where such advocacy is directed to inciting or producing imminent lawless action and is likely to incite or produce such action."

Free speech scholars believe that the *Brandenburg* approach differs from the clear-and-present-danger test in two ways. Stressing imminence seems to eliminate the possibility of "discounting" future dangers as the Court allowed in the Communist party case. And *Brandenburg* seems to focus more closely on the precise words the speaker uses than on the possible effects of the words: The speaker must use words that are fairly described as "inciting" law breaking.

Judge Bork was unable to explain, and Senator Specter unable to understand, these differences between *Brandenburg* and the classic clear-and-present-danger test. And perhaps there is nothing wrong with that. After all, neither was writing a judicial opinion, although Judge Bork hoped to do so soon. Instead, they were discussing the Constitution in front of the American people. We might see them as attempting to educate the people about the Constitution, which is different from attempting to educate the people about what the Supreme Court said the Constitution means. In a sense, they were *constructing* the First Amendment for public edification, not construing it. To criticize them for misunderstanding the Court's doctrine is itself to misunderstand the activity in which they were engaged.

A similar construction occurred in perhaps the most brilliant rhetorical move made in recent nomination controversies. The Supreme Court's abortion decisions have been the target of conservative criticism since they were announced in 1973. The Reagan administration's Justice Department wanted to overrule them. By 1987 the administration believed it could count four votes on the Court to overrule *Roe v. Wade*: Chief Justice William Rehnquist and Justice Byron White, who had dissented from *Roe*, and Reagan appointees Sandra Day O'Connor and Antonin Scalia. When Justice Lewis F. Powell retired in 1987, the administration saw its chance, and nominated Robert Bork.

Bork opposed *Roe*, but he also was a severe critic of an earlier decision, *Griswold v. Connecticut*, in which the Court found that a statute making it a crime to use contraceptives violated a constitutional right to privacy.[29] Like other distinguished constitutionalists such as Justice Hugo Black, Bork wondered where in the Constitution you could find a right to privacy. A reasonable question—for a legal academic. The political leaders opposing Bork's nomination appreciated that the public clearly regarded *Griswold* as unassailably correct by 1987. They made his opposition to *Griswold* a focus of their attack because they could not expect nearly as much public support for a direct challenge to Bork's position on the abortion cases. They managed to portray Bork, not entirely inaccurately, as an opponent of a constitutional right to privacy, without explaining clearly that he and the Supreme Court as well saw a tight connection between the right to privacy protected in *Griswold* and the abortion decisions.

Bork's nomination failed, and everyone learned the lesson. You had to support a constitutional right to privacy no matter what, and you could not say what you thought the connection was between privacy and abortion. It was a stunningly successful move on the part of abortion rights advocates.

Note, however, exactly what kind of success it was. One-time Yale law school dean Eugene Rostow wrote that the Court "is, among other things, an educational body, and the Justices are inevitably teachers in a vital national seminar."[30] The Bork nomination hearings, and some later ones, have been perhaps an even better seminar. The public has learned about the Constitution as it has listened to these nomination hearings—even though the learning took some time, and even though the public learned something different from what the Supreme Court was actually saying.

More generally, legislators can define the thin Constitution for the public as they examine judicial nominees. The treatment of the right of privacy in successive nomination hearings has taught the people that our constitutional rights are not confined to those specified in the document's text. And in doing so the hearings gave a firmer basis to such rights than the Court's own decisions had. It would be a mistake to think that the public's definitions have to be the same as the ones the Court offers, or even the same as the ones the nominees offer once they are placed on the Court. We should see the senators as constructing the thin Constitution, not as attempting to explore the Supreme Court's Constitution.

The Problem of Legislators' Incentives

Perhaps, then, we have less reason to rely on concerns about Congress's actual performance than we might initially think. But what about Congress's incentives? Judge Mikva argued that legislators would not take the Constitution seriously because they focused on the short run, on what it would take to get reelected, while the Constitution provides a structure for long-term policy-making.[31]

Here we have to sort out a number of difficulties. The first is straightforward. Students of Congress seem to agree that members are not exclusively concerned with reelection. They are interested in making good public policy, they want to make a difference, and they want respect from other members, which they can earn by demonstrating a sound grasp of the issues they face. These motives may not enhance the legislator's chance of reelection, but they may nonetheless lead a legislator to pay attention to constitutional values.

Even more, these motivations may sometimes appeal to voters, which gives legislators a *political* incentive to be serious about the Constitution. Candidates for office, and representatives once elected, would want to take constitutional rights seriously when the people themselves care deeply about constitutional rights.

Consider RFRA once again. As members of Congress saw things, constitutional values were at stake. The Court's peyote decision unjustifiably licensed legislative excesses that unfairly burdened religious practices. No doubt the coalition that lobbied to get RFRA adopted showed members that there were political advantages to advancing these constitutional values. On this dimension, then, Congress's incentives seem to work as the defender of populist constitutional law would hope.[32]

I doubt that anyone would claim that today's politicians *generally* have the incentives necessary to support the idea of populist constitutional law. Some do, of course: Some politicians satisfy their constituents' desires on lots of issues, thereby freeing up space for the representatives to act on their consciences; others gain political stature, an asset they can use to satisfy their constituents' desires on other issues, by getting a reputation as a person who takes the Constitution seriously. But, as a general matter, concern for the Constitution probably ranks relatively low in most politicians' calculations today.

Recall, however, the argument that this situation may have arisen in part *because of* judicial review. Neither the people nor their representatives have to take the Constitution seriously because they know—or believe—that the courts will. Political calculations might change if people knew that they were responsible for the Constitution.

The skeptic might reply that voters will not systematically care about the Constitution. Voters focus on the short-term: how the economy is doing, what the candidates promise to do in the next two years. We have constitutional rights, in contrast, because we worry that what we think we want in the short run is inconsistent with what we really want in the long run.[33] In a phrase familiar to constitutional scholars, the Constitution is an appeal from the people drunk (the people acting under the influence of short-term considerations) to the people sober (the people acting on their understanding of their deeper long-term interests).

Under the influence of a notorious bombing, for example, the people might support aggressive antiterrorist measures that violate constitutional rights, only to wake up a few years later to discover that they actually wanted to be protected from the government at least as much as they wanted to be protected from terrorists. A constitution, the skeptic might argue, is designed to keep us from doing things we would regret in the morning. But politicians will not have incentives to avoid constitutional violations precisely because we want the antiterrorist measures in the short run.

There is a very tricky question lurking here about spelling out exactly what it means to say that voters' long-term preferences differ from their short-run ones.[34] After all, when the people were thinking about adopting the antiterrorist measures, they surely "knew" that the statutes conflicted with some constitutional provisions. They decided that, as far as they were concerned at the moment, they preferred safety to constitutional rights. A few years later the people may have reversed their priorities. We might be able to say the new preferences are somehow "deeper" or more deserving of respect than the old ones if the new preferences reflected concerns arising out of the thin Constitution while the old ones did not. But, as we have seen, the asserted conflict between privacy and civic order arises *within* the thin Constitution.

One reason for giving the later preferences priority might be this: As a theoretical matter, the people can insist that the antiterrorist measures be repealed once their preferences have changed. In practice, however, it is much harder to repeal laws than enact them. We may find it difficult to change the laws we enact while drunk once we sober up. Nothing in this response requires that we give up on the idea of populist constitutional law. All we have to do is figure out ways to even the balance, so that it is no harder to repeal laws than to enact them. We could surely develop procedural devices to put repeal of constitutionally questionable laws on a fast track.

The skeptic might rely on the work of Yale law professor Bruce Ackerman to provide another reason for preferring the people's preferences as expressed—years ago, of course—in the Constitution to their preferences expressed in today's statutes.[35] Ackerman says that sometimes the people experience what he calls constitutional moments, in which a mobilized public reflects deeply and deliberately on fundamental questions of social order. He contrasts constitutional moments with ordinary politics. The skeptic might argue that the people's preferences during constitutional moments are better than their preferences during ordinary politics.[36] Legislators dealing with the daily grind of politics and responding to interest-group pressures are less likely to develop a decent set of rules than the mobilized people during a constitutional moment, when concern for fundamental questions allows people to extract themselves from their immediate circumstances.

The difficulty with this argument is that it shows why judgments made during times of high political mobilization and deliberation about fundamentals might be *different* from judgments made in ordinary politics, but not why they are better. Consider two examples.

Funding Artists. Law professor John Garvey's study of the judicial and congressional response to controversies over awarding federal money to support controversial artists led him to conclude that the courts and Congress dealt with the problem in different ways: "In framing the issues, Congress is more likely to personalize—to think about the equal treatment of groups rather than the equality of ideas. And in choosing a solution, Congress is more likely to compromise—to choose a kind of halfway house between censorship and laissez-faire."[37] I doubt that one could mount a strong challenge to Congress's compromises on the ground that they were constitutionally irresponsible—wrong perhaps, according to some normative criterion, but not irresponsible.

Controlling the Police. Today's conservatives argue that expansive interpretation of the Constitution's regulations of police conduct—restrictions on questioning, searches, and arrests—make middle-class liberals feel good while leaving inner-city residents subject to the depredations of criminals. Liberals respond that constitutional limits are necessary to protect everyone, including inner-city residents, from the depredations of the police themselves. I do not think it necessary here to decide which of these conflicting views is correct. My point in raising the example is that it seems quite wrong to think that a decision about regulating police conduct made in the abstract is likely to be better than one made while aware of what conditions in today's inner cities and police cars are like.

Legislators in ordinary politics are deeply embedded in the realities of public life. Interest groups make them acutely aware of the impact their proposals will have on daily life. They can make intensely practical judgments about the likely outcomes of policy proposals. Judge Mikva observed that constitutional rights are abstract and general. But there are costs to abstraction too. When the people during constitutional moments make abstract decisions, they are unaware of how their choices will actually affect people. Acting in ignorance they may make mistakes about the costs and benefits of the rights they create, or may misunderstand how those costs and benefits will be distributed.

Judgments in ordinary politics can be distorted by special interest group pressures or by excessive self-interest. Judgments made during constitutional moments may be distorted as well, by excessive enthusiasm at the prospect of developing rational rules that will permanently solve fundamental problems of social order. The general point is that decisions made in constitutional moments are different from, but not necessarily better than, decisions made during ordinary politics.

The skeptic might offer a variant of the "constitutional moments" argument. The variant does not claim that abstract decisions are better than concrete ones. Quite the contrary: Concrete decisions made with full awareness of their background and effects are better than ones made divorced from that awareness. But, the argument then goes, such concrete decisions are exactly what we get from courts deciding cases. A case is a real human situation in which someone has been hurt; the courts can examine the situation in all its detail and figure out what the best response is. Legislatures, in contrast, deal with general issues.

This contrast between courts and legislatures is so overstated as to be worthless for someone trying to argue against a populist constitutional law that focuses on democratic and legislative responsibility for enforcing the thin Constitution. Legislatures respond to real human problems too. Consider the origins of what is widely known as Megan's Law, requiring disclosure to the community that a convicted sex offender is living in their midst. The New Jersey legislature, and Congress soon after, responded to the abduction and murder of a child by a convicted sex offender. Similarly, the popular "three strikes and you're out" laws originated with the kidnapping and murder of Polly Klass in California. People can disagree about whether these laws are good ones, or whether they are constitutional: Critics would say that they show the inadequacy of law-making by anecdote. They show, however, that legislatures can respond to case-specific prodding just as courts do.

And courts can respond to general, abstract concerns just as legislatures do. Faced with a mountain of claims for illness due to working with asbestos, for example, the courts devised quite elaborate procedures to sort out the claims. Modern procedural devices, according to one scholar, sometimes convert court hearings into versions of a modern town meeting.[38]

Probably the best modern example of a court navigating between the abstract and the particular is the majority opinion in *DeShaney v. Winnebago County Department of Social Services.*[39] Joshua DeShaney's parents were divorced when he was one year old, and his father Randy got custody. When Joshua was three, social workers started getting information that Randy was beating Joshua. They noted the reports, and observed some suspicious injuries, but otherwise did nothing. When Joshua was four, Randy beat him so severely that Joshua had permanent brain injuries that left him profoundly retarded. Joshua's mother sued the social work agency on Joshua's behalf, asserting that the state agency's failure to protect Joshua from Randy deprived Joshua of his liberty in violation of the Constitution.

Chief Justice Rehnquist's opinion for the Court acknowledged that "[j]udges and lawyers, like other humans, are moved by natural sympathy in a case like this to find a way for Joshua and his mother to receive adequate compensation for the grievous harm inflicted upon them." But, the Chief Justice said, Randy, not the state, had beaten Joshua. Whether children at risk would be better off if Joshua won his case was, according to the Court, a complicated empirical question. Social workers would probably intervene more aggressively when they received information about child abuse if the agency was liable to Joshua. Then they would "be met with charges of improperly intruding into the parent-child relationship," charges that would be well-founded when the information was actually inaccurate or the child less at risk from his or her parents than he or she would be if removed from their custody.

Liberals were outraged by the *DeShaney* decision. The decision may be outrageous, but not because it was insensitive to Joshua's plight or the conditions of children at risk. *DeShaney* is wrong, if it is, because the Court's empirical—that is, legislative—assessment was wrong. The case demonstrates, however, that there is no sharp difference between the case-specific decisions courts make and the more general decisions legislatures make.

DISTRUSTING THE PEOPLE

We have been considering a group of *procedural* arguments for skepticism about claims for a populist constitutional law. The arguments are procedural because they focus on how the processes for creating laws and constitutions differ, or on how courts and legislatures have different procedures and capabilities. I have argued that none of the procedural arguments makes much headway.

The obvious next move is to make *substantive* arguments against populist constitutional law. I have suggested that the principles of the Declaration of Independence and the Constitution's Preamble would orient populist constitutional law. The people, that is, would evaluate policy proposals by comparing them with those principles and the Preamble.

But, the substantive skeptic would say, the people just will not do that— not because they cannot, or because their representatives cannot have the right incentives, or because daily life drives out concern for constitutional principles, but because the people of the United States are not really committed to those principles. That may be an unfortunate fact, the skeptic could concede, but a fact nonetheless.

Of course it is a fact that the people are not committed to the Constitution's principles *as the courts have understood them*. If they were, the courts would never find a law unconstitutional. And we can certainly expect mistakes to occur even if the people are committed to the Constitution's principles.[40] The skeptical rejection of populist constitutional law, however, is powerfully antidemocratic.

I doubt that the people of the United States have become so degenerate that the principles of the Declaration of Independence no longer mean anything to us. If the substantive skeptic is right, however, it seems wildly unlikely that the courts can save us from ourselves.

Chapter Four

THE CONSTITUTIONAL LAW OF RELIGION
OUTSIDE THE COURTS

QUESTIONS ABOUT RELIGION IN LEGAL RHETORIC

Columnist Armstrong Williams reported some comments by his friend Justice Clarence Thomas during the summer of 1995. According to Williams, Thomas invoked his religion to explain his position against affirmative action: "You cannot embrace racism to deal with racism. It's not Christian. . . . If I type one word in my word processor in one opinion against [white people], I break God's law. . . . If I write racism into law, then I am in God's eyes no better than they are."[1]

All Justice Thomas said was that his interpretation of the Constitution was consistent with his religious views, which is rather unremarkable. But his comments generated a flurry of responses suggesting that he had done something wrong. The thought seems to be that a public official, particularly a judge, should not connect the Constitution to religion quite so directly. The First Amendment says that "Congress shall make no law respecting an establishment of religion." Many people have come to think that the Amendment simply applies a much broader "nonestablishment" principle that ought to guide, not just Congress, but the president, judges, and voters as well. Justice Thomas's comments, his critics suggested, were inconsistent with this principle.

Law professor Stephen Carter finds such reactions all too prevalent. They reflect a "culture of disbelief," as the title of Carter's widely read book puts it. Although Americans are generally thought to be among the world's most religious people,[2] Carter finds elite culture at best indifferent and at worst hostile to religion.[3] And, Carter argues, that culture is reflected in a constitutional law of religion that sometimes disparages the presence of religious influences on our public life. Others who have sounded Carter's themes suggest that John Rawls, the most prominent contemporary philosopher of liberalism, similarly tries to cleanse public life of religious influences, through his effort to develop liberal principles that all *reasonable* people can agree on; they find Rawls's definition of who is a reasonable person to exclude many who hold deeply felt religious beliefs.[4]

This chapter presents a detailed discussion of these issues as an illustration of how we can talk about how legislators and ordinary citizens should act on the idea that establishments of religion are generally a bad thing because they are inconsistent with the thin Constitution's ideal of equal citizenship. How should a legislator or citizen interested in avoiding establishing a religion go about arguing for public policies that have some relation to religious beliefs? How can legislators, judges, and voters reconcile their religious beliefs with the thin Constitution's nonestablishment principle? In short, what might the Establishment Clause mean once we take it away from the courts?

Supreme Court decisions turn out to help in developing answers to these questions, because the decisions identify some considerations that a principle of nonestablishment outside the courts ought to take into account.[5] Political theorists have framed the issues of concern in this chapter more clearly, because they have been interested in seeing what they can say about how a good citizen in a liberal democracy ought to act. They offer principles of political morality or what political philosopher Robert Audi calls ideals of civic virtue to guide our actions outside the courts.[6] Examining what they have said deepens our understanding of the thin Constitution, particularly by showing how thin its prescriptions really are.

The Role of Purpose in Establishment Clause Cases

Judge Roy Moore of Alabama hung a wooden carving of the Ten Commandments in his courtroom. After a federal court dismissed a lawsuit challenging the practice, Alabama's governor and attorney general went to state court to get a declaration that Judge Moore's practice was constitutional. They were undoubtedly surprised when the state judge said that Judge Moore violated the Establishment Clause.[7]

The state judge relied on a Supreme Court case holding unconstitutional a Kentucky statute requiring the posting of the Ten Commandments in public school classrooms.[8] The Supreme Court found that case so easy that it did not even ask for full briefs. According to the Court, the Kentucky statute was unconstitutional because it had "no secular legislative purpose." Kentucky's legislators might have wanted students to reflect on the moral messages in the Ten Commandments, but that, the Court said, amounted to veneration of sacred texts, a religious exercise.

Lawyers could find reasons to treat Judge Moore's practice differently. A courtroom is not a public school classroom, and perhaps the people in a courtroom would be able to see that the plaque reflected Judge Moore's personal views rather than a government position. After all, no one could reasonably object if Judge Moore hung the carving in his office, even if lawyers and clients sometimes had conferences with the judge in the office.

But people in a courtroom are facing the state's coercive power, which might make posting the Ten Commandments even more dramatically a public religious exercise: Why put them up unless some official was trying to tell you that you ought to comply with them?[9]

Why would posting the Ten Commandments violate the Establishment Clause? The Supreme Court asked whether the practice had any "secular purpose." The word *purpose* is notoriously slippery. Sometimes the Court seems to use it to refer to what public officials had in mind. Judge Moore said that he posted the Ten Commandments "to acknowledge God." His subjective motivation was religious.

The Court seemed to use the same idea of purpose as subjective motivation when it invalidated a Louisiana statute requiring "balanced treatment" of evolution and what the statute called creation-science: If a public high school biology class covered the theory of evolution, it also had to present the theory of creation as a scientific theory. Again the Court found that the statute did not have a secular purpose. It relied in part on statements made by the legislation's sponsors that creation science "embodies the religious belief that a supernatural creator was responsible for the creation of humankind," that "the existence of God was a scientific fact," and that "this whole battle [is] one between God and anti-God forces."

Justice Antonin Scalia dissented in the creation-science case. He criticized the Court for relying on the legislators' subjective motivations. Individual legislators could have had a host of subjective motivations, ranging from "mak[ing] amends with a faction of his party he had alienated" to "settling an old score with a legislator who opposed the bill." If *individual* legislators had varying motivations, what exactly was the *purpose* of the legislature taken as a whole?

These criticisms of relying on subjective motivations really do not apply to Judge Moore. He was a single actor, and he told us exactly what he was trying to accomplish by posting the Ten Commandments. But another criticism of relying on subjective motivations to determine when the Establishment Clause has been violated applies as strongly to Judge Moore as it does to the Louisiana legislators quoted in the creation-science case: There is nothing wrong with a public official having and acting on a religious motivation to support legislation.

We could take up more than a few pages quoting prominent legislators who invoke religious reasons for supporting nearly any piece of legislation, ranging from laws extending capital punishment to more crimes, to laws reforming the welfare system. Supporting the 1964 Civil Rights Act, for example, the exuberant Senator Hubert Humphrey said, "As I have said, the bill has a simple purpose. That purpose is to give fellow citizens—Negroes—the same rights and opportunities that white people take for granted. This is no more than what was preached by the prophets, and by Christ Himself. It is no more than what our Constitution guarantees."

There has to be something wrong with a constitutional doctrine that tells us to be suspicious of laws enacted by legislators whose subjective reasons for supporting the laws were religious. And in fact the best way to understand the Court's decisions does not require us to look at the officials' subjective motivations, although the Court's statements have sometimes been sloppy.

Laws violate the Establishment Clause, the Court says, if they have *no secular* legislative *purpose*. All three of the words I have emphasized are important. To avoid Establishment Clause problems, a law must actually advance some public goal—must improve the world—by secular means. Secular means give people reasons to comply with the law in some way other than by inducing them to hold deep views about the afterlife or about the way the universe is ordered.[10]

The Court's standard is not hard to satisfy, which is why it has rarely invalidated laws because they failed the "purpose" test. True, many legislators will *have* religious reasons for supporting laws across an enormous range, and those reasons will surely play a part in what they do. But across almost that same wide range, there will be secular reasons as well. Religious reasons and secular ones frequently coincide, and when they do the laws that result do not violate the Establishment Clause. In upholding restrictions on public funding of abortions against an Establishment Clause challenge the Court said, obviously correctly, that the mere coincidence of a statute with particular religious beliefs "without more" did not violate the Constitution.[11]

The Declaration of Independence invoked "Laws of Nature and of Nature's God." Thomas Jefferson thought that secular laws (the laws of nature) coincided with religious laws (the laws of Nature's God). In several religious traditions, they do so because God offers secular reasons available to all humans, rather than reasons available only to those who accept God's authority. The views on public policy people in these traditions assert because of their understanding of God's will are consistent with views that ought to be held by people with quite different understandings, including atheists. So, when Justice Thomas cites the Declaration of Independence to support his position on affirmative action,[12] he is implicitly though indirectly offering a secular reason notwithstanding the fact that the Declaration's justification of its principle of equality invokes Nature's God.

If there is a problem with saying that laws are constitutional if they have some secular purpose, it is that the standard is too easy to satisfy. Dissenters in the Kentucky Ten Commandments case and the Louisiana creation-science case thought that both statutes had *some* secular purpose, even if their sponsors had religious motivations. Justice William Rehnquist thought posting the Ten Commandments might teach students about their moral and public responsibilities, because the Ten Commandments "have had a significant secular impact on the development of secular legal codes." Justice Scalia's dissent in the creation-science case noted that the statute's supporters called it an "academic freedom" statute. As he put it, providing balanced treatment might offset the indoctrination of students to believe a contested theory of human development without full consideration of a scientifically supported—and therefore secular—alternative.

Why aren't these good enough secular reasons? Mainly because they are too divorced from social reality. Puritans and others distinguished between the First and Second Tables of the Ten Commandments: The First Table contained purely religious requirements, such as "Thou shalt have no other gods before me," while the Second Table contained religious requirements that were the foundation of secular order, such as "Thou shalt not steal." The Kentucky statute placed the government behind the First Table, as the Supreme Court pointed out. Of course it may be true that both Tables affected the development of secular order. But there are so many other ways of helping school children understand the origins of the purely secular requirements of the Second Table that the claim that posting the Ten Commandments has a secular purpose rings quite hollow.

The creation-science case is harder. As with the Ten Commandments case, a balanced treatment requirement seems an overbroad response to any problem of indoctrination. The most direct response to that problem would be a directive that students should be instructed that the theory of human evolution is just that, a theory, on a par with other provisional theories with which science deals all the time. Second, if balanced treatment is presented as a remedy for indoctrination, the theory of human evolution and the theory of creation must have the same epistemological status. Despite heroic efforts to show that they do, however, the case has not been persuasively made that creation science is the same kind of theory that the theory of human evolution is.[13] The existence of God may be a fact, but it is not a scientific fact, at least as we ordinarily use the word *scientific*. And, if evolution and creation science are different kinds of theory, requiring that one be "balanced" by the other, cannot serve to remedy the problem of indoctrination; rather, students would be indoctrinated into two independent domains rather than one.[14]

But, more important, all this discussion of balanced treatment as a remedy for indoctrination is entirely unrealistic. In the real circumstances of Louisiana in the 1980s, there was in fact no secular justification available for the imposition of the balanced treatment requirement, whatever might be said about such a requirement in the abstract. The Constitution does not place out of bounds laws that result when legislators are actually motivated by religious views, if the laws themselves are independently justifiable by secular moral theories or by secular nonmoral considerations. But the justifications must satisfy a common-sense standard: They must really reflect what a detached—albeit populist—observer of the Kentucky or Louisiana legislatures would say about the public goals the laws advanced when the statutes were enacted.[15]

The Supreme Court's interpretation of the Establishment Clause, then, does not require religious cleansing of political discussion. According to the understanding of the Court's position I have offered, voters and legislators can refer to their religious views to explain their actions, and those references do not in themselves make their actions unconstitutional. All the Supreme Court requires is that there is a secular justification *available* for their actions, even if the legislators do not actually have that justification in mind when they act. Judge Moore's problem is that there does not appear to be a secular justification for posting the Ten Commandments in his courtroom. But Justice Thomas should not have run into trouble for noting the coincidence between his religious views and his interpretation of the Constitution.

RELIGIOUS DISCOURSE IN POLITICAL THEORY

The Supreme Court is not the only place where we interpret the Establishment Clause, of course. We do so as we develop standards for assessing how we ought to go about our ordinary political lives. So, even if Senator Humphrey's reference to the Christian justification for the 1964 Civil Rights Act properly did not lead the Supreme Court to hold it unconstitutional, perhaps he violated a nonestablishment norm that voters, legislators, and judges ought to adhere to. It certainly would have been jarring if a Supreme Court justice wrote an opinion upholding the 1964 Civil Rights Act by explaining that the Act was "no more than what was preached by Christ Himself." Are there some general nonestablishment norms we ought to adhere to? Do they differ for voters, legislators, and judges?

I address these questions by considering the work of Harvard philosopher John Rawls, whose political theory has generated a substantial body of academic commentary on the principles of political morality that ought to guide citizens and legislators even if they should not be enforced by the courts. Rawls is the late twentieth century's leading liberal political philosopher, whose books *A Theory of Justice* and *Political Liberalism* defined the terrain of serious discussion of liberalism as a political philosophy. Historically the idea of separation of church and state has been an important element in such a philosophy, and Rawls's account of liberalism offers a good opportunity to consider what principles of separation ought to regulate our ordinary political activity. This excursion takes us through a complex political theory, but I can state the conclusion at the outset: Rawls's approach, and that of those who have adapted it to the nonestablishment context, ends up describing principles that might regulate what some people ought to do—roughly, people who hold mainstream religious views—but those principles are too demanding for U.S. society as a whole, primarily because they speak only to some people in our religiously diverse society.[16] Adherents of mainstream religions might be persuaded to adopt the principles the theorists describe; religious fundamentalists will not. Yet even fundamentalists may come to understand that prudence, not principle, ought to guide what they do and say if they hope to get society to adopt the policies they prefer. And even if some fundamentalists are politically imprudent, a liberal society guided by a thin Constitution can probably put up with whatever sorts of political actions religious believers take. The thin Constitution's nonestablishment provision is thin indeed.

Political Liberalism begins by noting a simple fact about modern life: We live in a world in which people disagree deeply about "the Good," that is, about the best way for a person to live his or her life. Some of us are religious, some not; some religious people think that government has a duty to aid those in need, others do not; some religious people think that church and state ought to be kept rigidly apart, others do not; and so on, almost endlessly. And these disagreements are *reasonable*: In light of the limits on our ability to discern the Good, many reasonable views of the Good are available to us and each will be held by some.

For Rawls, this fact of pluralism poses a problem for political philosophy: In light of our deep differences about the good, how can we set things up so that we can just get along with each other? Rawls points out that disagreements about the Good have historically been the source of political violence and instability, and that liberalism as a political philosophy aims at guaranteeing stability in the face of deep differences. How can we achieve political stability when we disagree so much? Rawls describes a social process like this:

The Modus Vivendi. Each of us looks around and notices that lots of people disagree with us about things we think fundamental. We all realize that nothing good will come of trying to impose our own views, and that sometimes some very bad things will happen as combat breaks out. So we decide to try to get along by putting aside—for the moment—the things we disagree on. We adopt a *modus vivendi*—literally, a way we can live together. So, for example, we might set aside disagreements about what types of speech government can control or what religious beliefs government can support and concentrate on figuring out how the government can promote economic growth. But we have no principled commitment to free speech or nonestablishment. In principle we are each simply biding our time, awaiting the point when we can forcibly impose our views on others. The *modus vivendi* consists of ideas of free expression, nonestablishment, political participation, and some other minimal requirements for social stability in a world peopled by those with wildly divergent views: We can get along well enough if we live our public lives in accordance with such ideas, even though we think we would all be better off if everyone shared our own particular understanding of the Good.

The Overlapping Consensus. Rawls suggests that we can do better. We start living our public lives according to some purely strategic ideas about free expression, nonestablishment, and the like. We notice that we are getting quite a lot from the stable social order that results. We think about why that happens, and we realize that it happens *because of* those ideas. Then, according to Rawls, we might start thinking about our general belief-systems. And we can *revise* those systems so that they include principles of free expression and nonestablishment. Then, when we look around, we will discover that no matter how much we disagree with others about other things, nearly all of us agree that principles of free expression and nonestablishment are fundamental in everyone's belief-system. At that point, Rawls suggests, we can detach our principled commitments from within our individual belief-systems and convert them into what Rawls calls a free-standing conception of political liberalism. We have developed an overlapping consensus on those principles. From that point on, instead of asking whether a policy is required by or consistent with my individual view of the Good, I ask whether it is required by or consistent with the free-standing principles.[17]

There is a second process leading to the same conclusion. Sometimes, when we look around, we see that we are not entirely at loggerheads with everyone else. For example, some religious believers think that government should stay away from religion because God does not value religious belief resulting from public coercion; other religious believers think that government should stay away from religion because the only real religious beliefs are those that result from individual reflection on a person's place in the universe. Both groups may favor some rough notion of separation of church and state, but for different reasons, each from within their different belief-systems. And, because their reasons for that policy differ, they are likely to disagree about what precise outcomes follow from the policy: One group may think that ceremonial displays of religious symbols do not really coerce religious belief, while the other may think that such displays reflect the improper conclusion that government has any role at all in promoting reflection on religion.

A large number of value-systems in our society contain within themselves commitments to some equally rough ideas about many aspects of the society's basic structure: a rough idea of nonestablishment, a rough idea of free expression, a rough idea that people should have some say in determining the policies that affect them, and the like. We do not agree on some exalted principle of free expression, much less on the precise set of Supreme Court interpretations of the First Amendment. But we do agree that free expression is a good thing. And, importantly, we share that belief because each belief-system contains within itself some idea of free expression.

These shared beliefs let us arrive at a *modus vivendi*. But as time goes on, we realize that we are benefiting a great deal from the resulting stability. Stability and its benefits are always at risk as long as we stand ready to abandon the *modus vivendi* if circumstances turn in our favor. Can we reduce that risk? Again, we think about how we have achieved social stability, and come to understand that it results from the agreement we have that free expression, political participation, and the like are important. And again, we might then revise our own beliefs, converting our rough ideas of free expression and the like into principles of free expression.

What bearing does all this have on whether we can rely on religious reasons to support public policies? Rawls asserts that political liberalism in the West developed in large part out of reflection on the fact that governments' attempts to promote religion had produced enormous instability. So, he claims, people came to include the principle that a society's basic structure should rest on principles that all reasonable people can accept, in the list of free-standing principles of political liberalism. The basic structure must be justifiable by public reason. And public reason, as Rawls defines it, does not include religious argument.

But Rawls's claims about political liberalism are quite limited. Its principles apply, he says, only to a society's basic structure. The architectural metaphor is important. We have a wide range of public policies, about education, public assistance to the needy, capital punishment, and much more. These are erected on the base of our constitutional system, which includes provisions describing how laws get passed and provisions protecting individual rights. For Rawls, the basic structure is even more fundamental than a society's constitution: Some but not all of a constitution's provisions embody the basic structure.

One conclusion follows almost immediately from this construction. Political liberalism may well contain a principle of nonestablishment as an expression of the principle of public reason: Religious beliefs ought not be embedded in a liberal society's basic structure. But the principles of political liberalism are entirely irrelevant once we reach the stage of particular policies.[18] No principles of political liberalism insist on nonestablishment then. People can argue for or against social welfare policies, laws against race discrimination, and capital punishment using everything they have in their belief-systems, including their explicitly religious views. We will still have a stable society if we have a sound basic structure in place, no matter how contentious those issues are.

Rawls's conclusions are limited as well by a key assumption: that people's views are reasonable. In the present context this means that people are open to revising their views when they come to appreciate the benefits they are receiving from the *modus vivendi*.[19] Audi has elaborated a Rawlsian approach that makes a related assumption. Audi describes a "mature" religious believer, who seeks to align his or her beliefs grounded in secular reasons with those grounded in religious belief.[20] The very possibility of achieving such an alignment requires that sometimes the religious reasons be modified. Audi then describes a group of religious beliefs that provide theological reasons to "expect that there will be accessible, adequate, secular reasons for major moral principles."[21] On inspection these theological reasons characterize modern versions of mainstream religions—the kinds of views associated with the churches that constitute the National Council of Churches, the U.S. Roman Catholic church, and many Jewish congregations. But, notably, they do not characterize the beliefs associated with the dynamic evangelical churches whose political activism has provoked much liberal concern about the role of religion in politics.

Audi and law professor Kent Greenawalt use a Rawlsian approach to generate arguments that liberalism does require some restraint in using religious arguments. They distinguish three facets of a citizen's behavior.[22] (1) *Available reasons* are good reasons a person *might* have for supporting some proposed public policy. (2) *Actual reasons* might be called motivations, the reasons, good or bad, a person actually does have for supporting the policy. (3) *Arguments* are the things a person says in attempting to persuade people that the policy ought to be adopted.

Much of what Greenawalt and Audi have to say involves the distinction between motivations and arguments. Greenawalt argues that citizens can *act on* the basis of religious motivations but usually ought to *offer* secular arguments, while Audi argues that citizens ought not even act on the basis of religious motivations. Rawls himself, responding in part to these arguments, has concluded that people can make religious arguments freely, "provided that in due course proper political reasons [i.e., secular reasons] . . . are presented that are sufficient to support" the policy at issue.[23]

Consider first the question of arguments. Audi describes a principle of "secular advocacy," which requires that people offer only secular reasons for adopting the policies they prefer.[24] This principle is quite stringent, and insisting on it sacrifices some important features of political life that even secularists ought to think important.

Consider the citizen who speaks in favor of the abolition of the death penalty and expressly invokes religious convictions as a central part of the argument. The use of religious arguments can serve several functions.[25] A principle of political morality that cautions citizens against making religious arguments sacrifices these functions, and urging people to follow such a principle may give us a worse government overall, even from the point of view of a purely secular person.

Signaling Intensity. Stating that a position rests on such convictions may serve as a signal of the intensity with which the position is held, because for many people religious convictions are deeper than others. Theorists generally agree that intensity is relevant to figuring out the properly democratic outcome, although determining precisely how intensity of preferences should figure in the democratic aggregation of preferences is quite difficult.

Signaling Sincerity. Reliance on religious convictions can signal the sincerity with which the views are held. Perhaps the most striking recent example is Joseph Cardinal Bernardin's presentation of the official Catholic position on abortion as part of a "seamless garment" of Church teachings on many issues.[26] Unlike intensity, sincerity does not seem to be something that a theory of democratic aggregation must take into account. Rather, sincerity cautions other political actors about the kinds of trade-offs that the proponent might accept, and the kinds of overall political programs he or she might work to advance.

Witnessing. A religious person may be compelled by his or her beliefs to witness God's word by making religious arguments. The believer does not expect others to be persuaded by the act of witnessing, or even to modify the policy at issue because the witnessing demonstrates intensity or sincerity that secular people ought to take into account. Rather, the religious person witnesses because he or she can do nothing less.[27]

A secular person might want to make sure that religious people were comfortable in making religious arguments so that policy could be developed in ways that respond to the intensity (and perhaps the sincerity) with which people support or oppose competing policies.[28] Some secularists might think, however, that religious arguments serve different and less attractive secular functions. As law professor Martha Minow puts it, they can signal membership and exclusion as well.[29] The religious argument against capital punishment can say, *sotto voce,* "I am among the righteous, and those who disagree are damned."

The unattractive and historically dangerous attributes of religious arguments in public life lead Greenawalt and Audi to propose limiting the reasons people can offer for their political positions. As we will see, Greenawalt argues that people ought to offer secular reasons until they run out; Audi's principle of secular reason says that people ought to offer secular reasons only. Rawls's more modest position is that people can *offer* any arguments they want as long as they eventually give a secular reason. And there is an even more modest position, analogous to the Supreme Court doctrine described earlier: People can offer any arguments they want as long as there *is* a secular reason available for the proposal. But why should there be *any* requirement of political morality that a secular reason be available to justify public action?

One might simply stipulate that a liberal democratic citizen would have certain character traits, among which would be a refusal to make nonsecular arguments for public policies. Political theorists Amy Gutmann and Dennis Thompson, for example, describe "a distinctively democratic kind of character—the character of individuals who are morally committed, self-reflective about their commitments, discerning of the difference between respectable and merely tolerable differences of opinion, and open to the possibility of changing their minds or modifying their positions at some time in the future if they confront unanswerable objections to their present point of view."[30] Again we can hear resonances of a distinction between adherents of mainstream religions, who might be thought to have the qualities Gutmann and Thompson describe, and fundamentalists, who might be thought to lack those qualities.

These character traits are attractive to some, albeit perhaps more to the adherents of mainstream religions who they describe than to others.[31] A society populated with such citizens would probably be more stable than one lacking them. A liberal society in which such citizens predominated might well adopt noncoercive government policies designed to spread those traits more widely among the populace. Further, this set of character traits does capture something of what we mean when we speak of a "liberal" society.[32] Taken as a stipulation, however, the approach rather obviously conflicts with the assumption of diversity in the citizenry.

Gutmann and Thompson get off on the wrong foot when they characterize the point of the principles animating a liberal society as "eliminat[-ing] moral conflict from politics" and "remov[ing] decisions about [certain policies] from the political agenda." Those policies are ones as to which "there is no reasonable basis for resolving the moral conflict on an issue of policy." Their argument is designed to show that liberal principles of preclusion that "deny[] certain reasons standing in the policy-making process" cannot serve that goal effectively, because they "open up the political agenda to more moral disagreement than liberal theories usually allow." They must therefore be supplemented by principles of accommodation, which "govern the conduct of moral disagreement" and rest on "mutual respect," which "requires a favorable attitude toward, and constructive interaction with, the persons with whom one disagrees."[33]

The strategy adopted by Gutmann and Thompson seems inconsistent with the empirical premise on which liberal political theory rests, that differences about the Good are ineradicable. One can list character traits that would make a society more stable, but positing such character traits as the foundation of a liberal society asks that people as they actually are constituted give up important components of their views of the Good. At least some of those who believe that God prescribes a range of public policies as components of the Good are unlikely to believe as well that those who have tolerant characters—and therefore say, "Well, I believe that God prescribes those policies, but if you don't, that's all right with me"—really endorse their view of the Good.

These arguments seek to identify a principle of political morality that counsels people to avoid making religious arguments for public policies. None seems to me to capture the reality of political life in a diverse society, and to that extent none seems to me appropriate as part of the thin Constitution. But principle is not all there is to good citizenship. Prudence matters too, and perhaps the best arguments about the role of religious arguments in public life are prudential. The next sections argue that liberals often may have good prudential reasons for putting up with religious arguments, and that religious people often may have good prudential reasons for refraining from making religious arguments in public, whether they have secular arguments or not.

Before turning to my arguments, however, it is worth pausing to note a point related to my earlier discussions of constitutional crises. The entire Rawlsian argument rests on the proposition that social stability has very great benefits, as indeed it does. But stability is not the only important thing in life. When faced with an issue of transcendent importance—slavery in the nineteenth century, or abortion (for some) in the twentieth—people can reasonably say, "Getting the right answer to this question is more important than preserving a stable social order in which injustice prevails." Or, as Lincoln put it in his Second Inaugural Address, "Both parties deprecated war; but one of them would *make* war rather than let the nation survive; and the other would *accept* war rather than let it perish. And the war came."[34]

THE "PROBLEM" OF THE UNREASONABLE

Rawls confines his claim to the modest one that we can achieve stability in a society with lots of different views of the Good, as long as those views are reasonable. Again, reasonable views can be revised in principle as people holding them negotiate with others over the basic terms of social life. But what if the society has some unreasonable people in it?

Here some insights from the idea of federalism might be useful. Federalism is a way of dispersing power among groups based on where they happen to be. But we can take it to stand for a more general idea of dispersed power. Imagine a town composed of people with strong views about the Good, quite different from those prevailing elsewhere. Suppose that people in the town want to preserve its moral integrity, but also want to be as well off as they can. In the modern world they are unlikely to be able to do so without engaging in exchanges with people in the rest of the country.

Those exchanges will probably place some pressure on the townspeople. For Rawls, reasonable views of the good are those that can be revised after reflection on the importance of social stability, and unreasonable ones are those that are not in principle revisable. Sometimes such views are called *fundamentalist*, to suggest their connection to ways of thinking that focus on sacred texts whose meaning, once revealed, can never be changed.

Fundamentalist views are unrevisable in principle, but historical experience strongly suggests that they are revisable in practice. Adherents of such views have found it impossible to insulate their communities from the rest of the world. They need to engage in transactions with others if they are to attain a level of material well-being acceptable to the group's members. Those transactions in turn bring the group into cultural contact with the rest of the world, bringing information about what is going on elsewhere, and about what other people think, to the attention of some members. They experience the effects of what political theorist Michael Walzer somewhat ironically calls "the Four Mobilities"—geographic, social, marital, and political.[35]

History suggests two possible paths. The experience of the Amish in the United States is that members may drift away from the community. From inside the community it seems as if the fallen-away have been seduced by the attractions of the wider society. Those who remain will point out that transactions with the wider society threaten the group's identity. They will urge their compatriots to minimize those transactions, and to resist the cultural pressures that occur when the transactions do occur. As they see it, the pressures would diminish the community.

These concerns help identify the alternative path: The community can change from within, despite its stated fundamentalism.[36] Many in the community will think that the threat posed to their way of life by any particular transaction is small. They may prefer the concrete material benefits they get out of the transaction to the more abstract satisfaction of knowing they have resisted a small threat to their group's identity. Generations later, those who identify themselves as members of the same group will see that major changes have occurred, that their views of the Good have in fact been revised in the face of a stated fundamentalist doctrine.

Over time, these cultural pressures are likely to accumulate in ways that make sustaining the fundamentalist view as a whole extremely difficult. Although no one believes that the view is in principle revisable, in fact many people will come to believe that some modifications are merely adjustments to the facts of life as they have come to know it.

This process is likely to take a long time, and at any point those who hold fundamentalist views will appear to be unreasonable in Rawls's terms: They will not be willing to consider revising their views merely to achieve the benefits of social stability. The political activities of those who hold such views need not be worrisome as long as they remain a relatively small minority, perhaps no more than 10 percent of the population. Rawls's liberals can say to themselves, somewhat condescendingly, "Let them fulminate; in the long run they will come around." Such liberals may have an unattractive mind-set about fundamentalists, merely tolerating them rather than respecting their views as among those necessarily held by some in a pluralist society. Put in more attractive terms, liberals can see the terms of citizenship as constantly under negotiation. The negotiations are explicit among those whom Rawls calls reasonable, and they are implicit between the reasonable and the fundamentalists.

Mere tolerance may sometimes be enough, if the group wants only to be left alone and liberals are confident that the group's fundamentalist views will be undermined from within. Strikingly, however, liberals can go farther. They might sometimes accommodate the fundamentalists' views, adjusting public policy to give them exemptions from laws that burden their religious exercises, as long as the exemptions do not threaten social stability as the liberals see it. So, for example, a political liberal can support the Religious Freedom Restoration Act, even when some of its applications might seem to allow fundamentalists whom the liberal thinks unreasonable to get away with actions the liberals think really improper. Liberals confident that they will prevail in the long run can afford to be generous.

This view of liberalism means that liberals can accept a great deal of religious discourse about public policy. They can do so without hesitation when the religious discourse comes from those with reasonable views of the good. And they can put up with religious discourse from fundamentalists if they are confident enough about their society's stability.

What to Say?

According to Stephen Carter, "One good way to end a conversation . . . is to tell a group of well-educated professionals that you hold a political position . . . because it is required by your understanding of God's will."

You will "be challenged on the ground that you are intent on imposing your religious beliefs on other people."[37] Why is a statement that a position on a political issue results from a person's understanding of God's will sometimes a conversation stopper? Maybe, as Carter says, it is because listeners are hostile to religion. But maybe not. Exactly what sort of conversation does Carter imagine ought to occur after such a statement? "Oh, that's interesting. Could you explain to me exactly how you think your position is connected to God's will?" The listener might then get some greater appreciation for the basis of the speaker's position—a sort of multicultural education. But it is hard to figure out where the conversation might go next unless the speaker and listener already share beliefs about how people go about determining God's will and how to tell when you have discerned what God's will really is. Carter suggests one response might be, "Do you really imagine that your God would mandate something so fundamentally unjust?"[38]

Audi develops a similar point. If a citizen both relies on and makes religious arguments, it might elicit contrary religious arguments from people who believe deeply that the religious grounds being offered are wrong, even though both sides might have—and yet fail to discover— secular reasons for supporting the policy. Arguments based on religion, that is, might be "polarizing" and destabilizing.[39]

Here we can connect the question of appropriate motivation to the earlier discussion of religious argument. Audi begins by describing a "principle of secular rationale," that "one should not advocate or support any law or public policy that restricts human conduct unless one *has*, and *is willing to offer*, adequate secular reason for this advocacy or support."[40] He also states and endorses a "principle of secular motivation," that one should not promote public policies of the relevant sort unless one has secular reasons that are "motivationally sufficient for the conduct in question."[41]

Audi restricts his analysis to efforts to enact coercive policies, which creates two difficulties. Determining what is coercive may be difficult and controversial, as the example of Judge Moore's (mere) display of the Ten Commandments suggests.[42] Even more, Audi argues that religious people can support politicians and policies aimed at persuading others to join their camp.[43] But often the vehicle for persuasion may be advocacy of coercive policies—not in the hope that the policies will in fact be enacted, but because only by advocating such policies will people be brought along to agree with the principles that motivate the advocacy. So, for example, a person might think that the best way to reduce the number of abortions is to persuade them that the practice is wrong, and that the best way to persuade them of that is to advocate the adoption of restrictive abortion laws.

These difficulties aside, Audi defends his principle of secular motivation by suggesting that a citizen would not be acting appropriately if he or she had one kind of reason (a religious one) that, in his or her mind, justified the proposal, but offered for public consideration only another kind of reason (a secular one). He says that this "smack[s] of manipulation,"[44] because the citizen is saying, in effect, "Here are some secular reasons for this proposal. As a matter of fact, I do not find them compelling. Indeed, if these were the only reasons I could discover that might justify the proposal, I would not favor the proposal. That's what it means to say that I have a religious motivation for the proposal, and that the secular reasons I am giving are not motivationally sufficient. But, I have come to believe that you would be persuaded to support the proposal by reasons that I find inadequate, so here they are." For Audi, "there is a certain lack of respect implied in seeking my agreement to a policy by offering reasons by which one is not oneself moved."[45]

Yet the religiously motivated advocate could be saying something quite different, entirely respectful (though perhaps in a somewhat puzzled tone), and nonmanipulative. The advocate acknowledges that she lives in a liberal society characterized by ineradicable differences in views of the Good. She knows that some of those she is attempting to persuade will not share the religious premises that lead her to conclude that the policy she is promoting ought to be adopted. Still, she might think, others with different premises might conclude from *those* premises that the same policy should be adopted. Her secular argument, then, is, "In view of the premises you hold—though I do not—you ought to support this policy."[46]

In addressing his version of this point, Audi suggests that the audience might be suspicious of the claim, offered by someone who by hypothesis does not share the premises, that the premises compel support for the policy.[47] To take the easiest case, suppose Carter and his listener share the belief that God's will is revealed in the Bible. Carter will invoke some texts that, as he reads them, support his political position. The listener may dispute Carter's interpretation, or may invoke counter-texts. But this turns out to be a *religious* discussion, not a political one. If Carter's listener has a different view of how one finds out God's will—by reflection on personal experience, or by direct appeals for guidance, or by revelation, for example—the conversation will stop as soon as we find out that Carter's way of discerning God's will relies on interpreting the Bible. Further, if the believer questions the listener's credentials to talk about the *believer's* God, the dialogue is over.[48]

These considerations lead me to conclude that religious people often have strong reasons for refraining from making religious arguments, based in a prudent desire to be effective in political discussions.[49] This might not be terribly costly from the religious person's point of view. After all, it is often relatively easy to translate arguments made in religious terms into arguments resting on secular premises.[50] The Catholic Bishops' pastoral letters on the economy and on nuclear weapons were surely motivated by the Bishops' religious views and their interpretations of sacred texts, which the letters invoked. But they also included arguments that a secularist could detach from their religious origins. And yet, precisely to that extent, the pastoral letters do not show how *religious* arguments contribute to a dialogue with those who do not accept their premises.

Prudence in political action means thinking about the trade-offs that people have to accept. A person's use of religion in political discussions can signal the depth of feeling that person has, and even a nonbeliever might think such intensity matters in developing public policy: If the believer cares so much, and the nonbeliever thinks the issue not all that important, the nonbeliever might decide that a policy contrary to the believer's position is not worth the distress it would cause.[51] Sometimes, too, the believer's religious commitments might lead him or her to some insights that the nonbeliever accepts for nonreligious reasons, and that the nonbeliever might not have thought of, or might not have thought of so quickly, without the conversation.[52] Refraining from making religious arguments may sacrifice intensity, sincerity, and witnessing in exchange for political effectiveness.

Sometimes, however, making religious arguments does stop the conversation. The reason may be that the *believer* is not open to conversation. As a bumper sticker puts it, "The Bible says so. I believe it." And that is the end of the discussion. Or the reason may be that the *listener* is so hostile to religion that he or she simply "turns off" when someone else starts using "God language." The case for offering secular arguments, then, appears to be primarily prudential, and the case for requiring secular motivations seems unsupportable. What can be said about the weaker requirement that secular reasons be available? Such a requirement must be a principled requirement rather than a prudential one. Prudential arguments say, in effect, that things are likely to turn out badly if people do not behave in a certain way. Thus, Audi argues, people are unlikely to persuade their audience if they make secular arguments they themselves do not find compelling; or they may polarize the society if they have religious motivations. The requirement that secular principles be available cannot be defended on prudential grounds because it does not refer to action at all. According to that requirement, everyone involved in a decision could have entirely religious motivations and make entirely religious arguments, and yet what they do could be justified if there happened to be secular reasons available for their action. But, the mere availability of secular reasons cannot have the kinds of effects that are necessary for an argument based on prudence to get going, because the secular reasons play no role in what leads up to the action.

This means that the use of religious rhetoric in political discussions is largely a matter of prudence, not principle. Sometimes religious rhetoric works, from the point of view of the person using it, and sometimes it does not.[53] And sometimes omitting religious references would be imprudent, when it would lead listeners to suspect the speaker of having a hidden agenda. For example, the Catholic natural law tradition generates arguments against gay marriages that have a purely nonreligious form: Marriage is an institution in which people uniquely experience the human good of sexual friendship, and the possibility that offspring will result from sexual intimacy is an essential characteristic of sexual friendship. To make these arguments work you have to develop some explanation of why sexual intercourse among married people who can no longer have children, or who never could have children, is permissible. As the accounts develop they become increasingly strained, at least from the point of view of non-Catholics. A person who offered the natural law arguments against gay marriage without drawing on specifically religious arguments would probably come across as not revealing everything about the argument, and so would be less effective than someone who augmented the natural law arguments with religious arguments.

But it is not clear what an outsider to the religion has to say—or what the Constitution outside the courts has to say—if the question of whether to use religious arguments is largely one of prudence. Presumably religious leaders and citizens want to be politically effective, which gives them reasons to try to figure out what strategies of public advocacy will work best.

Should religious leaders and citizens make sure that their arguments are predominantly secular even if they include religious references as well? Even an outsider can suggest that the answer is pretty clearly, "Yes, most of the time." As a matter of social reality in the contemporary United States, which is characterized by religious pluralism, chances are that only such a strategy will succeed. Consider law professor Theodore Blumoff's observation based on his own experience: "[R]ecourse to the *Halakha* in general public conversation in middle Georgia as a political justification for a contested course of action is not likely to fare well."[54] As philosopher Elizabeth Wolgast puts it, "[A] wise citizen often will refrain from invoking parochial religious and moral values—values that will predictably divide—in order to maintain communication and even persuade someone who holds different values."[55] Often, but not always—and when the citizen decides not to refrain, he or she does not thereby demonstrate some failure as a democratic citizen.

A Note on Voters, Legislators, and Judges

It would be crazy to suggest that voters have to refrain from invoking religious reasons when they discuss politics. Greenawalt's arguments show why. He distinguishes between religious convictions and what he calls publicly accessible reasons and widely shared premises—the equivalent of what I have been calling secular reasons. He strongly prefers publicly accessible reasons and widely shared premises, with the liberal citizen justifiably relying on religious convictions only to provide broad perspectives on the evaluation of those reasons and premises or when those reasons and premises run out. For Greenawalt, then, the domain in which religious convictions may properly be relied on is a residual one. Only after the citizen is unable to come up with publicly accessible reasons to justify his or her position may he or she rely on religious convictions. Publicly accessible reasons will run out, in this motivational sense, before the possibility of *available* reasons—reasons that someone who thought long and hard about the policy in question might come up with—has been exhausted, because we are all limited in our ability to develop reasons for what we do. The typical citizen, then, might well reach the point of relying on religious reasons, and making religious arguments, relatively early in the course of political deliberations.[56] For such a citizen, secular reasons will indeed have run out. Greenawalt's arguments support the conclusion that the widespread invocation of religious arguments in ordinary discussions among U.S. citizens is consistent with his version of liberal political theory.[57]

Are public officials different? Law professor Michael Perry gives the lawyer's response: Public reason frequently runs out before it tells officials what to do, although perhaps it runs out a bit less frequently for them than for ordinary citizens.[58] The public official must rely on something else when public reason "underdetermines" the law. And that something else might be a religious reason.

We should put aside easy cases. Suppose a legislator represents voters who believe, for religious reasons, in race discrimination.[59] The legislator should refrain from representing the religious views of those constituents because those views are themselves inconsistent with the thin Constitution. The legislator would act wrongly in following the constituency's views not because those views were religious but because they were wrong.

In a representative system it is not clear why some requirements should be imposed on delegates and different ones on those they represent. Political philosopher Jeremy Waldron points out that "there ought to be continuity between whatever discourse is appropriate among the people and whatever discourse is appropriate among those whom they elect."[60]

Greenawalt hints that delegates may somehow shape public views more effectively than other citizens,[61] but surely that does not distinguish them from many other citizens, such as a deeply religious newspaper publisher who insists that the editorial pages of the newspaper reflect her religious views. Perhaps publicly accessible reasons run out later for the legislator, who has more time to develop available reasons, than for the ordinary citizen. Even then, however, the need for the legislator to connect with his or her constituents suggests that we ought not impose a strong requirement that the legislator avoid giving those religious reasons the constituents would find easiest to understand. My sense of the matter is that the most we could reasonably require is that legislators ought to do more work in developing publicly accessible reasons, and that they therefore ought to be more careful than ordinary citizens to ensure that they *include* such reasons in their arguments.

Legislators are constrained by the electoral process. We introduce what Greenawalt calls "a serious tension" between "proper grounds for election and proper grounds for legislative decision"[62] if we say that as a matter of political theory legislators may not take into account some considerations, such as religion, that lead voters to select one candidate over another. And, from the other side, if a legislator relies on religious views that his or her constituents do not share, their recourse is to the ballot box the next time around; they do not need to be bolstered by a political theory saying that the legislator ought not act on religious views.

Finally, Greenawalt suggests that a legislator who acts on particular religious views, shared perhaps by a majority of his or her constituents, may be demonstrating disrespect for the contrary views, religious or secular, of the rest of the constituency.[63] Somehow, the argument must go, the legislator ought to represent all the constituents, not merely those whose votes were necessary for his or her election. Yet, if this is a difficulty, it is a difficulty for representative government based on majority rule, not a difficulty particular to the domain of religion. A Republican who follows the party line demonstrates the same kind of disrespect for the views of the Democrats in the district.[64] The remedy, again, is not to place the delegate under constraints based on political theory but to go to the polls in sufficient numbers to assure that the delegate will worry about reelection if he or she continues to follow the party line.[65]

Hubert Humphrey acted properly: Legislators do not have to refrain from invoking religious reasons to support what they propose to do. Of course sometimes invoking such reasons will not be good political strategy. People may get their backs up if they think that someone is pushing a "religious agenda." But usually we think that politicians do a decent job of testing the political waters. Politics rather than political theory dictates sensible political strategy.

What about judges? Here the constraints of prudence seem to be stronger. Most people think that judges speak for "the law." And "the law," for most, includes statutes, prior court decisions, and much more, but not the Gospels, the Torah, or the Koran. As Greenawalt puts it, judges operate with "constrained sources."[66]

We go along with judicial decisions, when we do, because we think that the decisions rest on principles that everyone thinking about things in a reasonable way ought to accept. Two centuries ago perhaps judges could properly invoke the Gospels as a source of legal authority because they lived in a society where the Gospels were almost universally accepted as authority. That is no longer true in our pluralist society, which means that judges can no longer write opinions directly invoking religious principles: They are not part of the law any more.

Of course judges can implicitly rely on religious reasons that underlie the law. As we have seen, Justice Thomas did nothing wrong in citing the Declaration of Independence to support his position on affirmative action: He relied on the Declaration's commitment to the idea of human equality justified, in the Declaration itself, with reference to the laws of Nature and Nature's God. Chief Justice Warren Burger's invocation of "Judeo-Christian moral and ethical standards" to justify his conclusion that laws against homosexual sodomy were not unconstitutional seems more troubling.[67] Partly that is because the content of that tradition is more openly contested than Burger acknowledged. And partly it is because the tradition, such as it is, may be wrong. But Burger's language was not out of bounds because it relied on a religious reference.

Also, just as legislators can rely on—and explicitly invoke—religious premises when other reasons run out, so can judges. Suppose they are called upon to make a decision and find that conventional legal materials do not supply a single answer. I would think that the only thing a conscientious judge could say is something like this: "I can't give you an answer based solely on conventional legal materials. My answer, if you insist on it, will be based on my personal moral code, which for me is religious in nature." That might lead us to decide not to insist on an answer, of course—to withdraw the case from the judge's consideration and try to resolve it by our own moral resources.[68] We might want to do so because we are unsure what the judge's religious views are, and fear that we will not be persuaded to submit to public force by arguments from religious traditions that are not ours. But if the conventional legal sources underdetermine the law and the judge must say something, all the judge is left with is his or her moral code, which may be a religious one.[69]

How often do the conventional legal sources run out? Legal scholars disagree. My personal view is that they run out frequently indeed, and that judges will have to rely on their moral codes more often than many people would be happy with. A prominent alternative has been offered by law professor Cass Sunstein. According to Sunstein, quite often we can discover agreement on correct outcomes while disagreeing about ultimate justifications.[70] We need not be troubled by these incompletely theorized agreements, as Sunstein calls them, even when the judge's reason is a religious one if we think the outcome justified according to our own, perhaps quite different belief-system.

The depth of disagreement about religion might caution legislators— and judges even more strongly—to do what they can to explain their actions without invoking religious premises. But in the end if they find it appropriate to use such premises in public arguments, the Constitution outside the courts ought not limit them.

There *are* limits, however—not limits of principle, but political limits. Consider again the Religious Freedom Restoration Act. Justice John Paul Stevens thought RFRA violated the Establishment Clause because it singled out religion for preferential treatment.[71] And in some formal sense it certainly did: RFRA would not have let me get an exemption from historic preservation zoning no matter how sincerely I believed that my house is an artistic abomination, but churches might have been able to get such exemptions. But it is hard to see how RFRA posed a serious threat to the nonestablishment values of the thin Constitution. The reason is that it made its benefits available widely: Everyone with religious beliefs, no matter how odd, was entitled to claim that the government had to adjust its programs to accommodate their beliefs.[72] RFRA's scope illustrates an important point about politics in a religiously diverse society: Politicians have incentives to accommodate a wide range of views, which include the views of people who are skeptical about the role of religion in public life. Perhaps we can expect that the complex process by which public policy is developed will generate few policies that threaten the thin Constitution's values. The next chapter examines the incentives politicians have, to see the extent to which such complacency might be justified by the structure of our political system.

Chapter Five

THE INCENTIVE-COMPATIBLE
CONSTITUTION

THE IDEA OF INCENTIVE-COMPATIBILITY

So far I have argued against the position that the Constitution *ought* to be committed entirely to the courts, and that legislatures might do a decent job of implementing the thin Constitution. That still leaves open the question of whether legislatures actually *will* do a decent job. Will legislators run hog-wild if we leave them on their own? Do we need to make sure that they behave appropriately by subjecting whatever they do to the courts' scrutiny? An analogy drawn from economics may help clarify the issues here.

Suppose we have some goal we want to reach—selling as many new cars as we can, for example. And suppose we have to hire someone else to do the selling, perhaps because we are good at raising money to lend to car buyers but are not good at selling cars. How can we make sure that the sales staff we hire will actually sell as many cars as they can? All we can observe is the number of cars they sell, but that will not tell us how many cars they *could* have sold if they had tried harder. And, unfortunately, we cannot tell how hard they are trying precisely because they are good at selling and we are not.

The trick is to develop a way of paying the sales staff in a way that guarantees that they will try as hard as they can to sell as many cars as they can. Car dealers have figured this all out: They combine commissions on the sale of each car with a bonus to the person on the staff who sells the most cars in a month, or a year.[1]

Economists call this an "incentive-compatible" or self-enforcing arrangement.[2] We take the incentives the sales staff have to earn a living and harness the incentives to a different goal—selling as many cars as the car dealer can make a profit on, taking into account the fact that the dealer has to compensate the staff for its efforts. Extra effort increases the probability that a sales person will get the bonus. Many sales people will exert the extra effort if the bonus is large enough, and those who do not simply decrease their chances of getting the bonus. Taken as a whole, the sales staff pursues the goal of selling as many cars as they can even though each sales person might prefer to slack off a little and even though we could not tell whether any particular sales person had indeed slacked off.[3]

The important point here is that the car dealers get what they want without having to call on some outside party to determine how hard the sales people are working. The car dealers get what they want by piggy-backing on what the sales people want.

This chapter explores the extent to which the Constitution can be understood as an incentive-compatible or self-enforcing arrangement. The idea is the economists': We have some goals we want to achieve—here, advancing constitutional values—and we want to devise self-enforcing institutional arrangements.[4] If we can, we can take the Constitution away from the courts and still advance the Constitution's values.

The problem of monitoring the sales staff points to one reason for thinking seriously about a self-enforcing constitution. Suppose the car dealers really cannot devise a decent self-enforcing contract. They can try to write an employment contract saying, "I'll fire you if you don't try hard enough to sell cars." They are likely to find few people willing to sign up on those terms. The opportunities that contract gives the dealer to cheat are too big: The employer can fire someone who actually has tried really hard, just after the sales person has brought in buyers who are going to generate a lot of continuing business. The contract will have to say, "You can be fired if someone else—a judge or arbitrator—determines that you haven't worked hard enough." And now the problem is that the judge may not get the right answer: The judge may erroneously uphold firing someone who worked hard, or may direct the continued employment of someone who slacked off.

Judges are not perfect. We want them to enforce constitutional rights, but they can get those rights wrong, so to speak: They can find a constitutional right where the Constitution does not create one, and they can deny constitutional rights the Constitution actually protects. Perhaps we would actually get a higher level of compliance with the Constitution if we figured out ways to make it self-enforcing. This is not to say that a self-enforcing Constitution will be a perfectly enforced Constitution. We might be unable to develop ways of making some constitutional rights self-enforcing. The issue, though, is inevitably comparative: Will we get a better enforced Constitution if we rely on self-enforcing structures than if we rely on judicial enforcement, acknowledging that neither self-enforcement nor judicial enforcement leads to perfect enforcement.[5]

JAMES MADISON AND INCENTIVE-COMPATIBILITY

James Madison saw the Constitution as incentive-compatible. Judicial review played a relatively small role in his account of how we could be sure that the new Constitution's values would be honored.[6] Instead, Madison examined how people would act in response to their personal incentives within the structure created by the Constitution. As he saw it, self-interested action by voters, legislators, and the president would produce good public policy consistent with constitutional values.

Madison's argument was complex, and we need not explore all its details here. Rather, I select some portions to show how ideas of self-enforcement and incentive-compatibility worked their way into Madison's argument.

According to Madison, factions posed the most fundamental challenge to people trying to design a good constitution. Factions were groups "united by some common impulse of passion, or of interest, adverse to the rights of other citizens, or to the permanent and aggregate interests of the community."[7] Minority factions, which we might think of today as some special interest groups, could be controlled by requiring majority rule.

What about a majority faction, a majority intent on infringing minority rights? Madison argued that the new Constitution minimized the risk of majority faction in several ways. First, the country would be relatively large. That would make it hard for people sharing a common interest adverse to that of the nation as a whole to get together. Second, the Constitution created a representative rather than a direct democracy. The representatives would "refine and enlarge the public views," filtering them through their own interests. Madison knew, however, that representatives were not always going to be what he called "enlightened statesmen." Like the voters, representatives too would be self-interested.

Madison argued that we could reduce the role of self-interested action by representatives. First, they should be chosen from relatively large districts. He gave several reasons for thinking that would increase the probability that "statesmen" would indeed be chosen. The larger the district, the harder it would be for a candidate to "practice with success the vicious arts." Outright bribery would be more expensive and harder to conceal. More important, a candidate in a large district would find it hard to promise everything to everyone: The larger the district, the more likely that a promise to one group in the district would be inconsistent with the desires of another group in the district. Finally, Madison asked us to think about how a candidate would become widely enough known in a large district to be a plausible candidate. His answer was that the most reliable way was for the candidate to have been a public official already. But then, Madison said, the candidate's prior performance would give us a way of determining whether he or she would be self-interested or would instead serve our interests.

By this point Madison had established to his satisfaction that a large representative democracy would produce legislators who had a mix of self-interested and public-interest motivations, and who would probably be less self-interested than the voters themselves. That, however, would not be enough to ensure that the legislators acted in the public interest. They might be *less* self-interested than the voters, but they would be elected and reelected only if they were responsive to the voters. But that meant that the legislators would reproduce the self-interested desires of their constituents. How would that avoid the problem of majority faction?

Here Madison relied on the separation of powers within the national government. That system of checks and balances made it hard to get anything done without broad agreement. And legislators would want to get something done. In Madison's terms, they were going to be ambitious people. They would want a reputation for having accomplished something. True, they might really want to feather their own nests, or they might want to grab for their constituents as much as they could. But the checks and balances system meant they could not count on doing that. Legislators would enact laws in the public interest, if for no other reason than that they could not get a good reputation if they did nothing.

Finally, Madison noted that the system of separation of powers was self-enforcing. The Constitution created departments that were largely self-contained, and each had what Madison called "the necessary constitutional means and personal motives to resist encroachments of the others."[8] In a famous phrase, "ambition must be made to counteract ambition. The interest of the man must be connected with the constitutional rights of the place." To preserve his or her own power, a member of Congress would be alert to attempts by the president to make the presidency more powerful; and similarly for the president.

Law professor William Treanor has offered an intriguing application of the framers' ideas of incentive-compatibility.[9] Treanor examines the framers' allocation of the power to get the United States involved in military operations. He argues that the framers believed that political actors were strongly motivated by "the desire to achieve immortal fame." They were concerned, Treanor says, that a single president's desire for fame might lead him to commit the nation to war even when war was not in the national interest. But no individual member of Congress could win fame by committing the nation to war, even a successful war. Treanor argues that the framers drew the conclusion that "Congress alone could be trusted to decide questions of war correctly." The president's incentives skewed his assessment of the national interest; the incentives of members of Congress did not skew theirs.

Ideas about incentive-compatibility were part of the overall argument for the Constitution. And some of Madison's arguments still ring true. Political scientists have shown, for example, that at least as many important laws are passed when Congress is controlled by one party and the president leads the other party, as when we have a unified government.[10] The reason may well be Madisonian: People do not go to Washington to sit around accomplishing nothing, and when they must cooperate to get anything done, they will.

In some ways, however, Madison's arguments have an odd sound today. Not that we do not think that politicians' incentives may affect the way they behave, or that we might be able to design institutions that take advantage of politicians' incentives to advance the public interest. Rather, the difficulty is that Madison's arguments rest on empirical claims that seem at best out-of-date. For example, candidates can become well known by spending mounds of their own money, or by starring in television shows, or by being famous baseball players, rather than by serving as public officials before running for Congress or the presidency.

The disjunction between the empirical assumptions on which Madison's argument rests, which may well have been accurate in his day, and our own society points to a general question about whether we can design an incentive-compatible Constitution: Incentive-compatibility arguments may inevitably rest on empirical judgments that are both contentious and changeable. Can we get the stability we may want out of a constitution if we have to rely on institutions that work only under circumstances that may not exist for long?

INCENTIVE-COMPATIBILITY AND CONTEMPORARY LAW: FEDERALISM AND TERM LIMITS

Two modern examples of arguments about constitutional structure that invoke ideas of incentive-compatibility illustrate the nervousness we might have about the relation between the facts of modern life and structures designed to be incentive-compatible.

Federalism. Columbia law professor Herbert Wechsler published a classic article about the constitutional law of federalism in 1954. Its title was "The Political Safeguards of Federalism."[11] Wechsler picked up a Madisonian argument—members of Congress would respect the autonomous power of state governments—and reformulated it as an argument that the limits the Constitution placed on Congress's power in order to protect state autonomy were self-enforcing. The political incentives faced by members of Congress were enough to ensure state autonomy. Supplementing self-enforcement with judicial enforcement would not improve matters, because experience had confirmed that courts made mistakes too, giving the states more protection than the Constitution actually provided.[12]

Madison's argument rested on a combination of structural features and political predictions.[13] He pointed out that the original Constitution provided that state legislatures would elect senators, and would probably choose only people who would be deferential to state authority. Echoing a theme we saw earlier, he suggested that even the popularly elected members of the House of Representatives were likely to have served in state legislatures; their experience would lead them to appreciate the value of state autonomy. Madison thought that state governments would employ far more people than the national government would. They would deal with "all the more domestic and personal interests of the people," and the people in turn would have more "ties of personal acquaintance and friendship, and of family and party attachments" to officials of state government. All this, Madison argued, would lead national legislators to lean strongly in favor of state authority: "the members of the federal legislature will be likely to attach themselves too much to local objects." And, Madison pointed out, if the national government began to overreach, the states "still have the advantage in the means of defeating such encroachments." The people would refuse to cooperate with the national government, and they would organize political opposition with sympathizers in other states.

By 1954, of course, things had changed. The Seventeenth Amendment, adopted in 1913, eliminated the role of state legislators in choosing senators. The Great Depression and the New Deal substantially increased the scope of national authority, displacing state power over many aspects of economic regulation. Within a decade of Wechsler's writing, the Supreme Court's reapportionment decisions reduced the role of state legislators in structuring the House of Representatives in response to local interests.

But, Wechsler said, "Madison's analysis has never lost its thrust" despite the developments he acknowledged. For all that the national government did, there was much it did not do: The content of education remained determined at the local level; cities and states controlled zoning and therefore the general distribution of housing and industry. Institutions like the filibuster in the Senate gave representatives of small states disproportionate power in the national government. Candidates for the presidency could take advantage of the fact that small states and large each got two electoral votes in addition to the votes they got based on population, and might assemble a majority by paying particular attention to smaller states. The national government relies on state and local officials to administer a wide range of national policies, which gives those officials important leverage in the national legislative process. Finally, and perhaps most important, each national party was actually a loose coalition of parties based in the states, and national legislators depended at least as much on satisfying the demands of local party leaders as on going along with national party leaders, including even the president.[14]

The Supreme Court in 1985 adopted the Madisonian position, saying that "the principal means chosen by the Framers to ensure the role of the States in the federal system lies in the structure of the Federal Government itself."[15] Justice Harry Blackmun's opinion rejected a constitutional challenge to a national law requiring that state governments pay their employees the same minimum wages that private employers had to pay. Demonstrating that the idea of a self-enforcing constitutional provision includes the possibility that the Constitution actually prefers some specific results, the opinion pointed out that states had been quite effective in protecting their interests in Congress, obtaining statutory exemptions from many general laws and securing large grants of money from Congress.

The Supreme Court eventually abandoned the view that the Constitution placed only process-based limits on Congress's power with regard to the states. Three cases are instructive. The first held unconstitutional the Gun-Free School Zones Act of 1990, which made it a federal crime to possess a gun within 1,000 feet of a school.[16] The second case invalidated a provision of the Brady Handgun Violence Prevention Act, requiring local sheriffs to devote reasonable efforts to performing background checks on people buying guns, until a national computerized system came on-line in late 1998.[17] The Court said that Congress could not "commandeer" state officials to carry out national policy. Finally, there is the RFRA case.

The school-zone case certainly supports skepticism about the self-enforceability of federalism. Congress passed the statute without giving it much attention: There were no hearings or legislative findings explaining why the states needed help in this area, for example. The Brady Act and RFRA cases are different, though. In both Congress rather clearly made a deliberate, and reasonable, judgment that national interests ought to prevail over state interests, in a political debate that was not unfairly structured against the states. Many state law enforcement officials actually *wanted* to do background checks, for example, and those that did not had powerful allies in the National Rifle Association, which opposed the Act as a whole. The provision the Court invalidated imposed burdens on some state officers, but only for a short time.[18] Similarly, the Senate had a substantial debate over whether to impose RFRA's requirements on state prisons, in the face of lobbying by state prison officials, hardly a group who have a hard time getting a hearing in Congress. In both cases, of course, the states "lost," in some sense. But I think it hard to say that they lost because Congress was structured in a way that induced it to overlook state interests. They lost because Congress disagreed with the positions state officials were asserting.

The Supreme Court's opinions invalidating these three statutes did not even mention the Madisonian arguments, largely because they simply assumed that all constitutional provisions must be enforced by the courts. One reason for that assumption is this: The structural sources of state protection against national overreaching do indeed seem to have eroded. That leaves only political sources. Justice Blackmun relied on his evaluation of Congress's behavior to show that those political sources were indeed quite effective. Today we might point to the elimination of a national entitlement to public assistance, and the devolution of substantial authority to state governments to restructure public assistance programs, as a good example of what Justice Blackmun described. For many years constitutional conservatives claimed that the national government had irrevocably swept power into its own hands. But, it turned out, when the people thought that power would be used better at the state and local levels, they were able to get Congress to put power where they wanted. As Madison put it, the people were able to give "most of their confidence where they discover it to be most due."[19]

One difficulty with this argument is that it seems pretty vulnerable to political change. Lyndon Johnson and the Great Society come in, and states lose a lot of power; Newt Gingrich and the Reagan Revolution come in, and the states get more power. Even more, the argument depends on controversial political evaluations. For example, do states really have much power over industrial development when whatever industries they might want to attract have to comply with national environmental standards? Are educational policies effectively set by local school boards, or by national elites acting in teachers' unions, universities, and the national media? Even the Supreme Court's recent defenses of state authority might seem rather feeble. States might be able to control policy over whether guns can be carried near schools, but they have little power to deal with plant relocations, which one might think ultimately has a larger effect on what a state can do.

The general point is that the Madisonian argument in its modern guise rests the judgment that federalism is a self-enforcing constitutional structure on two shaky pillars: *controversial* assessments of *changeable* political reality.[20] We might wonder whether that is a sufficient foundation for important elements in a constitutional system.

Term Limits. Something of the same difficulty can be seen if we consider proposals to adopt limits on the terms legislators can serve as examples of reform proposals resting on ideas about incentive-compatibility. Proponents of term limits argue that legislators who can be reelected indefinitely become a class of professional politicians who act in their own interest rather than the public interest, and pass laws that benefit themselves while exempting themselves from laws that burden everyone else. By limiting legislators' terms, the term limits movement argues, we can make it more likely that citizen-legislators will seek to advance the public interest.

Term-limited legislators have different incentives, and they will produce better laws.

It is of course a matter of some controversy whether this argument is right. Noting some aspects of the controversy will advance the general argument about self-enforcement.[21]

1. Careers in politics versus careers elsewhere: Consider the question of whether term limits produce citizen-legislators. Serving as a legislator for a relatively short period means that some younger legislators have to interrupt their other careers. As one California politician put it, "I was working for a large corporation. It would have been difficult to sacrifice the benefits and ladder-climbing opportunities for a dead-end job."[22] This might mean that only people who do not have to rely on their jobs for their income—rich people, roughly—will be able to serve as term-limited legislators. Or, perhaps, large organizations such as corporations, law firms, and unions will give their employees special leaves of absence to serve in term-limited offices. Then the legislators might be delegates not of the people they represent but of the people they plan to work for again.

2. The "last period" problem: The incentives actually become perverse if a legislator is in his or her last term. Better to take the money and run than to promote the public interest, because what can anyone do to punish you afterwards? Term limits may not eliminate the class of professional politicians it was aimed at if this "last period" problem is met with the response that the legislator might want to run for some other public office.

3. Expertise versus a fresh look: Term-limited legislators might not be able to develop expertise in complex areas of public policy. The result might be the enactment of overly simple solutions to serious problems, or excessive reliance on unelected permanent bureaucrats in the civil service or on self-interested lobbyists from special interest groups, who do have the time to develop expertise.[23]

Again, the accuracy of the arguments for or against term limits is not our primary concern here.[24] This brief discussion identifies two important points. First, even today we find ideas of incentive-compatibility consistent with the way we think about designing a good constitution.[25] And second, deciding whether particular proposals actually will lead to good public policy often requires us to make complex and controversial judgments about how the political system actually does operate, given the incentives voters and politicians have under different structures.

Madison's arguments about government structure in general and federalism in particular and the term limits example all involve the structure of government rather than individual rights. By exploring additional structural examples, we can identify a number of considerations that will help in analyzing whether, or to what extent, or under what conditions, we might expect the thin Constitution to be self-enforcing as well.

THE POLITICAL QUESTIONS DOCTRINE AND SELF-ENFORCEMENT

Federal district judge Walter Nixon really was a crook. He was convicted of making false statements to a grand jury in connection with an investigation of his tax returns. Judge Nixon refused to resign, believing that his conviction was unjust. The House of Representatives adopted articles of impeachment, and the case went to the Senate. The Constitution says that "the Senate shall have the sole Power to try all Impeachments." Traditionally the Senate convened all the senators to hear the evidence in impeachment cases. Its procedure has been different recently. A full Senate hearing on the evidence was incredibly time-consuming and disrupted the other business the Senate needed to do, so the Senate adopted a rule allowing it to create a committee to take evidence and report on impeachment. In Judge Nixon's case, the committee heard ten witnesses over a four-day period. It sent the Senate a full transcript and a report summarizing the evidence. The Senate then voted to impeach Judge Nixon.

He thought he had not had the "trial" the Constitution guaranteed. A trial, as Judge Nixon saw it, was an event in which the people actually making the decision—the jurors or the senators—heard the evidence. We would not say that someone convicted of murder had had a real trial if four jurors heard the evidence and reported to the eight others what they had heard. How, Judge Nixon asked, was his impeachment "trial" any different?

The Supreme Court might have replied, "What you got was not dramatically different from a standard impeachment trial. You got a chance to put on evidence and to examine witnesses. You got a full hearing from a group of senators devoting their full attention to your impeachment, and a report to the other senators with a lot of detail. The Constitution gives the Senate some room to maneuver in developing procedures for impeachment trials, and the Senate did not come up with something that is so far removed from the standard impeachment trial that the Constitution was violated." That would be a holding that Judge Nixon got a "trial" within the Constitution's meaning.

But the Court did not do that.[26] Instead, it invoked the "political questions" doctrine.[27] Under that doctrine the courts will not decide what the Constitution means; they leave the task of interpreting a particular constitutional provision to the political branches. The Court held that Judge Nixon's claim that he had not been given a trial within the meaning of the Constitution was a political question. It is important to be clear about precisely what this means. It does *not* mean that the constitutional language—*try*—has no meaning. The Constitution is not indifferent as to the outcome of controversies over what its words mean. A political questions holding means that the language's meaning is determined by the Senate, not by the courts.

The political questions doctrine is obviously in some tension with the rhetoric of *Marbury v. Madison*, examined in chapter 1, that "it is emphatically the province and duty of the judicial department to say what the law is." And the Court has been rather reluctant to find that a constitutional question was a political question reserved to some other branch of government. Is there any justification for the doctrine?

We can begin with a skeptical question asked by Justice David Souter, who concurred in the Court's judgment in Judge Nixon's case: Suppose the Senate decided to convict Judge Nixon by flipping a coin. Surely, Justice Souter suggested, the courts would not refuse to find that he had been denied a trial within the meaning of the Constitution: "In such circumstances, the Senate's action might be so far beyond the scope of its constitutional authority, and the consequent impact on the Republic so great, as to merit a judicial response. . . ."[28]

Chief Justice Rehnquist's opinion for the Court did not respond to Justice Souter's suggestion. Justice John Paul Stevens did, in a short concurring opinion saying that "[r]espect for a coordinate Branch of the Government forecloses any assumption that improbable hypotheticals like [the one] mentioned by . . . Justice Souter will ever occur."[29] Justice Stevens was worried about the following problem: Any fool knows that tossing a coin is not a trial. If Judge Nixon's case presents a political question, the Senate determines the meaning of *try*. If the Senate decided by tossing a coin, it would be deciding as well that tossing a coin *was* a trial. How can a decent constitutional system tolerate a result so obviously inconsistent with what people think words mean? The answer for Justice Stevens was that the courts could not assume that the Senate would behave in such a ridiculous manner.

Justice Stevens refused to make such an assumption out of respect for the Senate. The courts could have respect for the Senate for two reasons. One is purely formal: The Senate is a coordinate branch of government, and as a normative matter the courts should not make assumptions that cast aspersions on the Senate, even if the aspersions are justified by the facts. The other is empirical: As a matter of fact the Senate is never going to behave in the way Justice Souter suggests (or if it does, our constitutional system will have broken down so dramatically that impeaching judges by tossing coins is going to be the least of our worries).[30]

I find it hard to take the purely formal argument seriously. The empirical one, however, seems to me correct.[31] Justice Stevens's response to

Justice Souter's concern then is rather straightforward. The Senate is highly unlikely to act irresponsibly by flipping a coin. The procedures it adopts may not be precisely the ones the courts would adopt for a "trial," but whatever they are, the Senate's procedures are almost certain to be reasonably fair and to support what Justice Souter called "the integrity of [the procedure's] results."[32]

Judgments about the Senate's likely behavior should matter a lot. In an astute analysis of Madison's political theorizing, historian Jack Rakove observes that Madison insisted that we ought to avoid thinking about the constitutional system "by pyramiding improbable contingencies that appeared 'more like the incoherent dreams of a delirious jealousy, or the misjudged exaggerations of a counterfeit zeal, than like the sober apprehensions of genuine patriotism.' "[33] What mattered to Madison, and should matter to us, is how the political system will probably operate in the ordinary course: not how it will act at its infrequent best, not how it will act at its infrequent worst, but how it will act on a moderately bad day.

We have to be careful in pointing to examples of moderately bad behavior, however. It is not enough to select some statute that you or I happen to think bad or even inconsistent with the thin Constitution. The point of populist constitutional law, after all, is to enhance the public's consideration of fundamental issues, and people will surely disagree over whether specific policies actually do advance the Declaration's principles. A moderately bad day, then, would have to be one on which the legislature enacted a statute that could not be understood by fair-minded people to be consistent with the thin Constitution.

Once we reach this point in the argument, it is impossible to avoid personal judgments, so I offer the following simply as my own evaluations of Congress's behavior in enacting statutes that I think inconsistent with the thin Constitution. I am convinced that a ban on burning flags as a political protest is inconsistent with fundamental free speech principles; indeed, I do not think it even a close case. Perhaps political leaders might see the point as well, and help the people understand our own commitments better. But perhaps not. Without judicial review, perhaps anti-flag-burning statutes would remain on the books and occasionally be enforced. A statute banning flag-burning as a method of political protest is in my view inconsistent with the thin Constitution, but I believe that fair-minded people could readily believe otherwise; a nation that enforces anti-flag-burning statutes does not strike me as, for that reason, setting down a path at the end of which is Stalinist Russia. I think the Communications Decency Act, which effectively barred distribution of "patently offensive" sexually oriented material over the Internet, presents a closer question about the thin Constitution (though not about Stalinism): The statute's breadth makes me think that a fair-minded person really could not believe that the statute advanced the Declaration's purposes.

Congress can make constitutional mistakes on a moderately bad day. But so too can the courts, which means that it is not enough to identify congressional errors; we need to compare official actions outside the courts that implicate the thin Constitution with judicial behavior before we can conclude that we should take the thin Constitution away from the courts by treating it as self-enforcing.

Will we get into trouble if we do? According to the argument developed so far, the constitutional provision requiring a Senate trial of impeachments is self-enforcing—or, as a classic article on the political questions doctrine put it, "self-monitoring."[34] But why is that? The answer must be that senators are committed to norms of fair procedure; they may push the limits of the Constitution's words to develop procedures that let most of them get on with the rest of the Senate's business, but they will not push the limits so hard as to deny fundamental fairness in impeachment trials. Senators will respect the values embedded in the Constitution's word *try* even if they adopt procedures that depart from traditional trial forms. As law professor Michael Gerhardt puts it, "[t]he political accountability of the members ensures . . . that they take due care in developing and applying standards."[35]

The next step of the argument is to generalize it: The political questions doctrine is justified with respect to particular constitutional provisions that are self-enforcing. Judicial review would not produce a higher degree of respect for constitutional values than remitting these questions to the political branches. Madison's argument about checks and balances relied on the Constitution's structural features to support its conclusion that the national government would respect constitutional values. The Senate's respect for constitutional values plays a central role in the argument about Judge Nixon's case. The argument is thereby different from Madison's. Senators' commitments to constitutional values *in themselves* explains why this constitutional provision is self-enforcing. We have here a *value-based* rather than a structure-based account of self-enforcing constitutional provisions.

Of course one could raise questions about the assumption underlying the value-based account. Perhaps senators—or the constituents to whom they respond—really are not committed to norms of fair procedure, or are not committed to them strongly enough to justify the complete judicial restraint that occurs under the political questions doctrine. One would have to be far more skeptical than I think sensible to assume that senators would routinely disregard the thin Constitution's values in this setting.

But—and here is the key point—if legislators are committed to *some* constitutional values in a way that justifies some aspects of the political questions doctrine, we have to consider the possibility that they might be committed to a wider range of such values than our traditional way of thinking about legislators assumes. Perhaps there are value-based reasons for thinking that other constitutional provisions might be self-enforcing as well.

Finally, it deserves emphasizing again that judges have *only* value-based incentives to respect the Constitution's division of authority between state and nation. True, politicians have *other* incentives as well, such as the desire for reelection, and those other incentives may distort the politicians' judgment. But judges are not entirely disinterested either, as chapter 1's discussion of the RFRA case showed. For example, they may want to build a reputation among one or another group of people they hang out with—legal academics, editorial writers, their former friends who remain active in political life. That desire may produce distortions parallel to the ones that affect politicians.

No doubt, a self-enforcing Constitution would only imperfectly advance the Constitution's values, because the incentives politicians have are not perfect: The Constitution is not perfectly incentive-compatible. Unfortunately, judges are not perfect either. They will make mistakes, or respond to imperfect incentives. So a judicially enforced Constitution will only imperfectly advance the Constitution's values too. The real question is which of these two imperfect ways of organizing a government gets us closer to what we want. The case for self-enforcement is stronger than our current legal culture thinks it is.

INCENTIVE-COMPATIBILITY AND POLITICAL STRATEGY

The distinction between value-based and structure-based incentives creates difficulties for the theory of self-enforcement.

Strategic Difficulties. We can use the theory of self-enforcement in two rather different settings. In the first the Constitution is completely indifferent as to the outcome of political bargaining. Whatever results from the political process is consistent with the Constitution. In this sense the Constitution is self-enforcing with respect to these issues.

Some prominent arguments about the distribution of warmaking authority between Congress and the President treat the Constitution in this way. The Constitution's words give Congress the power to "declare War," make the president the commander in chief of the armed forces, and give him the general "executive Power." There is a large scholarly literature about the extent to which these words specify what military actions the president can take without explicit congressional authorization. Some authors argue that the Constitution does not give *any* answer here—or, perhaps more accurately, that the Constitution permits whatever choices the president and Congress work out in their political negotiations.[36]

The second setting is more interesting. Here the Constitution does prefer a particular outcome—the protection of state interests, for example—and achieves that outcome by ensuring that politicians' incentives are structured to produce it. The Madisonian argument about federalism, and even more Justice Blackmun's argument, have this form. What happens when some people think the Constitution is indifferent as to the outcome, and others think it prefers an outcome?

The Senate Judiciary Committee's hearings on the nomination of Clarence Thomas to the Supreme Court illustrate this problem. One issue in the hearings was exactly what sort of hearings they should be. Anita Hill accused Thomas of misconduct. To vote against Thomas, should a senator be persuaded by Hill's charges beyond a reasonable doubt, or would it be enough to think that she probably was telling the truth? Could a senator vote against confirmation on the ground that Hill's charges had raised sufficient questions about Thomas's character that it would be inappropriate to have him on the Supreme Court even if the charges were not "proved" in some moderately strong sense? In fairness to Thomas and Hill, should there be some constraints on the order in which testimony was given or the length of the investigation and hearings?

According to the best account of the Thomas hearings, Democratic senators led by Joseph Biden thought that these questions had substantive answers.[37] For example, they thought it important to conclude the hearings rather quickly, which made it difficult for them to process the information available to them. Their decisions probably affected the hearings' outcome. Neither senators nor the public had enough time to develop nuanced understandings of the characters of Hill and Thomas in ways that would make it possible to see how their competing accounts might each be correct, and then to evaluate Thomas's suitability in light of these more complex understandings.

Thomas's Republican supporters, in contrast, appear to have treated the hearings as entirely political. For them the Constitution simply created a framework within which purely political considerations would play themselves out. The Democrats took a value-based view of the Constitution, the Republicans a structure-based one. The positions had been reversed when Judge Robert Bork was nominated to the Supreme Court. Then Republicans took a value-based view, asserting that the only issue fairly open to the Senate was whether Judge Bork was qualified for the Court by reason of his experience and talent—which, on those grounds, he clearly was.[38] Democrats took a structure-based view, arguing that the confirmation process was purely political.

Notice now that in both case those who took the structure-based view prevailed: Democrats defeated Judge Bork, and Republicans confirmed Justice Thomas. This suggests that those who take a value-based position, that is, those who act on the view that the Constitution actually prefers a particular outcome, may be at a systematic strategic disadvantage when faced with those who think that the Constitution accepts whatever outcome the political process produces. The reason for this disadvantage seems clear: Senators who think that the Constitution tells them what they should do will rule out of bounds purely political arguments. So, for example, a senator who thought that fairness demanded a prompt resolution of the Hill-Thomas conflict could not say, "If we stretch this thing out, my constituents will weigh in with their views, and I'll be in a better position to decide what is politically expedient." The senator is thus deprived of a political resource that is available to someone who thinks the process completely political. Sometimes this will not cause a problem. Republicans could have pushed for prompt hearings on fairness rather than political grounds, and they would have secured what they thought politically advantageous too. But, overall, it seems likely that conflicts between those holding value-based views and those holding structure-based ones will tend to come out in favor of the latter.[39]

This gives legislators a strategic reason for taking the position that they should respond only to political incentives in developing their constitutional positions, rather than trying to work out a substantive interpretation based on the Constitution's text, structure, history, or whatever. To this extent the argument here fits nicely together with the arguments made in the preceding chapters, all of which were skeptical about the utility or importance of such considerations outside the courts.

There is, however, one important limit. Suppose the legislator's constituents demand that their representative act on principle. They might say, for example, that once the representative has protected their particular parochial interests, he or she ought to be free to act on principle, to do whatever the representative thinks best for the country, or most consistent with the Constitution. Indeed, these voters might penalize a representative who seemed to abandon principle on matters of little direct interest to the district. At this point the strategic problem reproduces itself: Political considerations demand that the legislator take a position that rules out direct consideration of politics, and that leaves the legislator at a political disadvantage.

History may provide some guidance in the particular setting of confirmation hearings. The framers ensured that the politics of the day would define the politics of confirmation by building politics into the confirmation process. When politics consisted of backroom deals, Supreme Court justices were nominated and confirmed on the basis of such deals. Now, when politics is more heavily dominated by interest-group lobbying, so is the confirmation process.

This may suggest a more general conclusion, although I would not urge it forcefully. Perhaps the entire Constitution is self-enforcing on a deeper level: In any historical period we get out of our Constitution and our politicians what we want.

Rhetorical Difficulties. Sometimes the disadvantage is on the side of the structure-based position. The reason is that it may seem *overly* cynical, political in a pejorative sense. The people who pay attention are likely to want to think that a constitutional provision means *something*, and will want to hear arguments about what it means, not an argument that its meaning is determined by a purely political process. They will gravitate to the other side if they hear a purely political argument, and the proponents of the structure-based position will not have enough political power to accomplish what they want—and what, on their own views, they can achieve only by having enough political power.

Article III says that federal judges hold their offices "during good Behaviour." In the late 1960s Republicans filed a resolution to impeach Justice William O. Douglas, citing among other things articles he had published in *Playboy* magazine, in which he expressed sympathy for some of the 1960s movements. Is that an example of impeachable bad behavior? House minority leader Gerald Ford offered a definition: The permissible grounds for impeachment were "whatever a majority of the House of Representatives considers them to be at a given moment in history." More recently, Representative Tom DeLay revived the idea, although without quite as pithy a statement as Ford's.

That is a pure structure-based position. Justice Douglas's critics would cite anything they thought inappropriate. His defenders would have two responses: What he did was just fine, and anyhow, it does not count as bad behavior within the meaning of the Constitution as revealed by the framers' intent, the historical background, and the like. Representative Ford and the Republicans never got anywhere with their impeachment charges, partly because they were the minority party opposing someone widely admired within the Democratic party, but partly because their attack—and Representative Ford's constitutional defense of their position—seemed inappropriately political.

Not every substantive position on what the Constitution means is a rhetorical resource, however. A lot depends on what the position is. Public support drives the argument here, and it is easier to get public support for some constitutional positions than others, not because of their content but because of their form.

Law professor Robert Nagel wrote a scathing criticism of what he called the formulaic Constitution.[40] *That* Constitution, he said, was filled with three-part tests like this: "When 'speech' and 'nonspeech' elements are combined in the same course of conduct. . . a government regulation is sufficiently justified if it is within the constitutional power of the Government; if it furthers an important or substantial governmental interest; if the governmental interest is unrelated to the suppression of free expression; and if the incidental restriction on alleged First Amendment freedoms is no greater than is essential to the furtherance of that interest."[41] The Supreme Court often has good institutional reasons for developing constitutional formulas. They make it easier for lower court judges to figure out what to do, for example.[42] But formulas rarely provide rhetoric suitable for generating wide public support. No one is going to make a movie about the First Amendment I have just described, for example, but there are many movies about the First Amendment that says, "Congress shall make no law . . . abridging the freedom of speech," celebrating the fact that, as Justice Hugo Black used to say, " 'No law' means 'no law.' "[43]

Another typical constitutional argument may be equally unhelpful in public rhetoric. This is the balancing test: Enumerate all the considerations that bear on a sensible resolution of the constitutional problem, give each one its appropriate weight, and figure out what the best thing to do is on balance. This is not a bad way to decide, in the abstract, but it may not work well in practice.

Sometimes legislators will speak in balancing terms because of the judicial overhang we examined in chapter 3: They use the terms the Supreme Court has used. But, as with formulas, courts use balancing tests for institutional reasons. Here the reasons are rather different from those for using formulas: Formulas help the Supreme Court guide lower courts; balancing tests keep power in the Supreme Court's hands, for who except the justices can tell us how the balance comes out. Commenting on a balancing test adopted by Justice Powell, for example, a law clerk once wrote, "[I]t [was] hard to tell whether . . . [lower courts had] 'misread' [a Powell opinion], since nobody knows what that opinion stands for now that Justice Powell has retired."[44] Widespread criticism of Justice Sandra Day O'Connor's affection for balancing tests has rested on similar grounds: Under such tests the Constitution appears to mean what Justice O'Connor thinks it means, and nobody knows what that is until we ask her.

Balancing may not be useful in public rhetoric even if one thinks that balancing is the right way to think about a constitutional provision independent of the judicial overhang. The listing of considerations and the assignment of weights may give the argument a ponderous air, leaching it of the kind of passionate commitment that can generate real public support.

These rhetorical difficulties can be avoided quite readily. One solution is *procedural*. The Constitution may give people rhetorical resources only if the Supreme Court has not spoken, or has spoken in ways so opaque that every participant in a later discussion can fairly say that the Supreme Court is on his or her side. We can generate a vibrant public rhetoric about the Constitution if we get the Supreme Court to say nothing—or to say too much.[45]

Another solution is *substantive*. Value-based positions will be rhetorically helpful if they are simple. And they will be simple if they have clear links to the Declaration's principles. The Constitution outside the courts should be a thin Constitution if it is to be self-enforcing through a political process that combines structure-based and value-based incentives.

INCENTIVE-COMPATIBILITY AND THE PRESIDENT'S DUTY TO ENFORCE THE LAW

Constitutional questions about the president's powers provide a useful way of exploring the idea of a politically based system of incentive-compatibility, in which the president's political incentives lead him or her to act in a way consistent with constitutional values. The examples typically involve provisions in the thick Constitution, but the analysis points the way to understanding how the thin Constitution might be self-enforcing.

After Paula Corbin Jones sued President William Clinton for sexual harassment, the president attempted to block the suit by saying that the Constitution gave the president an absolute right to delay lawsuits against him until his term of office ended.[46] There is almost no constitutional text to go on here: The Constitution's reference to "*a*" President, the decision to make a single person the repository of all executive power, is just about all there is. From that decision, the president argued, we can infer that the president's ability to manage his or her own time is essential to the functioning of this unitary executive. So, the president argued, courts could not order the president to show up for a trial or even to show up for the kinds of pretrial interrogations that are routine in modern litigation. Jones responded that our constitutional tradition rested on the idea that no person, not even the president, was above the law, and that any problems the president faced could be handled by careful scheduling decisions made by the trial judge handling the lawsuit. The president answered the latter point by saying that it would be inappropriate for a trial judge to say to a president, "I don't agree with you that the NATO meeting you say you have to attend—or the political fund-raiser you say you have to go to—is more important than giving the deposition we have scheduled."

The Supreme Court agreed with Jones that the lawsuit could proceed while Clinton remained in office, although it emphasized that the trial judge should "manage" the trial to avoid "interference with the President's duties." How could we look at this problem from the perspective of incentive-compatibility? Consider the following rule: The president is not entitled to a complete suspension of lawsuits until he or she leaves office, but the president has an absolute right to refuse to attend any particular court session for any reason whatever. The court must accept the president's decision if the president says, "I can't show up for a deposition today because I have a more important meeting," or even, "I can't show up but I can't tell you why."

How would such a rule work in practice? The president would be able to continue to conduct his ordinary work, but would have to take some political heat each time he objected to showing up in court. People might understand that a NATO meeting was really important, but the president might lose more political points for refusing to show up because of a conflict with a political fund-raiser. The president would have to calculate whether the political costs associated with objecting were worth the gains he gets from delaying the lawsuit. He would also have to worry about crying wolf: If he objects too often, he may lose so much political esteem in the public's eyes that he might be unable to get away with objecting when there really was a crisis demanding his full attention. Giving the president this sort of absolute privilege might simultaneously protect the presidency and the rule of law, not because judges figure out the correct balance themselves but because the president's political incentives are likely to lead to a decent solution.[47]

Controversies during the Reagan and Bush administrations pose more serious problems. They are all variants of a more general question: What may a president do when faced with a statute with which the president disagrees? The question identifies a tension between the Constitution's general provisions about how something becomes law and the president's duty to "take Care that the laws be faithfully executed." The conventional way of putting the problem is to ask whether the "laws" the president must faithfully execute are the statutes enacted by Congress, or the entire body of law that includes the Constitution.[48] The idea of incentive-compatibility suggests that the answer to the question about what a president can properly do, "Whatever the president thinks politically expedient," will produce a resolution that advances, or at least does not impair, constitutional values.[49]

Variant One: Disregarding a Law by Exercising a "New" Power. In the late 1980s the Bush administration came under pressure from conservatives, supported by the editorial page of the *Wall Street Journal*, to exercise a line-item veto by refusing to spend money for particular projects even though Congress appropriated money for them.[50] The conventional wisdom was that the president could veto entire bills, but could not "veto" or otherwise ignore particular provisions. The *Wall Street Journal* and other conservatives developed an argument that the president had the power to exercise a line-item veto under the present Constitution. The argument, in bare outlines, was that the Constitution requires that "Bills" be presented to the president for signature or veto, that at the time of the framing "Bills" dealt with single subjects, that the present practice of presenting the president with multi-topic, large-scale appropriations measures should be understood as a method of packaging many "constitutional Bills" into one group, and that the president may veto any "constitutional Bill," that is, any single-subject matter contained within the new form of packaging.[51]

President Bush's legal advisers told him that this argument was inadequate. The president declined to exercise a line-item veto, suffering some political loss among conservatives for his decision. Imagine what would have happened if President Bush had gone ahead anyway.

—There would have been an outpouring of statements from members of Congress that the president was ignoring the Constitution. Some might even come from members who actually agreed that money would be wasted if the project the president vetoed went forward, because even they would be interested in preserving Congress's power over appropriations. Critics would say that we had gone two centuries without a line-item veto, that no president had ever even come close to thinking that he had the power, and would point out that proponents of a line-item veto had repeatedly introduced proposed constitutional amendments to give the president that power. One can readily imagine the statement from a Democratic senator's office, "Who does President George Herbert Walker Bush think he is? King George III?"

—Newspapers all over the country would echo these sentiments.

—The political outcry would be even more substantial if the president had line-item vetoed a project in a way that made it extremely difficult to get a court to decide whether the president really did have the power he tried to exercise. Critics would say that a president should not take extreme constitutional positions without giving the courts a chance to tell us whether he was right or wrong.

—The situation would be exacerbated because the president would have ignored his own legal advisers. The president's critics would ask, "Why should a mere politician, even the president, decide for himself what the Constitution means?"

Contemplating the prospect of such reactions, President Bush decided against exercising a line-item veto. The Constitution was self-enforcing in this instance. The political concerns the president faced combined substantive disagreements with the items he would have to have vetoed, structure-based concerns regarding the distribution of power between the president and Congress, and value-based concerns regarding the kind of government we have.

Variant Two: Ignoring a Law the President Thinks Unconstitutionally Invades Presidential Authority. President Bush acted against a background of controversy in the Reagan administration. The Reagan administration held a strong theory of executive power, which it sought to advance in many forums. The Reagan administration decided that an obscure statute called the Competition in Contracting Act unconstitutionally infringed on the president's prerogatives: The statute directed the executive branch to refrain from awarding a contract if it was notified by the Comptroller-General, an official located in the legislative branch, that there were questions about the proposed contract. This, the administration said, amounted to a legislative invasion of executive authority.

Prominent Democratic legislators took out after the administration. If the administration thought the Act unconstitutional, they said, the president should have vetoed it. That would have given Congress a chance to override the veto. If Congress did so, the president would have a duty to enforce the law. Otherwise, it would be silly to have a veto provision in the Constitution: The president could disregard any law he thought unconstitutional, so why bother to give him the power to veto laws as unconstitutional? Notably, the legislators who criticized the administration were powerful committee chairs. The administration needed their cooperation to enact other parts of its legislative program. In the end the administration retreated. Somewhat shamefacedly it said that it really did not want to provoke a constitutional confrontation. All it wanted to do was get a judicial ruling on the constitutionality of the Competition in Contracting Act. It took the position it did, the administration's statements said, simply to set up a lawsuit.[52]

Madison's insight seems directly relevant here. These cases show what happens when the "interest of the man"—the president and congressional leaders both—is "connected with the constitutional rights of the place." The Reagan administration's retreat shows how powerful structure-based political concerns can be—how, that is, they provide real incentives to which politicians respond.

The process is simple: Political conflicts occur, the parties explain their positions to the public, and some resolution is reached.[53] We might be troubled if we thought that the Constitution dictated the correct resolution. But the political resolutions of these controversies seem entirely acceptable if we think that the Constitution requires only that the principles of the Declaration of Independence be respected.

Variant Three: Ignoring a Law Because the President Disagrees with It on Policy Grounds (the Overridden Veto). So far we have been dealing with presidential claims that a statute invades the president's constitutional prerogatives. Suppose next that the president vetoes a statute because he or she disagrees with the policy it embodies, and Congress enacts it over the veto. Can the president refuse to enforce the statute nonetheless? It is hard to see how that course is consistent with the Constitution's assumptions. Again, why give Congress the power to override a veto if the president can still refuse to enforce the law? It is at least plausible to think that a president's constitutional prerogatives exist—that the Constitution gives the president some powers that Congress cannot take away—even if Congress denies that the president can continue to act on policy grounds after Congress has overridden a policy-based veto.

This position too may be self-enforcing. A substantial political controversy erupted when President Richard Nixon refused to spend money Congress had appropriated because he thought the expenditures unwise. It was ultimately resolved when the courts held that the president lacked *statutory* authority to withhold the funds. The administration acquiesced, in large measure because the political costs of continuing to impound the funds were far too high. And, if a statute as obscure as the Competition in Contracting Act can lead to real political difficulties for a relatively popular president like Ronald Reagan, it seems likely that the value-based view that the president must enforce all laws, even those with which he or she disagrees on policy grounds, is self-enforcing through the political process.

An example from the Clinton administration is instructive. Late in the extremely contentious process of enacting a budget in 1996, Representative Robert Dornan introduced an amendment requiring the armed forces to separate from the service all service members who tested positive for HIV. High-ranking military leaders unanimously condemned the amendment: They believed that it would deprive the services of valuable members, some of whom had contracted HIV under circumstances for which the military ought to take responsibility. President Clinton signed the budget containing Representative Dornan's amendment, largely because the entire package resolved the political confrontations over the budget. The administration's lawyers then took a complex position. They would begin the process of separating HIV-positive members from the armed forces, fully anticipating that some would challenge the Dornan Amendment's constitutionality. When such attacks occurred, they would take the position that, in the eyes of military leaders, the provision not only had no military justification but actually interfered with the military's efficient performance. They would inform the courts of that view, and let the courts apply judicially developed standards to decide whether the amendment was constitutional. The administration informed the House and the Senate of this position. Congress repealed the Dornan Amendment when it learned of the administration's position.

The case is interesting for two reasons. It involves a situation in which the administration objected to a statute on policy grounds but was unable to exercise a veto, for political reasons. And it involves a situation in which the administration did *not* assert that the statute was unconstitutional but rather laid out the military's position, leaving it to the courts to decide whether the statute was constitutional, given the apparent differences between military leaders and Congress over whether the statute was justified. President Clinton's assessment of the political lay of the land was borne out when Congress repealed the statute.

Variant Four: Ignoring a Law Because the President Disagrees with It on Policy Grounds (the Outdated Law). Policy disagreement can occur in a different form. A president arrives in office and finds that Congress earlier—a year before, or decades ago—enacted a statute with which the president disagrees. The president has two choices: ask Congress to repeal the statute, or disregard the statute. The president has to use up some political capital either way. Getting a statute enacted means not doing something else; ignoring the statute means attracting adverse public and political comment. Here, however, it seems unlikely that the political consequences of either choice differ dramatically. Perhaps a modest, and largely prudential, preference for stability would suggest that the president would do well to try to get the statute repealed.

The president might reply that he or she has recently gone to the people, who endorsed the president's political program, which includes disagreement with the statute in place. The people's more recent views ought to have some weight in deciding what the better course is. Putting it more starkly, the president might claim that requiring enforcement of the earlier statute means giving the status quo a preference it does not deserve. Sometimes, of course, departing from the status quo disrupts a lot of settled expectations. In the present context, though, we can observe that in those circumstances we can expect the adverse political effects of disregarding the existing law to be rather substantial. Once again, it seems reasonable to think that the president's political calculations will lead to an acceptable resolution of the policy disagreement between the president and the now-departed Congress that enacted the statute.

Variant Five: Ignoring an Unconstitutional Law. The case of a veto on constitutional grounds unrelated to presidential prerogatives, which Congress then overrides, is more complex. Suppose Congress passes a law banning flag-burning, which the president believes unconstitutional under the First Amendment. The president can veto the statute. May the president refuse to prosecute someone who burns a flag if Congress overrides the veto? Presidents have taken the position that they have the power to ignore unconstitutional statutes of this sort, but that they should do so only when the unconstitutionality is gross and apparent.[54]

Again a recent example illustrates how the Constitution can be self-enforcing. The Communications Decency Act regulated distribution of information on the Internet. One provision banned distribution of information regarding the availability of abortions. President Clinton signed the Act, stating that he had no intention of enforcing that provision. In many cases, such an action would be unseemly and politically costly, because the question, "Why not veto the bill?" would have real political bite as the bill's sponsors attacked the president for hypocrisy. Not here, though. The Act's sponsors were concerned primarily about the distribution of sexually explicit material on the Internet, and the abortion provision seems to have slipped into the bill almost by mistake. The president could refuse to enforce it at almost no political cost. It would take a fanatic about the president's obligation to "take Care that the laws be faithfully executed" to think that President Clinton's actions were constitutionally problematic.

Fanaticism is misplaced here because the political costs were properly low. But that is to say that the "take care" clause is self-enforcing through the political incentives the president faces. What if the political costs were higher? Again self-enforcement is relevant. The presidential standard for nonenforcement—gross unconstitutionality—identifies situations where it seems likely that the political costs will be low. Congress itself has responded to the traditional presidential position by requiring the Attorney General to notify both the House and Senate when the administration is going to take a position in court that a statute is unconstitutional. Again this is a political accommodation designed to protect both the general process of enacting statutes and the president's authority to enforce all the law. In light of this statute, a president runs a real risk if he or she refuses to enforce a statute that is, in the president's view, unconstitutional, but not grossly so.[55]

I have accumulated a number of examples that show how political considerations help resolve constitutional controversies. There may be other examples showing that political considerations operate in ways that produce outcomes that *are* constitutionally problematic. We have to decide whether judicial intervention improves things overall, taking all the cases into account and being constantly aware that courts make constitutional mistakes too. In the cases I have presented, uncertainty about the Constitution's meaning—or disagreement between the branches about its meaning—fuels the controversies, but it also makes constitutional argument a rhetorical resource as each side claims that the Constitution properly read supports its position. Judicial intervention in *these* controversies would destabilize the political process by purporting to impose one interpretation on the contending sides.

The Real Politics of Incentive-Compatibility

Those who believed that the Constitution, properly read, does not give the president the power to exercise a line-item veto discovered that the Constitution was self-enforcing in that respect. President Bush did not think that, on balance, the political benefits he would gain from conservatives who liked executive power and others, both conservatives and moderates, who wanted him to take control of the budget, would outweigh the political costs he would suffer from the constitutional controversy he would provoke.

I must note one complication. The episodes I have discussed have all occurred in a legal universe where political actors ordinarily think that the courts stand ready to resolve their disputes. The possibility of judicial review becomes a resource in the political bargaining between the branches. And perhaps the outcomes I have described, and have suggested are generally satisfactory, occur precisely because the president and Congress have anticipated what the courts would do if they ever got hold of the problems.

How exactly might the possibility of judicial review affect outcomes? Suppose the president says, "My constitutional position is correct, and the courts will go along with me." One possibility, of course, is that Congress will reply, "No, our position is correct, and the courts will agree with *us*." If both sides sincerely believe their assertions, the possibility of judicial review actually makes it impossible for political bargaining to produce an agreement: Each side will hold out for what it (optimistically) thinks the courts will give it, although one of them must be wrong.

If each side is somewhat pessimistic—if each thinks it *might* lose—they might prefer a sure compromise deal now rather than taking their chances going to court, with outcomes they cannot be certain of. The difference between Congress's assessment of the risk of losing and the president's defines the range within which a deal can be struck.[56]

What would happen if the courts were not available? Instead of a real court, the president and Congress appeal to the court of public opinion. The public might want *some* agreement, which gives the president and Congress some reason to agree. But there might be a rather large range within which the deal could be struck, determined by each side's assessment of how likely it is that the public will eventually endorse its position. Again the difference in assessments of how likely a loss is defines the range within which a deal can be struck. That range might be larger than the one that exists when a court decision might be rendered. Finally, perhaps any result within the narrower range is satisfactory—consistent with the thin Constitution—while some results outside it might be unsatisfactory. In this way, the fact that courts are ready to intervene improves the likelihood that bargaining will produce good outcomes.

There is another possibility. Perhaps the president's underlying statement really is, "Well, I've appointed most of those people, and I'm confident they will go along with me." If the president is right, he is asserting that he has the sheer power to get away with what he wants because he has the powerful weapon of the courts on his side. It is not clear to me that we ought to be comfortable with the use of courts as mere weapons in a power struggle. But, to the extent that the prospect of judicial review operates in this second way, we cannot conclude that satisfactory outcomes would result if everyone knew that the courts would stay out of the fight.

In light of these possibilities, I cannot establish that satisfactory outcomes would generally result in a world without judicial review. I *think* that the results were produced more by pure bargaining power than by bargaining power in light of the possibility of court intervention, in part because technical legal doctrines such as rules about who can bring a court case and when a challenge is ready for decision made the actual prospects of a definitive court decision quite small in nearly every case. Both sides should have been quite pessimistic about prevailing in a court showdown, which implies that the bargaining range was in fact nearly as large as it would have been without the possibility of judicial action. But, in the end, one's conclusions about the relation between the possibility of judicial review and the fact that bargained outcomes have generally been satisfactory must be a matter of judgment.

Suppose then that President Bush worked through the textual, historical, and other arguments about the line-item veto, was persuaded that his legal advisers were right, but nonetheless thought that it would be good for the country for him to exercise a line-item veto. Chapter 2 argued that he would not act in a constitutionally irresponsible way if he tried to exercise such a veto. Of course he would do so recognizing the political costs he would incur, but he would exercise the veto only if he thought that the political costs were worth it. He might even think that the political controversy would be so great that it could fairly be described as a constitutional crisis. But, as we saw in chapter 1, there is no reason in principle to reject acts that lead to constitutional crises. What matters are the political stakes: A politician can provoke a constitutional crisis when he or she thinks the stakes are high enough.

But, as we saw, the politician should recognize some constraints.

Prudential Constraints. The Reagan administration recognized that it could turn down the political heat by structuring the controversy in a way that would lead to a judicial ruling on its position. More generally, part of the political calculation ought to be: Are there ways of sustaining our position that would impose smaller political costs on us? In particular, if the politician thinks there are good reasons to believe that courts would sustain his or her position, that is a reason to try to get the courts to resolve the controversy.

Principled Constraints. Constitutional crises ought to be unusual, reserved for situations where the principles of the Declaration of Independence are at stake—or, at least, for situations where those who provoke the crisis can persuade the public that those principles are at stake. Less need be at stake if the politician can structure the constitutional controversy in a way that lessens tension, for example by ensuring judicial review. Note that the courts play a role here for essentially political reasons. It is not that our *constitutional* system demands that courts resolve all constitutional questions, but that in our *political* system, as people now understand things, letting the courts decide constitutional questions sometimes reduces political contention.

In the cases we have examined, I doubt that either the Reagan or Bush administrations could persuasively have made out the case that the Declaration's principles were at stake in their situations, but they surely could have claimed persuasively that what they wanted to do was not *inconsistent* with the Declaration's principles. Their actions would have been justified if they fell short of producing a constitutional crisis.

As these discussions show, figuring out whether some constitutional provisions can be self-enforcing will often require making difficult and controversial empirical judgments. Does the necessity for such judgments introduce an undesirable instability into thinking about the Constitution?

I think not, for two reasons.

1. Slippery-slope arguments: One form of empirical argument pervades our constitutional rhetoric already. It is the slippery-slope argument: "If we let the president get away with this, next time he'll try something worse and maybe he'll get away with it, until we end up with Hitler's coup." Or, "If the courts uphold a statute against flag desecration, next time we'll discover that they are upholding laws against holding demonstrations against the president." Sometimes these are good arguments, sometimes not. But surely they are basically empirical, resting on predictions about how the president, legislators, and the courts will actually behave when faced with new circumstances. It is hard to see how empirical arguments would destabilize the system if slippery-slope arguments do not.

Slippery-slope arguments simply illustrate the more general phenomenon of courts' routine use of empirical judgments as they develop constitutional doctrine.[57] Another example is the Supreme Court's concept of a "chilling effect" in free speech doctrine. The Court develops rules that protect more speech than is absolutely necessary because it has made the empirical judgment that people who know what the legal rules are will "steer far wider of the unlawful zone" to make sure they do not get into trouble.[58] Maybe so, but maybe the American people are so resolute in their attachment to free expression that we will always walk right up to the line between permitted and prohibited expression. The Court's own doctrines often rest on empirical judgments. It would seem just as reasonable to rest our more general thoughts about the Constitution on such judgments as well.

2. Empirical arguments and judicial review: Even more, the ultimate issues involve comparisons between a regime of self-enforcing provisions and a regime of judicial enforcement. Determining whether judicial enforcement is effective requires making precisely the same kinds of empirical judgments.[59] Empirical judgments, far from introducing instability into a constitutional system, are the only way to see whether the system is defensible.

THE POSSIBLE SCOPE OF AN INCENTIVE-COMPATIBLE CONSTITUTION

I have developed the view that a combination of value-based and structure-based incentives makes it sensible to think of the Constitution's provisions dealing with federalism and separation of powers as self-enforcing: The constitutional values protected by those features of our Constitution would not be threatened by eliminating judicial review, particularly when we recognize that the courts might themselves mistakenly bar our representatives from adopting policies that are in fact consistent with the Constitution. The constitutional provisions I have discussed might be located in the thick Constitution, however. What about self-enforcement of the thin Constitution?

Dissenting in the state minimum wage case, Justice Powell took the majority to be arguing that the courts should refrain from enforcing federalism limits on national power because the states were represented in Congress. He responded, "One can hardly imagine this Court saying that because Congress is composed of individuals, individual rights guaranteed by the Bill of Rights are amply protected by the political process."[60] The Madisonian argument, of course, is more complicated than Justice Powell thought. Its claim is that the values of federalism are adequately protected by the self-enforcing mechanisms built into our political structure and public values.[61] The claim is therefore specific to federalism: There is no particular reason to think that structures and values will protect individual rights just because they protect federalism.

Elitists tend to think that the people could not possibly care enough about individual rights to protect them through politics. And yet there are some dramatic examples of popular respect for what the people understand to be constitutional rights.

The Second Amendment. Gun control legislation is hard to enact because large numbers of people are convinced—wrongly, in the eyes of many scholars—that the Constitution guarantees an individual the right to own a wide range of guns.

Abortion. In 1992 the Supreme Court made it substantially easier for the states to adopt regulations restricting the availability of abortion.[62] It said it would allow regulations so long as they did not place a "substantial burden" on the woman's right to choose. It was not entirely clear in describing what a substantial burden might be, but there is no doubt that the decision allowed states a much wider range of action than before. The legislative response to this decision was dramatic: For all practical purposes—that is, from the point of view of women seeking abortions, and of those who think that abortion is always unjustifiable murder—essentially nothing happened. There were a few efforts to expand regulation substantially, and more to tinker with existing regulation at the edges, but there was no rash of legislation seeking to make it significantly more difficult for women to obtain abortions.[63] The reason appears to be political: Enough people think that women ought to have a right to choose that it is very difficult to get legislatures to enact laws making it much harder for them to exercise that right.

These two examples rest on values. Enough people will vote against legislators who support gun control or restrictions on the availability of abortions to give the legislators political incentives to respect these constitutional rights. Are there structure-based incentives that might work in the context of individual rights?

There is an obvious structural device to support those who think that constitutional values are threatened only by laws the government enacts: Make it hard to enact laws. More subtly, sometimes people will come to adopt specific values because they find themselves within institutions with particular characteristics. The classic example is deliberation: We might induce our representatives to rely somewhat more on reason and somewhat less on mere calculations of political advantage if we structure our legislatures to require some degree of open debate and deliberation.

We examined in chapter 3 one prominent argument that we cannot structure our institutions to give representatives incentives to *protect* constitutional rights, although we may be able to make it harder for them to *violate* those rights. The argument was that voters focus on the short run while the Constitution deals with the long run. We can look at this argument here from another perspective.

We might think that voters would care about the long run, about constitutional values, because each voter has to worry that in the long run he or she will be the target of some law that seems sensible in the short run: Give the government the power to aggressively investigate domestic terrorism, in the form of bombings of government buildings, and you may find that the people in charge of the government think that you are a domestic terrorist because of your political views.

Short-run considerations might of course overwhelm this more speculative long-run concern. Law professor Cass Sunstein has suggested that we ought to develop judicially protected constitutional rights where we think that the political incentives facing legislators are likely to make them inattentive to fundamental values.[64] So, he argued, the nations in Eastern and Central Europe formerly under Communist rule should not write protection for welfare rights into their constitutions, but should protect rights to private property; nations in Western Europe, in contrast, might reasonably protect welfare rights in their constitutions and not private property rights. The historical circumstances of Eastern and Central Europe make it likely that legislators will not care enough about private property, while those of Western Europe make *legislative* protection of private property far more likely.

Again, this is a value-based account. But it introduces a key point: The incentives legislators face depend on the historical circumstances in which they find themselves. Constitutional restrictions on legislative power become increasingly inapt if the incentives change as the years go by. The Constitution written in 1789 will restrain Congress with respect to matters where we can count on the people's values to give legislators incentives to respect fundamental rights. And, perhaps worse, the Constitution written in 1789 will not restrict Congress with respect to matters where the people today will be inattentive to fundamental values.

This shows why the apparently attractive strategy of combining self-enforcement and judicial enforcement probably will not work. In the abstract, we would want to make sure that courts enforced constitutional values where politicians did not have either structural or value-based incentives to do so, and would leave to self-enforcement the constitutional values where politicians had the right incentives. But we cannot hope to do that with consistent success. Incentive structures change as values and political problems change. For the allocation strategy to succeed, we would have to make sure that courts would start enforcing the right constitutional values at the right time, then stop when circumstances change.

The test we would be asking courts to apply would be, "As an empirical matter, what are politicians' incentives with respect to this particular constitutional question?" I doubt that judges will get the right answer very often. To some extent, judges with political experience might have some sense of the political realities, at least for a few years after they become judges. But their grasp on the realities of politics will fade. In any event, recently we have seen a rapid decline in the number of Supreme Court justices with substantial political experience. No one presently on the Supreme Court, for example, has anything like the political experience Earl Warren and Hugo Black—or even lesser figures like Harold Burton, Tom Clark, Arthur Goldberg, or Abe Fortas—brought to the Court. Even more, as the RFRA case showed, judges have something like a self-interest in finding that politicians' incentives are not "right," because that conclusion gives the judges themselves more power.

The question of whether the Constitution is self-enforcing, then, probably is an all-or-nothing proposition: Either we have a Constitution that the courts enforce entirely (with a minor exception for a problematic political questions doctrine) or one that is entirely self-enforcing (again, perhaps, with some minor and problematic exceptions). The conventional assumption is that of course we get a higher rate of compliance with constitutional values if the courts enforce the Constitution. That assumption often rests on the unstated, and largely indefensible, belief that the courts never make mistakes. But they do. The peyote case showed that courts may underenforce some values that legislatures would vigorously enforce,[65] and the RFRA decision showed that they may "overenforce" some values, thereby depriving the people of our power to govern ourselves without promoting any value the Constitution actually seeks to promote.

There are some procedural ways of addressing these difficulties.

Clear Statement Rules. We could require legislatures to be quite specific when they enact laws restricting fundamental rights. Legal scholars refer to this sort of thing as a "clear statement rule." We can make sure that legislators at least focus on what is at stake by insisting on a clear statement. This gives those who think that fundamental values are at stake a chance to make their case to the public. And it gives the public the chance to accomplish what it desires, so long as the legislation truly reflects those desires.

Constitutional Amendment. The problem we are dealing with is constitutional rigidity in the face of changes in the historically specific value-based incentives legislators face. But perhaps the Constitution does not have to be all that rigid. We could make it relatively easy to amend.[66] Scholars have shown that the mechanisms of constitutional amendment in the U.S. Constitution are among the most stringent in the world.[67]

Of course there are many ways to make amending the Constitution easier. Some nations allow amendment by popular referendum. Others allow amendment by simple majorities in the national legislature in successive sessions.

Canada has a particularly ingenious device. The legislature can override some of Canada's constitutional provisions by a simple majority, but the override can last for no longer than five years, which means that an election has to intervene before an override can be renewed. Canadian legislatures have rarely used their override power. The reason is again value-based. Shortly after legislatures got the power to override, the legislature in Quebec used the power to protect a law requiring the use of French on public signs from constitutional invalidation. The Quebec sign law was intensely controversial in Canada as a whole, because it symbolized Quebec's separatist impulses. The use of the override compounded the controversy, because it seemed to many like an indirect way of promoting separatism when direct methods either had failed or were constitutionally out of bounds. The Canadian Supreme Court upheld Quebec's use of the override, but the episode appears to have discredited the power—in the sense that the Canadian people think that, as a general matter, their legislatures should not expressly violate their existing constitutional rights.

Taking Responsibility for Constitutional Values. As we saw in chapter 3, some prominent constitutional scholars have argued that judicial review itself diminishes the political incentives legislators face. Legislators—and voters—need not care much about protecting constitutional values precisely because they know that courts will enforce the Constitution. Judicial review, that is, may be a structural *impediment* to self-enforcement of individual rights. Michael Gerhardt observes that the absence of judicial review of impeachment questions appears to have given legislators "a peculiar mix of freedom . . . and responsibility" that seems attractive.[68] Elite skepticism about popular commitment to constitutional values may then accurately reflect current circumstances, but those circumstances need not tell us anything about the basic commitments of the American people.

Constitutional Content. Recall the earlier discussion of the formulaic Constitution. Perhaps people would be deeply committed to constitutional values, and would penalize their representatives for infringing those values, if the values were easy to grasp. The people can be deeply committed to the thin Constitution of the Declaration's principles. What is more, historically the American people have been committed to those principles, at least as aspirations.[69] And, I have argued in chapter 2, it is not at all clear why we ought to be deeply committed to the details of the thick Constitution we actually have.

CONCLUSION

Should we begin to think of the Constitution as incentive-compatible or self-enforcing in general? This chapter has argued that traditional methods of constitutional interpretation support the conclusion that *some* constitutional provisions are self-enforcing. I do not believe, however, that the same traditional methods lead to the conclusion that the entire Constitution "is" self-enforcing. My argument operates on a different level.

If we accepted the controversial empirical judgments about how the political system actually operates, and

if we thought that a stable constitutional system could be founded on such judgments, and

if we were able to free ourselves from our obsession with courts, and

if we paid attention to the thin Constitution of the Declaration's principles,

then we would find that the idea of a self-enforcing Constitution describes an attractive way of distributing constitutional responsibility throughout the government.

Chapter Six

ASSESSING JUDICIAL REVIEW

Constitutional Heroes?

Political scientist Peter Irons wrote a book about sixteen people who took their constitutional claims to the Supreme Court. They included Mary Beth Tinker, who successfully challenged her school board's policy barring her from wearing a black armband to protest the war in Vietnam, and Barbara Elfbrandt, a Quaker teacher who refused to take an oath supporting the Constitution. Irons called his book *The Courage of Their Convictions*.[1]

Recently the winners in important Supreme Court cases upholding First Amendment claims have been James Buckley, brother of publisher William F. Buckley who became a United States Senator and federal court judge, the Colorado Republican Campaign Committee, and the First National Bank of Boston.[2] Perhaps someone writing a book like Irons's today should call it *The Color of Their Money*.

The preceding chapters have argued that legislators freed from the judicial overhang might not do such a bad job of interpreting the thin Constitution. This chapter and the next turn to the other side of the necessary comparison, and argue that the courts actually have not done such a wonderful job as to distinguish them sharply from legislatures. Many people, particularly liberals, have warm and fuzzy feelings about judicial review. Admiring the Constitution inside the courts, they are nervous about taking the Constitution away from the courts. Defenders of judicial review hope that the Supreme Court will give them victories they cannot win in the political arena. Liberals with this view may think that the Supreme Court under Earl Warren—who left the Court in 1969—is the Supreme Court today. Or they may think that the Court's recent performance is a mixed bag, but still beneficial to liberals on balance. Or they may think that the Court's recent conservatism is a deviation from the Court's historic role.

None of those perceptions is accurate. This chapter explains why.[3]

The Political Tilt of Free Speech Law

We can begin with a quick look at free speech law. Does it tilt in favor of liberals or conservatives?

The Warren Court during its peak years of 1963 to 1968 upheld free speech claims in about thirty cases.[4] Almost all the cases involved what we might think of as classic free speech problems. Some involved political protests, against the war in Vietnam or in favor of civil rights. Even as late as the mid-1960s, a few involved claims by people whom government officials believed to be subversive. Others involved people who were criticizing the government in other ways. And some involved picketing by unions.

Contrast that with the cases decided from 1989 to 1996. The Supreme Court again upheld about thirty free speech claims. Some of the cases involved traditional claims. The Court held unconstitutional the exclusion of crosses erected by the Ku Klux Klan from a public square near a state capitol. Another case involved a political pamphleteer who distributed a pamphlet anonymously, and yet another involved a woman who wanted to hang a flag protesting the Gulf War from her window. A fair number involved religious proselytizers. And in probably the most famous, the Court held unconstitutional laws banning flag-burning as a form of political protest.[5]

Margaret McIntyre, the pamphleteer, Margaret Gilleo, the protestor against the Gulf War, and Joey Johnson, the flag-burner, might someday appear in a new version of Professor Irons's book. But then there are other cases. The Court now devotes a fair amount of attention to protecting the commercial interests of businesses. Sometimes those businesses are media enterprises—cable television operators, for example, or, in another case, the publisher of a weekly handout consisting entirely of commercial advertising. Since 1976 the Supreme Court has developed an extensive set of rules that severely limit our ability to regulate campaign financing.[6]

In the 1960s free speech protection tilted fairly strongly to benefit liberals and critics of the government.[7] Today that tilt is not nearly as strong. And, if the commercial advertising cases and the campaign finance cases deal with issues with greater social impact than the distribution of anonymous pamphlets, free speech protection tilts somewhat—not strongly, but somewhat—to the right, aiding people who are already pretty well fixed for political and economic power. As law professor J. M. Balkin put it in 1990, "Business interests and other conservative groups are finding that arguments for property rights and the social status quo can more and more easily be rephrased in the language of the first amendment."[8] His observation remained accurate as the decade progressed.

The Supreme Court's recent decisions are more libertarian than liberal. A fair number of justices appear to like unregulated markets. They oppose government regulation of economic markets, and they oppose government regulation of the marketplace of ideas. We tend to think that people with economic power are likely to have an advantage in politics. They may have an advantage in the marketplace of ideas as well. Free speech libertarianism may reinforce the existing distribution of economic and political power. The Court's campaign finance decisions may be particularly pernicious in this connection. They block us from taking steps to reduce the influence of economics on politics.[9]

Why do liberals still celebrate the First Amendment when it benefits their political opponents? Liberals typically like to use the government's power to ameliorate the effects of the current distribution of economic power on food and housing. Why don't they like to use the government's power to ameliorate the effects of the current distribution of economic power on the dissemination of ideas?[10]

We can begin with the proposition, borne out by history, that the American Civil Liberties Union and most other liberal defenders of free speech used to defend it because free speech protections helped liberals. In the 1950s and 1960s, for example, conservatives mounted an anticommunist crusade that had the effect of weakening domestic liberal forces; invoking the First Amendment to deflect the anticommunist crusade helped liberals indirectly. In the 1960s free speech law helped civil rights protestors continue their activities in the face of efforts to repress them.

Why stick with free speech when it seems to help the other side now if liberals were attracted to free speech principles because they helped their side? Balkin calls this the problem of ideological drift.[11] Liberals started out holding some principles, which had a particular political tilt, and they stick with those principles even though they do not have that tilt any more.

Why does ideological drift occur? One possibility is that young radicals actually have become old conservatives. That is, the underlying political values of the people involved in discussions of free speech and politics have changed. These people used to tilt to the left, and they liked free speech then because it tilted to the left. Now they tilt to the right, and they like free speech because it tilts to the right. This is a real possibility, but it does not seem to me to describe many people.[12]

Another possibility is that social changes force new issues to the fore, but people get stuck in the past. They do not like to have to rethink the positions they have become comfortable with. So, for example, controversies over regulating racist speech are simply slotted into old categories. This may be just an example of natural human laziness.

Balkin suggests another perspective on ideological drift. Instead of thinking that the free speech principle has drifted away from liberalism, we might decide that liberalism itself has changed. This is most clearly true in recent controversies about the regulation of pornography and hate speech, where people who describe themselves as liberals find themselves on opposing sides.[13] The term *liberalism* has become contested, so people can support regulation of pornography—and campaign finance—without losing their credentials as liberals despite what the ACLU might say.

Proponents of regulation say that we protect free speech to ensure that it is as widely available as possible. They claim that their proposed regulations actually enhance the availability of speech—when they overcome the "silencing" of women and racial minorities, for example, or when they reduce the ability of the rich to "drown out" the voices of the poor. Their opponents can make a strategic point. They may argue that the proposed regulations actually will not work that way: Regulation of pornography will lead to the suppression of feminist literature rather than misogynist pornography. Or the opponents can defend free speech as a principle: People ought to choose for themselves from what they hear. The strategic and principled objections, however, are disagreements about *liberalism*, not about free speech.

There is a different and perhaps better explanation for ideological drift. The ACLU member can say, "Look, we know that a lot of free speech law today gets in the way of the liberal political causes we also favor. Sometimes you may be overestimating how bad the tilt to the right is. It may not be such a big deal that the tobacco industry is going to be able to get regulations of their advertising overturned, because there are other ways to get at the social problem—a public campaign against smoking, higher taxes on tobacco, and stuff like that. But maybe you're right that there is a slight tilt to the right."

"But," the ACLU member continues, "we have to be vigilant in protecting free speech principles. If we let them erode in connection with campaign finance regulation, for example, there's a risk that the new revised principles will get applied to core political speech. The theory that lets government restrict contributions to political campaigns might be used to let government restrict the distribution of anonymous pamphlets. If we treat campaign finance as something the government can regulate to equalize contending voices in the society, we might end up discovering that government was being allowed to restrict the use of public spaces, streets and parks, again purportedly to promote equality."

This argument has the right form. There is no ideological drift at all. Rather, there is a change in the tilt on the surface if we look at a few cases—important ones to be sure—but no change if we look at the underlying structure. We are enthusiasts about the First Amendment, the ACLU says, because it has to be defended everywhere if it is going to be strong enough to protect the political interests we do care about.

This argument might not be accurate even though it has the right form. Consider three problems.

Campaign Finance. Making it hard to regulate campaign finance almost guarantees a permanent tilt in the political playing field to the right, in the direction of the rich and already powerful. They can spend money on politics, and purchase policies in their favor, while the less well-off cannot.

Libertarianism. Liberals ought to be quite nervous if the Court protects free speech because it is a libertarian court that opposes government regulation of anything. The defense of free speech against the charge of ideological drift was that defending free speech for businesses was necessary to make sure that it would be available to political protestors. But a libertarian court is going to generalize somewhat differently: Instead of saying "protect free speech here, there, and everywhere," the libertarian court will say, "Keep the government out of here, there, and everywhere." Liberals cannot like that idea.

Balancing. The Court might adopt an approach to free speech law in which it balances competing interests—a cable operator's interest in making quasi-editorial decisions about which channels to keep on the system to attract the widest audience, against the government's interest in keeping cable channels available to people who cannot afford to start up their own channels. But balancing interests can cause real problems. Judges can unconsciously smuggle in their political preferences as they evaluate the interests and figure out which ones are weightier than others. When a basically conservative court balances interests, the court may invoke the First Amendment a lot, but in the end, when the interests are balanced, conservative interests win and liberal ones lose.

The Supreme Court and the Election Returns

This short overview introduces more general questions about how to assess judicial review. We could continue with a survey of other areas of constitutional law such as race discrimination. We would find that the Court's position in recent years ought not comfort liberals.

Liberals asked the Court to uphold affirmative action programs and race-conscious redistricting because the Constitution prohibited only race-conscious programs that disadvantaged racial minorities. The Court replied that, to the contrary, the Constitution prohibited all race-conscious programs unless the programs had exceedingly strong justifications, which a majority of the Court had not found by 1998.[14]

Liberals asked the Court to prod school districts to continue dealing with the effects of de facto segregation by adopting generous—and perhaps disingenuous—definitions of improper school board decisions. The Court responded by relieving school boards of continuing obligations.[15]

One set of decisions appears—but only appears—to show the Court acting to support racial minorities. Overruling a decision rendered by the Warren Court, the Supreme Court held it unconstitutional for a prosecutor to exclude African-Americans from juries because of their race alone. Later cases extended the holding to bar defense attorneys from doing so, and to civil cases. Then the Court made it easy for a prosecutor to show that his or her decision was based on some factor other than race, gutting the initial decision. And, more generally, those who think that people with different racial backgrounds bring different ways of looking at the world into the jury room might think as well that sometimes it is useful to allow attorneys to try to construct a jury composed of people with these distinctive views.[16]

These examples suggest that it would be helpful to see what we can say about judicial review in more general terms.

The limitations of judicial review were given their classic expression by the journalist and humorist Finley Peter Dunne. Writing shortly after the United States had begun to govern foreign territories, Dunne had his alter ego Mr. Dooley comment on a controversy over whether U.S. occupying forces had to comply with the Constitution. As the question was put at the time, did the Constitution follow the flag? After the Supreme Court decided that constitutional limitations applied, but in a rather restricted form, Mr. Dooley said, "No matter whether the Constitution follows the flag or not, the Supreme Court follows the election returns."[17]

A half century later political scientist Robert Dahl examined the Court's record more systematically, and came to roughly the same conclusion. According to Dahl, the Supreme Court rarely holds out for an extended period against a sustained national political majority.[18] Later studies have qualified Dahl's conclusions by stressing the importance of the words *extended*, *sustained*, and *national*, as we will see. But with those qualifications Dahl's conclusion remains accurate.

No one should be surprised that the Supreme Court follows the election returns, at least in Dahl's sense. Another political scientist, Martin Shapiro, made the point in the large. Shapiro points out that courts everywhere are parts of the national political system.[19] A political system with one part consistently at odds with other parts, Shapiro argues, would be a system routinely in crisis. In stable political systems, then, we should expect to find the courts and the other national political organs in rough correspondence most of the time.

The United States Constitution tries to guarantee this sort of correspondence. We like to think that our judges are independent of political pressure. They are, in the sense that they rarely respond to telephone calls from political figures. But they are also selected through a political process—nomination by the president and confirmation by the Senate. And, although federal judges serve for life terms, mortality means that there is a reasonably regular turnover in the Supreme Court's membership. The

Supreme Court is likely to fit in with the national political majority, with something of a time lag.

This is particularly true when that majority sustains itself over an extended period. So, for example, by the 1960s the New Deal political coalition had controlled national politics for so long that the Supreme Court's justices were simply another part of that coalition. And by the 1990s the transformation of American politics that began with Richard Nixon's presidency and extended through the Reagan-Bush years—and, to many, into the Clinton years—produced a Supreme Court whose moderate centrism corresponded almost precisely to the national center of political gravity.

All this means that judicial review is likely simply to reinforce whatever a political movement can get outside the courts. Sometimes, however, judicial review might make it harder for political movements to accomplish their objectives.

THE POLITICS OF SUPREME COURT DECISIONS

Immediately after the Supreme Court announced its decision in the 1992 abortion case, lawyers and spin doctors on both sides of the issue congregated on the Supreme Court's plaza to interpret the decision. Remarkably, both sides went out of their way to emphasize how serious a blow the Court had dealt to their position. Pro-choice advocates insisted that the Court had severely impaired the protection available to the right to choose by abandoning the proposition that the right to choose was fundamental; anti-choice advocates bemoaned the fact that the Court had reaffirmed rather than overruled *Roe v. Wade*.

These press conferences illustrate part of the political dynamics of judicial review. The advocates believed that winning a legal victory in court was less important to their goals than winning in the arena of public opinion, and their comments showed that they believed they could gain more public support by persuading audiences that they had *lost* in court. There is no necessary connection between winning legal victories and advancing political goals. Winning legal victories either does not advance political goals or actually impedes them, more frequently than most lawyers think.

To begin with, we should distinguish between *short-term* and *long-term* effects of Supreme Court decisions. Merely getting a judgment from the Supreme Court that constitutional rights have been violated may not amount to much unless that judgment is enforced. The Supreme Court's 1954 decision invalidating school segregation is one of the prime examples for those who celebrate judicial review. But the history of school desegregation litigation illustrates the importance of the long-term/short-term distinction. The Supreme Court's 1954 decision was so widely disregarded in the deep South that only a tiny number of schools there were desegregated by 1964. In this sense *Brown v. Board of Education* was a short-term victory (the short term being the days following the Court's decision) and a long-term irrelevancy (the long term being the ensuing decade).

Of course that view of *Brown* is distorted in several ways. Why, for example, should the long term be a decade rather than a generation? If we take a longer perspective, *Brown* was successful in eliminating legally sanctioned explicit racial school segregation.[20] And, why should the measure of success be actual desegregation rather than the public assertion by the nation's highest court of a principle, arguably with large-scale though long-term effects on public opinion about race?

Another way to think about the relation between legal victories and political ones is to distinguish between *ideological* effects and *material* ones. The Court's statement that segregation was unconstitutional could be an ideological victory in court even if it had no material effects on schools in the deep South. And, ideological victories can have material effects over the long run; the principle the Court articulated in *Brown* might have become embedded in the nation's self-understanding in ways that affected race relations much more generally.

If we start with the simple distinction between legal outcomes and political outcomes, there are four possibilities: (1) Winning a legal victory and winning politically; (2) winning a legal victory but losing politically; (3) losing in court but winning politically; and (4) losing in court and in politics too. There are interesting and important examples in all four categories.

1. Winning and winning: *Brown v. Board of Education* may be problematic as an example of winning material victories by winning legal ones, but it certainly is an example of winning an ideological victory. Beyond an authoritative statement about segregation, *Brown* was a demonstration to the entire nation that one of its major institutions took the claims of African-Americans to equal treatment seriously. More generally, ideological victories in court can constitute the entry of previously excluded groups into one of the most important forms of discourse in United States society, that is, the discourse of rights.

Legal victories can of course also be material ones. Canada's Supreme Court invalidated the country's regulation of abortions on what could have been taken as rather narrow procedural grounds. As a matter of law a legislature might easily have designed a new abortion law that satisfied the court's requirements. The political context into which the decision was inserted, though, meant that no alternative proposal could obtain a parliamentary majority. As a result, Canada has *no* regulation of abortion (aside from its general regulation of medical procedures). The legal victory in Canada, narrow on its face, turned out to be more effective in securing the right to choose than the apparently more sweeping legal victory in the U.S. abortion litigation.

The political context plays a large part in explaining why the legal victory in Canada was also a material one. This points to a broader issue. Sometimes it may be hard to figure out whether the legal victory, or something else, really mattered in bringing about the material change. Often so much else is going on in the culture that change might have been inevitable. A controversial example is the suggestion, made by political scientist Gerald Rosenberg and others, that in 1973 changes in public policy about abortion were already occurring, and the Supreme Court's abortion decision did relatively little even to accelerate those changes.[21] Consider as well the suggestion that *Brown*, even as an ideological victory, made a smaller contribution to national opinion about race by the early 1960s than was made by the desegregation of the armed forces and of professional major league baseball, which had occurred before *Brown*.[22]

2. Losing and losing: Probably the best recent example of losing and losing is the welfare rights movement. Public sentiment about "welfare" was so adverse in the late 1960s that the courts were the only place advocates of expanded public assistance programs could expect a fair hearing. For a brief period it seemed possible that the Supreme Court would take an aggressive stance in vindicating the claims of recipients of public assistance. When the Supreme Court rejected welfare rights claims, were those advocates and their constituents any worse off?

Claims of rights occupy an important place in the constitutional and legal culture of the United States. Something special happens when those claims are vindicated: Political actors and the public are supposed to take those claims much more seriously than before. Formally speaking, nothing special ought to happen when such claims are rejected: The claims should become political demands, no different from the entire range of ordinary political demands made by defense industries, organized labor, and the like.

One serious adverse possibility does exist. If a social movement places all its bets on a rights strategy—even if it does so because no other strategy has any prospect of success—when its claims of rights are rejected the public may think that the claims need not be considered *at all*. The rejected claims of rights simply drop out of political consideration instead of becoming ordinary political claims like any other. Successful rights-claims are extremely important in political rhetoric, while rejected ones are not ordinary policy claims but are, instead, completely unimportant.

Balkin has described this process by identifying what he calls the idealized Constitution, a Constitution that answers every important question correctly.[23] *That* Constitution, however, is not the one we live under. Rather, we live with constitutional rights specified by the Supreme Court, which does not answer every question correctly. Balkin suggests that idealizing the Constitution runs the risk that we will adjust our understanding of the correct answer to conform to the Supreme Court's decisions. When people lose in the Supreme Court, they really lose, because the rest of the society may come to think not merely that their claims lacked constitutional force, but that their claims had no moral justification whatever.

3. Winning and losing: Consider next cases where groups that win legal victories nonetheless are *worse* off. The basic dynamic here is simple. Consider how proponents and opponents of social change can respond to winning their constitutional case. Having won, the proponents can turn their attention to another part of their political agenda. They will invest less than they had before in securing or protecting this particular claim. Meanwhile, their opponents may continue to invest as before. Facing constant pressure from the opponents and reduced pressure from supporters, the courts may whittle away at the prior legal victory. Further, having won in court, supporters of change may think that they no longer have to be as worried, and can turn their attention from political and legal matters to other things, such as raising children or making money. On the other side, their opponents may have been outraged by the legal victory, and they may devote even more energy than before to opposing social change. The result of winning the legal victory can be losing the political battle when supporters become complacent and opponents mobilize.

Consider the following version of the history of abortion litigation in the United States. The Supreme Court struck down most states' abortion laws in 1973. Its decision provided some opportunities for anti-choice forces to try to enact restrictive legislation. Pro-choice activists, though, believed—correctly, for two decades—that the courts would strike down restrictive abortion laws. Sensibly enough, they devoted their political energies to other issues, relying on the low-cost courts for protection against restrictive abortion laws. Meanwhile, their opponents mobilized around the abortion issue,[24] but their political concerns were broader. Their efforts to enact and enforce restrictive *abortion* laws were unavailing, but they had real influence over other issues. That is, pro-choice forces found themselves facing stronger forces on issues *other than* abortion than they had faced before their legal victory in the abortion cases.[25]

Pro-choice forces prevailed on abortion issues, but lost on the other issues they hoped to advance. The overall composition of the federal judiciary was among those other issues. The pro-choice legal victories contributed to the right-wing transformation of the federal courts. Conservative

Republicans did not control the presidency because of the abortion issue; obviously, economics played a much larger role. But conservative activists in the Republican party gained control over judicial appointments, and insisted on appointing only right-wing judges. The pro-choice victories themselves eroded with that transformation. Perhaps on balance the benefits for pro-choice forces, measured by what happened on the abortion issue over the years since 1973—including the erosion but not the overruling of the initial victory—exceeded their losses on other issues. But examining the abortion decisions standing alone does not show that judicial review was a good thing even for advocates of women's rights.

We should note as well that a legal defeat may energize proponents of social change. For example, the Canadian abortion litigation had an early defeat. Dr. Henry Morgantaler challenged Quebec's abortion regulation and, remarkably, was acquitted by the jury even though he had unquestionably performed the procedure. Canadian law allows prosecutors to appeal acquittals, and the appellate court reversed the jury's judgment. The appellate court invoked a rarely used provision and actually entered a judgment convicting Dr. Morgantaler instead of sending the case back for another trial. Morgantaler served a jail term, which must be counted as a legal defeat. Yet, the sequence of events, and particularly what seemed to many Canadians the appellate court's overreaching, gave pro-choice forces a powerful political boost. This dynamic explains why both sides sought to call the U.S. Supreme Court abortion decision in 1992 a defeat.

The political dynamic of demobilization after a legal victory is the largest component in assessing judicial review. But there are others. Legal victories can be ideologically or culturally significant, particularly in offering support from important social institutions to claims that no such institution had taken seriously before. Like the victories themselves, however, the ideological significance may erode.

As we have seen, when a court recognizes a claim as a legal *right*, and particularly as a *constitutional* right, it treats the claim as really important: Rights outweigh ordinary policy concerns, for example. People on the other side of the issue then have to respond. They can say, as they often do, that the court made a mistake. But that may not be a promising strategy, at least in the short run. They can argue instead that, although the court found a right on the other side (and so overrode mere policy objections), it did not consider whether that right was countered by some other right. The rhetoric of rights generates a rhetoric of counter-rights: against the right to choose, the right to life; against affirmative action, the language of discrimination against white men.

Proponents of progressive social change tend to treat the rhetoric of counter-rights as phony; for them it is a distortion of the language of rights to say that white men have rights infringed by affirmative action.

Counter-rights are invoked so often, however, that they should be under-stood as systematically bound up with the rights themselves.

Two things happen once counter-rights come into play. First, and less significant, the framework of legal analysis changes. Rights may outweigh mere policies, but the outcome when a right is arrayed against a counter-right is far less clear. The rhetoric of counter-rights, that is, may assist the courts if they want to whittle away at the initial legal victory.

Second, and more important, at the outset rights may seem to be partic-ularly powerful claims on society. For example, sometimes such powerful claims might seem to be needed because they are asserted on behalf of those previously excluded from serious consideration; having been ex-cluded before, these groups not only should be allowed to take part in ordinary politics, they should receive special consideration because of their prior exclusion. The special force attached to the language of rights dissipates as rights proliferate and generate counter-rights. The distinction between rights and mere policies weakens, and proponents of rights-claims become just another interest group in the ordinary play of politics. Of course, to the extent that the real benefit of recognizing their rights was ideological, in validating their participation in politics, this transfor-mation should be expected. It is likely to be experienced, however, as a betrayal of the promises made when rights, those especially powerful claims on society, were recognized.

The dialectic of rights and counter-rights has another effect. Because rights seem to be especially powerful claims, discussions of rights and counter-rights tend to get particularly heated. Really fundamental matters seem to be at stake when rights are involved. Losing then seems tremen-dously damaging, something to be avoided at almost all cost. Compro-mises may seem unacceptable in principle because something fundamen-tal is involved: How could pro-choice (or anti-choice) activists compromise to accept a legal regime in which women's access to abor-tions was impeded (restricting the fundamental right to choose) but not made impossible (contrary to the fetus's fundamental right to life)? Yet, if compromise is ruled out, either one side will face a permanent defeat on an issue it regards as fundamental (which could have bad effects on social stability), or policy will swing wildly from protecting one right and denying the counter-right to protecting the counter-right and denying the initial one.

Of course people would not worry if they were sure that they would end up on the winning side in this dialectic with permanent victories. In the long run, however, the chance of wild swings may be great enough that people ought to be willing to accept compromises that are, from their point of view, favorable on balance; the losses during the periods when their opponents are in control may be large enough to outnumber the losses that happen under the permanent compromise regime.

The Underside of Constitutional Rights

The distinction between material and ideological effects of judicial review raises another question. Some of the most important progressive advances in this century occurred through judicial review: *Brown*, the 1973 abortion decision, restructuring the law of gender equality. And, even if the legal victories alone were insufficient to vindicate the material interests at stake—insufficient, that is, to achieve racial or gender equality—still they had something to do with alleviating the worst inequalities of race and gender.

We should not overestimate judicial review's significance, however. The persistence of segregation after *Brown*, for example, cautions advocates to distinguish between the short term and the long term, and between material accomplishments and ideological ones. To say that *Brown* was more significant as an ideological victory than as a material one does not mean that it was unimportant; it means only that we ought to be careful in thinking about the way it was important.

In addition, we have to remember that we buy judicial review wholesale: In getting the decisions we like, we run the risk of decisions we despise.[26] So, for example, those who celebrate *Brown* as the exemplar of judicial review have to live with Supreme Court decisions restricting affirmative action and campaign finance reform.

This sort of caution is particularly important for lawyers, and for a public in the United States with its distinctive constitutional and legal culture. Lawyers are likely to overestimate the contributions we can make to social progress, for obvious and understandable reasons. Cautions about what we can actually accomplish help deflate our sense that we are essential contributors to social change.[27]

The U.S. constitutional and legal culture matters, too, because in that culture the simple statement by a court that someone has a right—in itself only an ideological victory—can too easily be taken, by the public if not by progressive lawyers and their allies, as a complete victory. It takes work, in our culture, to connect ideological victories to material outcomes, to explain why *Brown*'s condemnation of school segregation is betrayed when African-American children still attend schools with almost no white children. The cautions remind us that such work continues to be necessary.

The constitutional and legal culture may be even more important. Sometimes winning a legal victory can actually impede further progressive change. This argument comes in a narrow and a broad version. The narrow version points out that some ways of articulating rights have ideological implications that work against change. For example, Catherine MacKinnon argues that the Supreme Court, in protecting a woman's right to choose to have or not have a child as an aspect of her right of *privacy*, helped define a sphere of private life into which the government could not intrude. According to MacKinnon, this way of approaching the abortion issue helped immunize the "private" sphere of domestic relations from government regulation even though women are severely disadvantaged within that sphere, as when they are beaten by men they live with, or are coerced into having sex with those men.[28]

This narrow argument once again offers a caution: Lawyers ought to be careful in articulating their legal claims, so that if the courts adopt their arguments the long-term prospects for change will not be impaired by the ideological implications of the *way* in which the legal claims were made. So, for example, perhaps it would be better to defend the right to choose as an aspect of women's equality, as essential to their full participation in social life in all its aspects, rather than as an aspect of privacy.[29]

The broader version of this argument asserts that these cautions almost certainly cannot succeed. In part this is because advocates frequently lose control over the arguments they make once courts accept them; what privacy means, or what equality means, is substantially determined by courts, which are almost certainly not going to be as progressive as the progressive advocates would like. The experience of the Bork nomination, where advocates constructed a public understanding of the Constitution that was substantially at odds with what the Court had done, is unusual.

More important in the broad version of the argument, though, is the claim that legal rights are *essentially* individualistic, at least in the United States constitutional and legal culture, and that progressive change requires undermining the individualism that vindicating legal rights reinforces. The argument's conclusion is that the long-term ideological consequences of winning victories in courts are almost certainly going to be adverse to progressive change.

Why, though, are rights-claims so essentially individualistic? After all, we can easily *define* rights that attach to groups; contemporary international human rights law, for example, recognizes rights of cultural minorities for preservation of their cultures, or of linguistic minorities for preservation of their languages.[30]

Rights-claims are individualistic, nonetheless, not because of something inherent in the concept of rights, but rather because of the historical development of the language of rights. The central image of "rights" in our culture is, as MacKinnon's critique suggests, of a sphere within which each of us can do what he or she pleases. This image, in turn, reinforces the distinction between law and politics. Politics is the domain of pure will or preference, not subject to discussion and deliberation except as each individual chooses to be influenced by others. Rights—or law—protect the domain in which political preferences are formed. If, however, a critic believes that making politics truly social is an important task, it might be important as well to fight an ideology, the ideology of rights, that leads people to think of themselves as disconnected from others in important ways.

This broader argument about the individualistic ideology of rights is not an argument about the *concept* of rights. Rather, it is an argument about the way the language of rights actually functions in contemporary U.S. constitutional and legal discourse. Even more, the argument does not assert that the individualistic ideology of rights is the *only* one available in contemporary legal discourse. The argument does assert, however, that the individualistic ideology is the predominant one. Like the narrow argument, it could be taken as simply cautioning against hoping for too much from rights-based arguments, particularly emphasizing the adverse ideological consequences that such arguments might have. Because it relies on quite general concerns about contemporary constitutional and legal culture, the broader argument suggests a deeper skepticism about the ability of progressive advocates actually to formulate arguments that will not succumb to these ideological perils.

THE LIMITATIONS OF VICTORY

Even winning by winning may cause problems for the apparent victors. What of losing in court and losing in politics too? The political loss shows that investing in a failed legal campaign would not have changed the result, although on a rare occasion or two switching the resources devoted to a legal strategy into a nonlegal one would have changed the political loss into a political victory.

More important, judicial review is often the last resort of a social and political movement that lacks political power. People rarely go to court—choose a legal strategy—unless they are pessimistic about what they could accomplish through political action. Judicial review *must* help these people—or so liberals think.

Here we should return to the idea that the Supreme Court follows the election returns. *Brown v. Board of Education* stands as a powerful objection to critics of judicial review: The Supreme Court appears to have accomplished something—perhaps not desegregation, but at least an important statement about racial equality—that neither Congress nor the president could have, constrained as they were by politics.

A quick look at *Brown*, the abortion decisions, and the Supreme Court's 1996 decision finding for the first time that gays and lesbians enjoyed significant constitutional protection allows us to assess judicial review in contexts where political liberals generally approve the Court's results. In what follows I do not pretend to provide a comprehensive account of the Court's decisions, nor even one that is so compelling that any reasonable reader would have to accept it. Rather, I offer an account of the Court's decisions that has enough going for it to undermine the view that the Court's decisions actually made a big difference for groups that could not secure their claims in the political arena. The idea, once again, is not that judicial review is meaningless, but only that the differences it makes are rather small.

Dealing with "Outliers." One place to begin is with the Supreme Court's family privacy decisions. *Griswold v. Connecticut* provided the doctrinal foundation for the abortion cases.[31] The Court in *Griswold* found that Connecticut's ban on the use of contraceptives infringed on a constitutionally protected right of privacy. Later the Court invalidated a city zoning ordinance that had the effect of barring a grandmother from living with all her grandchildren.[32]

For our purposes, what is most notable about these decisions is that they hardly stand as examples of the Supreme Court acting against the will of the people of the United States. When *Griswold* was decided in 1965 only two states banned the use of contraceptives. The zoning regulation was unique and its adverse effects on extended families probably resulted from a mistake by the city council rather than a considered democratic decision.

The Supreme Court often acts on behalf of a national political majority that has not yet worked its will through legislation. It can act against real aberrations, as in the zoning case. Does judicial review help in dealing with these problems? Justice Robert Jackson suggested that it did. Writing in a slightly different context, Jackson said that such laws "are individually too petty, too diversified, and too local to get the attention of a Congress hard pressed with more urgent matters."[33] Perhaps more important, a Supreme Court that eliminates aberrational regulations plays an interesting political role but, precisely because the regulations are "petty," hardly a major one.[34]

The relation between *Griswold* and the abortion cases suggests, however, that decisions wiping aberrational laws off the books may have broader effects. The Supreme Court, after all, has to explain why an unusual regulation is unconstitutional. In doing so it articulates a legal doctrine that has effects both as precedent and, as we have seen, as ideology. These effects may swamp the rather minor consequences of getting rid of an aberrational law. People might sometimes conclude that the benefits of this sort of judicial review are outweighed by the costs of these precedential and ideological effects of constitutional doctrine. The cost-benefit calculation is at least more complicated than we might think.

Dealing with Regional Majorities. Brown is of course a more interesting case. There the Court may have acted against a regional majority at odds with a national political majority. By 1954 segregation was an embarrassment to a national political elite concerned about how the United States looked to the rest of the world. Communists in the United States, and supporters of the Soviet Union around the world, pointed to Southern apartheid to demonstrate that what they described as the democratic Soviet system was superior to the fake democracy in the United States. Eliminating segregation would advance the national interest by combating these arguments. But Congress could not act. It was organized on the basis of seniority, which meant that long-serving members from the one-party South had a lot of power. They could block anti-discrimination legislation. More important, they could use their positions to thwart initiatives unrelated to race put forth by liberal Democrats and Republicans, if the liberals pushed too hard on antidiscrimination issues. The Court's decision in *Brown* might best be understood as enforcing a national political view against a regionally dominant one that happened to have excessive power in Congress. As law professor Derrick Bell has pointed out, the Supreme Court typically has acted to benefit African-Americans only when African-American interests converged with the interests of whites.[35] *Brown* is a good example.

Gerald Rosenberg and law professor Michael Klarman have argued against overestimating the effects of *Brown*.[36] As we have seen, rather little desegregation occurred in the deep South before 1964. That date is important, because in 1964 Congress enacted a Civil Rights Act with teeth. Congress had recently started to give federal funds to elementary and secondary schools. The 1964 Civil Rights Act provided for a cut-off of those funds to schools that continue to discriminate. The federal agencies administering the funds took their charge seriously enough to induce Southern school systems to desegregate out of fear of losing federal money. Then, a year later Congress enacted a Voting Rights Act that transformed Southern politics.

By 1970 the political obstacles to enacting federal antidiscrimination laws had essentially disappeared. African-Americans were an important political force in the national Democratic party, and had substantial influence on the development of national policy. And, notably, around that time the Supreme Court began to withdraw from exercising judicial review aggressively on behalf of African-Americans.

A defender of judicial review might attribute these political changes to *Brown*. African-Americans gained political power, according to this defense, because they had won their constitutional case in *Brown*. The civil rights movement received a real emotional boost from *Brown*, and participants became more enthusiastic as they realized that they had the Constitution—and the courts—on their side.

The Freedom Rides of 1961 provide one symbol of the relation between *Brown* and later direct action mobilization. The Freedom Rides challenged continuing segregation of interstate bus travel and bus terminals, which was clearly unlawful by 1960. Freedom Riders took buses and refused to comply with segregation requirements. They were beaten and the first Freedom Ride never reached its destination. That destination was New Orleans, and the Freedom Ride was planned so that it would arrive there on May 17, the anniversary of *Brown v. Board of Education*.[37]

The connection between *Brown* and the civil rights movement seems reasonably clear.[38] The connection between the civil rights movement and the achievement of political power by African-Americans is more complex. Klarman describes the connection as paradoxical. According to him, *Brown* produced a sharp shift to the right among Southern white politicians. Governor Orval Faubus, for example, had run as a relative moderate on race issues before *Brown*, but afterwards took a strong segregationist stance. Southern white politicians resisted desegregation strenuously as they shifted to the right. Their resistance produced violence, in Little Rock and later elsewhere in the South. Northerners seeing the violence began to support the civil rights movement in increasing numbers. In addition, the continuing migration of African-Americans from the South to the North made them a potent political force in the North. By the mid-1960s a national majority was ready to endorse serious civil rights laws.

The unanswerable question is whether that would have occurred without *Brown*. It seems quite likely that something would have happened in the South without *Brown*. African-Americans were increasingly unwilling to accept Southern apartheid, and some sort of civil rights movement was probably inevitable. It might well have met with the same violence that actually occurred. And the effects of migration on African-American political power in the North would have happened no matter what.

Klarman and Rosenberg suggest that the political landscape in the mid-1960s would have looked the same even if *Brown* had been decided differently. I am inclined to agree, although I believe that Rosenberg underestimates the role *Brown* played in energizing the civil rights movement and that Klarman attributes too much of the South's violence to reaction to *Brown* rather than to the mere fact of challenges to apartheid. Others disagree with their bottom-line conclusions about *Brown*.[39] No matter how one comes out at the end, however, it seems reasonably clear that we ought not celebrate the Supreme Court's role in *Brown* as a strong demonstration of how the Court can bring about change on behalf of those who lack political power.

Acting for a National Political Majority. The abortion cases show the Supreme Court acting on behalf of a latent national political majority even though the 1973 decisions invalidated abortion laws throughout the nation.

As we have seen, the political context of the abortion decisions is complex.[40] By the early 1970s abortion law reformers had achieved some success in eliminating outright bans on abortion. States were beginning to adopt modern abortion laws, which allowed abortions when doctors found they were necessary to protect the woman's life or health. Abortion rights advocates were becoming disillusioned with experience under these reform laws in practice. The reformed laws set up an obstacle course that abortion rights advocates came to believe only middle-class women could get through. Their political agenda shifted to repeal rather than reform. Repeal would allow doctors to set up easily accessible clinics rather than confining abortions to hospitals where committees had to approve them. Simultaneously, abortion-rights opponents began to mobilize against both reform and repeal.

Much had happened before the Supreme Court's abortion decisions in 1973. While purporting to avoid the "abortion on demand" position taken by the most vigorous advocates of abortion rights, the Court's decisions actually went very far in that direction. Yet these were decisions by the supposedly conservative Burger Court. The supposedly more conservative Rehnquist Court modified the holdings in the abortion cases, now allowing states to regulate if they do not impose an "undue burden" on the right to choose, but expressly said that the "core holding" of *Roe v. Wade* remained good law.[41] How could this happen?

The Supreme Court responded to the construction and gradual disintegration of the New Deal coalition. The Warren Court's decisions responded to the interests of the New Deal and Great Society coalitions: organized labor, African-Americans, and liberal intellectuals. Those coalitions gradually disintegrated during the 1970s. As historian William Berman puts it, they had been held together by the Democratic party's ability "to serve as the champion of both corporate America and social decency." Stable and sustained economic growth made it possible for the Democratic coalition to satisfy the demands of working-class Americans and African-Americans through a social welfare system financed by progressive taxes. Changes in the position of the United States in the world economy destroyed this "growth coalition." The "new politics of austerity all but precluded legislative deals that included benefits for the rich, the middle class, and the poor alike." Two other commentators observed, "In the context of slow and erratic growth, . . . a gigantic squeeze began to develop on social spending. This . . . constrained [the Democrats'] ability to deliver the social benefits that had long secured them a real mass base."[42]

By the early 1970s the Democratic coalition began to fracture into interest groups competing with each other for their shares of a no-longer-expanding economic pie. The Warren Court's agenda of expanding rights exacerbated the Democrats' difficulties. Paying for the rights articulated by the Court meant increasing taxes. In journalist Thomas Edsall's words, "Insofar as the granting of rights to some groups required others to sacrifice tax dollars and authority, to compromise longstanding values, to jeopardize status, power, or the habitual patterns of daily life, this new liberalism became, to a degree, a disruptive force in American life, and particularly so within the Democratic party."[43]

The party's leaders were unable to develop a program that would unite the declining labor movement, African-Americans, environmentalists, and feminists. Republican leaders saw their opportunity to exploit these emerging divisions within the Democratic coalition. The political outcome was a shift in the presidency from Democratic to Republican control.

Republican presidents appointed relatively conservative justices to the Supreme Court. Consider again Martin Shapiro's argument that courts are political institutions. Like other political institutions, they seek to develop constituencies that support them. The disintegration of the New Deal coalition freed up political space, but during Burger's tenure—and perhaps to the present—no alternative coalition replaced the New Deal coalition. That gave the Court an opportunity to act relatively freely to develop its own constituency of support.

Women became such a constituency. The social welfare basis of the New Deal coalition disappeared, replaced by a pluralist interest group coalition. For Democrats, the emergence of women as an interest group, with claims made by an aggressive political leadership, did not pose a dramatic problem. They simply had to accommodate women's interests in the general pluralist bargaining that characterized the Great Society.

During Burger's tenure, Republicans as a party were divided over the claims asserted by the organized women's movement. The Republicans on the Supreme Court, however, were not—or at least there were enough Republicans on the Supreme Court responsive to those claims to make it relatively easy for the Court as a whole to develop women as a constituency of support.

The reason is that the Court's conservatives represented a class of Republicans—country-club Republicans—that has nearly faded from memory.[44] They accepted the basic contours of the New Deal and the welfare state, were concerned about the fiscal consequences of New Deal policies, and, notably, could identify the claims made by the organized women's movement with their own class interests. That segment of the Republican party had historically supported the Equal Rights Amendment, for example. Key Supreme Court justices appear to have the same views. Justice Harry Blackmun came to his position on abortion partly through his experience as general counsel to the Mayo Clinic and partly through the messages his daughters—representative of modern professional women—sent him. Justice Lewis F. Powell, a Republican appointee although nominally a conservative Virginia Democrat, was affected by his daughters' views as well.[45]

Country-club Republicanism accounts for the pattern of the Court's results in abortion cases. The Court's decisions made it possible for middle-class women accustomed to navigating their way through complex regulatory schemes to obtain abortions when they wished. They also made it possible for states to make it more difficult for less well-off women to do so, most dramatically by allowing states to refrain from providing public assistance for abortions.[46]

Once again we can understand the Court's decisions in Mr. Dooley's terms: The Court was following the election returns, although the returns in the 1970s and 1980s were sufficiently unclear that the Court had some space to pursue its own political agenda. It thus seems appropriate that the major *constitutional* victory for women in the 1990s has been a decision finding unconstitutional sex-segregated public education at one of only two such institutions that remained operating.[47]

Acting for National Politicians. Political scientist Mark Graber identified another way in which the courts respond to national politics—or, more precisely, to national politicians.[48] Playing with the word usually used to describe judicial restraint, Graber calls this category "legislative deference to the judiciary." According to Graber, sometimes national politicians notice a "no-win" issue: No matter what position they take on the issue, they will lose politically. And sometimes they rely on the courts to bail them out of this political problem: They defer the issue to the courts. They can use the courts' decision to test the political waters. They can climb aboard the courts' bandwagon if it turns out that enough people support the decision, and they can attack the courts for making the wrong decision and taking the issue away from the people if it turns out that enough people dislike it.

Graber argues that the Supreme Court's decision in the notorious *Dred Scott* case resulted not from a judicial power-grab or the justices' calculation that they could resolve the slavery issue, but rather from a decision by national politicians to send the slavery issue to the courts: "[I]n deciding *Dred Scott*, the Court was carrying out the wishes of Jacksonian moderates who desperately hoped that persons aggrieved by whatever decision the justices eventually made might nevertheless be more disposed to accept constitutional principles announced by a 'neutral' judiciary than public policies enacted by elected officials." More recently, Graber argues, the abortion decisions resulted from similar legislative deferral of decision to the courts: Politicians "encouraged judicial resolution of an issue that threatened existing partisan alignments," splitting traditional country-club Republicans from newer social-issue Republicans, and dividing elite Democrats from their traditional working-class, Catholic, and union allies.

Predicting the Future. Law professor Alexander Bickel was a critic of the Warren Court's aggressive judicial liberalism. He was puzzled by the fact that the Court seemed to be getting away with its decisions. Even decisions that seemed quite unpopular when made rapidly settled into the public consciousness as permanent fixtures in our constitutional scheme.

Bickel explained why that happened. The Court, he said, sometimes took on the task of predicting the future.[49] The Warren Court's successful decisions, Bickel concluded, rested on good predictions: The Court had spotted an emerging trend, perhaps not yet supported by a national majority but soon to have that support. It then endorsed the emerging position. Perhaps the Court's decisions might give the emerging majority a slight boost, somewhat accelerating the pace of change. But, according to Bickel, the Court's successes lay in guessing right about a future that was going to happen no matter what the Court did.

Bickel's argument explains the Supreme Court's 1996 decision in *Romer v. Evans*.[50] The Court held unconstitutional a provision in the Colorado constitution, adopted by a 56–44 percent vote in a referendum, barring the state or any city from adopting policies banning discrimination on the basis of sexual orientation. Strikingly, the Court would have invalidated the amendment even if neither of President Bill Clinton's appointees voted on the case; in addition, the justices appointed by presidents Reagan and Bush divided evenly.

The fact that *Romer* supported the gay rights position is more interesting here than the decision's legal analysis. Public opinion surveys nationwide showed high levels of support for the proposition that employers should not discriminate against gays and lesbians. Within a few months of the Court's decision, a Republican-controlled Senate came within one vote of adopting the Employment Nondiscrimination Act to bar such discrimination, and it seems sure to pass within a few years. The best explanation is Bickel's: The Court was predicting the future.

Justice Antonin Scalia's dissent in *Romer* excoriated the majority for enacting the views of a cultural elite. Although the Senate vote on the Employment Nondiscrimination Act shows that Scalia overstated the point, there surely is something to it. The justices are members of the cultural elite, and they are likely to see the future moving in the direction the elite wants. And yet, one thing that gives a cultural elite its status is precisely the power to shape the future. The Court could do worse than follow the views of cultural elites if it wants to predict the future.

Of course the Court does not have a perfect crystal ball. The 1857 *Dred Scott* decision sought both to predict and shape the future by resolving the slavery controversy. In taking the South's side, the Court failed. The Court's decisions restricting legislative ability to regulate campaign finance seem to continue to be at odds with what both cultural elites and the people generally believe appropriate. A decade before *Romer v. Evans* the Court upheld state laws making homosexual sodomy a crime (*Bowers v. Hardwick*, 1986).[51] The decision was badly received among elites at the time. The future had arrived by 1996, and the Court was so embarrassed by its earlier decision that its opinion in *Romer* simply—and therefore eloquently—did not so much as mention *Bowers*.

Acting Against a Real National Majority? Brown is important in another way. Whatever its effects were, we know that it did not transform the material conditions in which most African-Americans live. African-American participation in the national political process has not produced public policies that have eliminated discrimination and the disproportionate poverty affecting the African-American community. The reason is that a national majority believes that such policies would be too expensive.

The point to note here is that judicial review has not addressed these problems either. Again following the election returns, the Supreme Court has shifted gears. It now uses the rules it developed to assist African-Americans to strike down affirmative action programs. Perhaps this is a more complex case of the Court predicting the future, as the Court seems more opposed to affirmative action than cultural elites and more even than the American people, who reveal in polls more even ambivalence about affirmative action than the Court's decisions express.

This look at the Court's recent history questions claims by progressives and liberals that judicial review makes a big difference in defense of their political positions. It follows, of course, that precisely the same point can be made from the perspective of political conservatives. For example, the Supreme Court has been quite ambivalent about affirmative action since 1976, and yet affirmative action programs remained deeply entrenched in society well into the 1990s. The conservative judicial victories did not translate into substantial political gains in reining in affirmative action.

The Court's actions fall into two broad classes. Sometimes the Court has acted against outliers, those who persisted in policies a strong national majority rejected. And sometimes it chose sides when the national political majority was closely divided. In this second group of cases, we might say that the election returns sometimes followed the Court, when the Court successfully predicted the future. At other times, however, the election returns followed the Court in another sense, when a political constituency upset by the Court's decisions mobilized against the Court and its supporters. On balance, the question of whether judicial review benefits progressive and liberal causes more than it harms them seems rather difficult.

TAKING A DIFFERENT VIEW OF JUDICIAL REVIEW

But is whether liberals or conservatives benefit from judicial review the right question? We might try to evaluate judicial review in a principled rather than a political way. We would ask, Does judicial review as an institution have characteristics that make it a good part of a well-designed constitutional system?

As we saw in chapter 3, constitutional scholars have two basic answers to that question.[52] They invoke the judges' independence and their focus on particular cases. We saw as well that the contrasts between judges and legislators are often overdrawn, and do not always show that judges are better than legislators. Here we need to consider a different point.

Judicial review in the United States is, by design, connected to ordinary politics. Justices are nominated by the president and confirmed by the Senate; they are not chosen by legal professionals on the basis of their legal qualifications, although professionals are consulted and professional opinions carry some weight. The overall arrangement is undoubtedly a good thing, but it creates fairly close connections between ordinary politics and judicial review. The nomination and confirmation process is political to the very ground. It will mirror the political process that occurs when we decide agriculture policy or foreign policy. At times presidents will rely on the judgments of respected lawyers about who the best nominee is, and at times presidents will calculate how nominating one person will appeal to political interest groups. In both cases the president is concerned about how the nomination will affect his or her political standing with important constituencies. At times senators will defer to a president's choices and at times they will vigorously interrogate the nominee. In both cases the senators are concerned about how their behavior will play with their constituents. At times interest groups will mobilize their constituents around a nomination, and at times they will not. Nomination politics are politics, after all.[53]

The effect is to bring judicial review into alignment with politics elsewhere. The very structure of judicial review in the United States thrusts the "Who benefits" question to the fore. More generally: Judicial review is an institution designed to help us run a good government. It cannot be defended except by seeing how it operates—whether in fact the government is better with it than without it.

Conclusion: Noise around Zero

Many people think we need courts to protect free speech because the Mary Beth Tinkers and Barbara Elfbrandts whom government regulates are not able to protect themselves. Somehow, though, that no longer seems quite right. Margaret McIntyre might be in trouble in the legislature, but surely not James Buckley or the Republican party.

Looking at judicial review over the course of U.S. history, we see the courts regularly being more or less in line with what the dominant national political coalition wants. Sometimes the courts deviate a bit, occasionally leading to better political outcomes and occasionally leading to worse ones. Adapting a metaphor from electrical engineering, we can say that judicial review basically amounts to noise around zero: It offers essentially random changes, sometimes good and sometimes bad, to what the political system produces. On balance, judicial review may have some effect in offsetting legislators' inattention to constitutional values. The effect is not obviously good, which makes us lucky that it is probably small anyway.

AGAINST JUDICIAL REVIEW

ENDING THE EXPERIMENT?

Suppose the Supreme Court issued the following statement one October morning:

> In 1803 we launched a great experiment—judicial review. We believe the nation benefited from judicial review over the past two centuries. Today, however, the gains from further exercises of judicial review no longer exceed the losses. We have therefore decided to end the experiment in 2003. We will no longer invalidate statutes, state or federal, on the ground that they violate the Constitution.

What would happen after such an announcement? Of course there would be a rush to get any possible constitutional challenges to existing laws in under the wire. Politics might take some curious turns as proponents of laws they think might be held unconstitutional try to delay consideration of their proposals, while opponents use the time to build opposition. And of course the Court would be denounced from all sides. This chapter asks, would taking the Constitution away from the courts make much difference to society or to the liberties of the American people?

As we saw in chapter 6, the historical record and considerations of constitutional theory and structure suggest that judicial review does not make much difference one way or the other. On balance, eliminating it is likely to help today's liberals a bit more than it would hurt them. True, without judicial review, liberals would have to give up the prospect of further constitutional gains for gay rights and run the risk that they would be unable to defend abortion rights in the political arena. But without judicial review, conservatives would have to give up the prospect of further erosion of affirmative action programs and would have to fight campaign finance reform in the political arena. The effects of doing away with judicial review, considered from a standard liberal or conservative perspective, would probably be rather small, taking all issues into account.

Doing away with judicial review would have one clear effect: It would return all constitutional decision-making to the people acting politically. It would make populist constitutional law the only constitutional law there is.

Solving the Problem by Getting the Right Judges

Two straw objections have to be gotten out of the way at the start. One is minor: People with vested interests in using the courts to challenge official action—public interest law firms of the left and the right—are bound to oppose doing away with judicial review. Judicial review has been good to them, whatever its effects on everyone else, and they can hardly be expected to give up a good thing without a fight.

The second straw objection is that everything wrong with judicial review occurs because we do not have the right judges. People routinely counter arguments against judicial review by saying that judicial review is not the problem, but that particular judges are. They offer variants of the following argument: "If only we could get judges who

—respected the original understandings of the Constitution,

—or were true liberals,

—or, in general, agreed with me all the time,

everything would be fine."

Of course I have many views about what the Constitution means. So do you. And of course if I could guarantee that five justices held exactly the views I have, I would be wildly in favor of judicial review. So would you. The problem, of course, is that your views and mine might be rather different, and neither of us can guarantee that the judges will agree with us all the time.

A lot of scholarly writing about the Supreme Court, and a lot of op-ed articles as well, seems to assume that if academics and journalists natter at the justices long enough, they will wake up and see the light we are offering them—original understanding jurisprudence, true liberalism, or whatever. Arguments about what courts should do are not completely ineffective, but our nation's experience with judicial review gives little reason to believe that such arguments have a substantial impact on what the justices do.

There are two general problems with arguments attempting to induce judges to get it right.

Too Many Theories. There are simply too many approaches to constitutional law rattling around to guarantee that you or I will be able to persuade judges as a class to choose the approach that you or I think is right.

The arguments about what courts *should* do frequently point in quite different directions, and generally have enough substance that a judge can pick and defend *any* theory he or she wants. The question then is on what basis a judge would choose a theory. The historical record suggests that a judge is rather more likely to pick the theory that points where he or she wants to go anyway, than to pick a theory and reluctantly find that it leads to conclusions he or she would have preferred to avoid.

Theories do sometimes lead judges to conclusions they are uncomfortable with. Justice Anthony Kennedy provided the fifth vote to strike down laws against flag-burning. Simultaneously asserting and denying his personal responsibility for the result, Justice Kennedy said that the case involved "a clear and simple statute to be judged against a pure command of the Constitution. The outcome can be laid at no door but ours." He continued, "The hard fact is that sometimes we must make decisions we do not like. We make them because they are right, right in the sense that the law and the Constitution, as we see them, compel the result."[1]

The question, however, is how common this phenomenon is. Again, the historical record strongly suggests that it is rare. Overall, the justices seem to pick the theories that lead them where they want to go anyway, and drop a theory pretty quickly if it seems to force them to unacceptable conclusions.

Two dramatic examples come from conservative adherents of a jurisprudence of original understanding. (1) *Brown v. Board of Education*: These originalists have a problem with *Brown v. Board of Education*. In the modern era you cannot defend an approach to constitutional law that leads to the conclusion that *Brown* was wrong. The Supreme Court invoked the Fourteenth Amendment's guarantee of equal protection of the law in *Brown*. One difficulty for adherents of a jurisprudence of original understanding is that the very Congress that submitted the Fourteenth Amendment to the states for ratification also supported segregated schools in the District of Columbia. Another is that the Amendment's opponents routinely said that it would lead to integrated schools, and its supporters routinely replied that it would not.

Originalists have ways to deal with these objections. Indeed, one prominent conservative constitutional scholar has argued ingeniously though unpersuasively that the historical record shows that the framers of the Fourteenth Amendment actively opposed segregated schools.[2] The real problem for originalists, however, is *Bolling v. Sharpe*, the companion case to *Brown* involving segregation in the District of Columbia's schools.[3] The Fourteenth Amendment applies only to *states*, not to the national government that supports the District's schools. The only relevant constitutional provision the Court could invoke was the due process clause of the Fifth Amendment, adopted in 1791. And, whatever we can say about Congress in 1868, it is surely impossible to believe that the framers of the Fifth Amendment, many of whom owned slaves, thought they were somehow making segregation by the national government impossible.[4]

Faced with this difficulty, conservative originalists give up the fight. The best they can do is assert that some decisions, while perhaps wrong when announced, have become so entrenched in our constitutional order that they cannot be abandoned. This means, however, that they have to supplement their theory of original understanding with a theory of precedent and *stare decisis* that allows them to explain, for example, why they would adhere to *Bolling* and *Brown* but would reject the assertion by Justices O'Connor, Kennedy, and Souter that *Roe v. Wade*, while perhaps wrong when decided, had become so entrenched in our constitutional scheme that it cannot be abandoned.[5] They have not yet done so.

2. Takings: Justice Antonin Scalia describes himself as a faint-hearted originalist.[6] He also thinks that government regulations can so destroy the value of a person's property as to amount to a "taking" of that property for which the Constitution requires the government to compensate. Unfortunately, the historical record is about as clear as these things get: The Framers simply did not think that there could be what we now call a regulatory taking. To them, takings were physical invasions of property, and they happily imposed regulations that destroyed the value of a piece of property without offering the owner any compensation. Faced with this history, Justice Scalia declared it "entirely irrelevant." What mattered were the "historic understandings" of the American people.[7] This faint-hearted originalism is hard to distinguish from non-originalism. Justice Scalia appears to become faint of heart when a full-blown originalism would stand in the way of the results he prefers.[8]

The theory class might respond to these objections by once again asserting that the difficulties arise because judges have not gotten the message. There is nothing wrong with the theory, only with the judges. I think we are entitled to be skeptical when a hundred years of constitutional theory has not yet persuaded judges to follow where principle—as defined by the theory class—leads.

Theories That Do Not Work. The second difficulty with academic efforts to ensure that judges always come up with the right answers requires an extended discussion. Suppose that somehow we managed to get all the judges to agree on a single approach to interpreting the Constitution. Even so, we would find judges reaching wildly divergent results.

A full-scale demonstration that this objection is correct would take a book.[9] Instead, here I will sketch how the problem arises in connection with an approach to constitutional interpretation most compatible with the idea of populist constitutional law.

Populist constitutional law rests on the idea that we all ought to participate in creating constitutional law through our actions in politics. To do that, however, political life has to satisfy some preconditions. Three seem particularly important. (1) Voting: People who are not allowed to vote will be unable to help construct populist constitutional law, or even the less exalted policies that are the meat and potatoes of everyday political life. (2) Criticism of government: People who are not allowed to criticize the government will be unable to change the government and so will be unable to secure what they believe to be better policies or to construct what they believe to be better constitutional law. (3) A place to form independent views: People need some private space in which they can develop their own views about good policy and constitutional law. Otherwise, political life will routinely reproduce the status quo.

In addition, there may be an overarching category. (4) Dealing with real crises: A determined political majority can enact laws that repudiate fundamental constitutional principles. We can argue against those laws until we are blue in the face, but if we do not have judicial review what else can we do about them? The Supreme Court's record may not be all that wonderful, but it is all we have to deal with these situations, which have unfortunately occurred with some regularity in our history.

Judicial review confined to securing these prerequisites to populist constitutional law would surely be a good thing. Unfortunately, there are several difficulties with getting just this sort of judicial review.

—The proper domain of judicial review according to this approach is quite a bit smaller than the domain of judicial review today.

—The number of real problems of disfranchisement, limitation on criticisms of government, and government domination of private thought is rather small today—perhaps because we have developed a constitutional tradition in which ideas of voting, free expression, and privacy have powerful support in our political culture.

—Once we tell judges that they ought to exercise the power to judicial review to secure the preconditions of populist constitutional law, we are going to find that they will be doing much more than that.

These three difficulties are connected. I will give a broad outline, but presenting the argument in its full glory would be extraordinarily tedious.

Formal exclusions from the vote are unusual in today's society. Basically, the only people who cannot vote are resident aliens, children, some felons, and the mentally incompetent. Most people think that those exclusions have pretty good justifications. There may be a few minor exclusions from the vote that could not be justified, and judicial review to eliminate them would indeed secure the foundations of populist constitutional law. But not having judicial review would not be a big deal in this area.

Formal exclusions are one thing, informal ones another. Constitutional theorist John Hart Ely developed the most sophisticated justification for judicial review to deal with informal exclusions from the vote, although he did not put it in quite these terms.[10]

Ely focused on the following problem: Your political adversaries, who are a majority, let you vote, but they do not take your votes entirely seriously. They regularly use their power as a majority to override your interests, and do not care about what happens to you. The jargon of constitutional law calls you a "discrete and insular minority," using a phrase introduced in a footnote to an opinion by Justice Harlan Fiske Stone in 1938.[11] Judicial review, on this account, can protect minorities who are unable to protect themselves through the political process.

But why can't minorities protect themselves? It cannot be enough to point out that they are a numerical minority. Somebody loses whenever a vote is taken: Every law overrides the views of the minority that loses. No one thinks, however, that burglars deserve special judicial protection because legislatures have made burglary a crime. We have to distinguish between *mere* losers and minorities that lose because they cannot protect themselves in politics.

The problem, Ely said, was not that minorities lose, but that some minorities lose because of *prejudice*. Prejudiced majorities systematically place too little value on the harm they inflict on minorities; that is precisely what prejudice is. Laws against burglary do not underestimate the adverse impact on burglars, so we end up with a correct calculation of social costs and benefits from making burglary a crime. Laws adversely affecting minorities against whom the majority is prejudiced, in contrast, do not strike a correct balance of costs and benefits because the prejudiced majority has undervalued the costs. Judicial review in these circumstances could produce better laws.

The difficulty with this argument is that it overlooks politics. Consider first a group that is a 10 percent minority in the population. It can muster only 10 percent on up-or-down votes on issues it cares about, and it will lose all the time. But it is pretty easy to see how such a minority actually can get quite a bit of what it cares about. Its leaders have to find some issue on which the majority is closely divided—45 percent pro-environment to 45 percent pro-logging, for example—and then say to both sides, "We will deliver our votes on *that* issue to whichever side votes for *our* issues."

Religious parties in Israel, representing a small minority in parliament, advanced their political program for decades in just that way. Israel has a system of proportional representation, which makes this sort of deal almost transparent as political leaders try to put together coalition governments. But the same thing happens in the United States, though less visibly: It is basically the story of the political achievements of the African-American community. By becoming a core constituency in the New Deal and Great Society political coalitions, African-Americans have been able to obtain a fair amount of legislation that they sought. They have not obtained everything they want or should have, but then, that is what happens in politics. African-Americans are sometimes mere losers rather than a group at a systematic disadvantage in politics.

This sort of political bargaining is available to almost everyone, although success does require the minority group to develop political leaders who can promise and deliver the votes.[12] As with formal exclusions, judicial review confined to real informal exclusions would be a rather small institution.

Informal exclusions can take many forms. Terrorism kept many African-Americans from voting in the South earlier in this century even though the Constitution formally secured the right to vote and even though the Supreme Court did a reasonably good job of striking down formal evasions of that command. Today many people do not vote because they find it too difficult to make a living and simultaneously learn enough about the issues to be comfortable with casting a vote; under the circumstances, they think they have better things to do with their free time.

Consider what judges would have to do to address the limitations terrorism and economic conditions place on the ability to exercise a right to vote that the Constitution and laws formally guaranteed. They would have to deploy police forces and reorder the economy. If judicial review confined to eliminating formal exclusions from the vote is no big deal, judicial review dealing with these informal exclusions would go far beyond anything the courts have done. We can be sure that it is never going to happen, whatever its theoretical merits.

Note, however, the structure of the argument. We began by observing that courts might remedy *formal* exclusions from the franchise. But that did not seem to capture many of the problems in the real world. So we expanded judicial review to allow judges to deal with *informal* exclusions. But figuring out what an informal exclusion is turned out to be inherently controversial: Does pluralist bargaining actually work? Should restrictions on bargaining arising from economic circumstances count as informal exclusions from the franchise?

To summarize: In principle judicial review ought to be available to guarantee the preconditions for populist constitutional law such as voting. But if we follow that principle we are likely to get judicial review that is really small, dealing only with formal exclusions and pariah groups, or really big, dealing with informal exclusions resulting from economic circumstances. The theoretical approach we began with generates quite contradictory results in particular cases depending on how expansively the judges understand the approach.

The argument about free expression has the same structure as the argument about voting. We might want judges to strike down laws restricting criticism of government officials, because otherwise we would find it hard to kick them out of office: Any opposition might be taken as violation of a law prohibiting criticism of the government. And we might want to extend the analysis to strike down laws restricting criticism of the policies government officials have adopted, because the most effective way to criticize government officials is to criticize their policies.

In the jargon of First Amendment scholars, the populist justification of judicial review in free speech cases seems to allow restrictions of speech as long as the subject matter is not political in a fairly ordinary sense.

Now consider the problem of libel law. A newspaper publishes a false statement that damages the reputation of a celebrity or, even worse, some ordinary citizen, perhaps a wealthy corporate takeover raider. It does so to increase its circulation—that is, to make money. The Supreme Court has made it hard for victims of these libelous statements to recover damages. It seems quite mysterious what this has to do with making sure that criticism of government officials and their policies goes on unimpeded. Why should the Constitution require celebrities and takeover artists to subsidize newspapers by protecting the newspapers' quest for circulation through articles impugning the celebrities' reputations?

The answer appears to be this: Courts have to develop legal doctrines they can readily administer. The Supreme Court, in particular, has to articulate doctrines that tell lower courts and newspapers how to behave. But, as we saw in chapter 2, this means that the Supreme Court will almost certainly articulate doctrines that are simpler than their underlying justifications. Newspapers and lower courts will fight over who counts as a public official if the Court tells newspapers they cannot libel public officials. Sometimes the newspapers and lower courts will allow libelous statements about people the Court thinks are public officials. To avoid that problem, the Court says, "You have to be really careful about what you publish about *anybody*, public official or celebrity." That is a rule that does the job, as the Supreme Court sees it. But it also protects more than the preconditions of populist constitutional law.

Populist constitutional law can justify judicial review of laws restricting criticism of government officials and of current public policy, and it can perhaps justify a few other constitutional rules. The constitutional law the courts have created is quite different, however. Constitutional protection for speech ranges well beyond criticism of government officials and their policies. We might say that from a populist point of view the Supreme Court has given us the worst of both worlds: We do not get enough protection of speech critical of the government, because the Court has protected only directly critical expressions and has not responded adequately to problems of limits on expression arising from the distribution of wealth, and we get too much protection of speech that has nothing to do with such criticism, because the Court has protected commercial speech and libelous statements about private people.

As with voting and free expression, so—even more briefly—with privacy. There may be good reasons for judges to protect a domain of privacy within which people can form their own views about matters of public importance. It is quite unclear, however, that this justifies the Court's decisions protecting autonomous choice in matters of sexual privacy. It is much easier to defend them on general libertarian grounds than on the ground that judicial review makes sense because it preserves the preconditions for populist constitutional law.

The question of real crises deserves a bit more attention, because it explains why even well-intentioned judges devoted solely to the principle of securing the preconditions for populist constitutional law might generate a lot of judicial review.

It will help to distinguish between truly *extreme* cases of oppression—slavery and the Holocaust—and *ordinary* ones. As Ely pointed out, in extreme cases all bets are off.[13] In the Holocaust Germany's political leaders, supported by a majority of the nation's people, were willing to exterminate other peoples. It was not a country whose judges could resist in the name of the Constitution had there been one. Nor should we expect that judges in such a situation would be so out of line with the rest of the nation that they would want to resist. We can look around the world for examples of such resistance, and we will not find enough to take heart from.[14]

The experience in the United States, while limited, is not encouraging either. The Supreme Court began to develop the modern law of free expression in cases involving critics of the government's involvement in World War I and its aftermath in the Soviet Union. The Court upheld the convictions. It similarly upheld the convictions of leaders of the Communist party in the early 1950s. As the anticommunist crusade abated, the Court began to say that the First Amendment might limit government prosecution of subversives. But the Court did not stand strongly in favor of free expression when tensions were at their height.[15]

The Brandenburg case, discussed in chapter 3, did limit the government's power to prosecute its critics during the war in Vietnam even though it involved a member of the Ku Klux Klan, not an antiwar protestor. The Court's decision may have inhibited the Johnson and Nixon administrations from moving against antiwar protestors. The antiwar movement had enough political support, however, that it seems likely that political constraints and value-based judgments by federal officials played a more significant role in restraining government prosecutions.[16]

We also have to think about the consequences of having judicial review in order to guard against extreme cases of oppression. The problem is that judges will not sit around waiting for such cases. They will instead exercise the power of judicial review routinely. And, indeed, if we want a vigorous institution able to stand up against the powerful in extreme cases, we probably want the judges to get used to the idea of exercising their own power.[17] But, if they do, they will invalidate statutes in less-than-extreme cases (what else could they do with their power?).

Preserving judicial review to deal with extreme cases, that is, means allowing it in ordinary cases. And that has costs. We have to assess the risk we run of truly extreme cases, how great is the possibility of successful judicial resistance in such cases, and what are the costs of routine judicial review. In the end we have to decide whether on balance the risk of extreme cases and the possibility of successful resistance is great enough to justify routine judicial review. I doubt that it is.

This section's argument, then, is that we cannot justify judicial review by invoking the hope that it will produce the results we desire—whatever those results are—because we can guarantee what judges will do. We cannot guarantee that judges will act "appropriately" when we appoint them, or by offering them a constitutional theory so compelling that it will induce them to routinely support outcomes they think unwise. Under these circumstances, the argument against judicial review cannot be met simply by hoping for a better class of judges.

A WORLD WITHOUT JUDICIAL REVIEW?

What would a world without judicial review look like? It might look like Stalinist Russia. Or it might look like Great Britain, which does not have a written constitution, or the Netherlands, which has a written constitution that the courts do not enforce.[18] Our vision of what is possible without judicial review has been shaped by our own political history, in which judicial review has played such a large role. But suppose we had several years to adjust, as my imaginary Supreme Court announcement would give us. Our political behavior might change in ways that could enable greater self-government.

The examples of Great Britain and the Netherlands show that it is possible to develop systems in which the government has limited powers and individual rights are guaranteed, without having U.S.-style judicial review. Part of the reason is that we can have *legal* restraints on government without having *constitutional* ones. The difference is that legislatures can override legal restrictions but not constitutional ones.

A great deal of what we in the United States know as constitutional law parades in Great Britain as administrative law. The British courts have developed a reasonably robust law of *ultra vires*, a doctrine that denies any legal effect to acts by a government official outside the bounds of authority granted the official by the law. So, for example, an undercover police officer might be said to act *ultra vires*, beyond his or her authority, if the officer arrested a person for driving with a broken taillight; as an undercover officer, the court might say, the officer lacked authority to arrest for traffic offenses. An important study by law professor Seth Kreimer demonstrates that the overwhelming bulk of the constitutional decisions of lower federal courts involves challenges to actions by low-level bureaucrats, including police officers, which could easily be handled by sensible nonconstitutional theories like these.[19] And the provisions in a written constitution can influence the way in which a court interprets a statute: The greater the tension between the statute and the thin Constitution's values, the more reason a court would have for interpreting the statute in a way that reduces the tension.

These can be powerful doctrines. A court that took them very seriously could end up finding any official action unauthorized unless the legislature specifically authorized it. Mere general police authority, for example, might not be enough to justify intrusive searches. Adopting this approach, the Netherlands Supreme Court suppressed evidence obtained by continuous covert video surveillance of a suspect held in jail because it was such a "drastic measure" that it had to be authorized by a specific statute. In a related move, a court might interpret statutes authorizing searches narrowly, so that a statute authorizing searches of automobiles might not authorize searches of cars in the police department's impound lot, or searches of mobile homes. Similarly, courts could regulate prison conditions by asking whether the legislature had authorized the conditions as they actually existed.[20]

There is nothing inevitable about this aggressive use of the *ultra vires* doctrine, or of similar doctrines regarding statutory interpretation.[21] And a court that does not have the power to invalidate statutes can do nothing when the legislature steps in and does everything the court demands: authorizes the searches in language so specific that the court cannot invoke the *ultra vires* doctrine or interpret the statute away.

We must remember, however, that there is nothing inevitable about an aggressive interpretation of constitutional restraints on police behavior either. The U.S. Supreme Court allowed searches of impounded cars based on precedents that could easily have been read to rest on the sensible observation that the police have to have the power to search cars they stop on busy highways, so that people simply do not drive off having successfully hidden the evidence of their crimes.[22] Read in that way the precedents would not authorize searches of impounded cars. The Court, that is, was not very aggressive in asserting its power here.

Sometimes, indeed, decisions upholding police techniques may *result from* the existence of judicial review. In 1996 the Supreme Court held that Washington, D.C., undercover narcotics officers did not violate the Constitution when they stopped a car whose driver, they said, had violated a traffic regulation requiring drivers to pay full attention to driving.[23] Washington's police regulations actually said that undercover agents should not make traffic arrests, for rather obvious reasons: If you were a woman driving at night and someone in an unmarked car, dressed like everyone else, signaled you to pull over, what would you do?

The case is a perfect one for invoking *ultra vires* ideas. But doing so would sound decidedly odd in our constitutional system. How, critics would ask, could a person's *constitutional* rights depend on whether a police department's regulations happened to authorize an arrest or search?[24]

The courts might be reluctant to develop detailed constitutional restrictions on police power for another reason. The United States is a large country. The problems police face vary widely. We abandoned our experiment with a nationwide speed limit because a sensible speed limit of 55 miles per hour in the congested Northeastern corridor was ridiculous in Wyoming. Similarly, sensible restrictions on the power of Washington, D.C., police officers might not make sense as restrictions on Wyoming state troopers. Courts invoking the *ultra vires* doctrine can fairly easily develop ways that would allow Wyoming's legislature to explicitly authorize searches, while making it difficult for a city council to do so. Such an accommodation is much harder to develop if the restrictions on the police are rooted in the Constitution.

The courts might be *more* willing to regulate police activities if they could do so without invoking the Constitution. In this odd way, the existence of judicial review may actually *reduce* our protection against government overreaching.[25]

Constitutional Rights without Judicial Review

Eloquent voices from the African-American community have spoken in favor of the Constitution. United States Representative Barbara Jordan electrified the country with her statement at the hearings considering whether to initiate impeachment proceedings against Richard Nixon, "My faith in the Constitution is whole. It is complete. It is total." Law professor and social critic Patricia Williams described the role rights have played in her community's self-understanding and social transformation:

> To say that blacks never fully believed in rights is true. Yet it is also true that blacks believed in them so much and so hard that we gave them life where there was none before; we held onto them, put the hope of them into our wombs, mothered them and not the notion of them. And this was not the dry process of reification, from which life is drained and reality fades as the cement of conceptual determinism hardens round—but its opposite. This was the resurrection of life from ashes four hundred years old. The making of something out of nothing took immense alchemical fire—the fusion of a

whole nation and the kindling of several generations. The illusion became real for only a few of us; it is still elusive for most. But if it took this long to breathe life into a form whose shape had already been forged by society, and which is therefore idealistically if not ideologically accessible, imagine how long the struggle would be without even that sense of definition, without the power of that familiar vision.[26]

The important thing to note here about Jordan's and Williams's statements is that they are about the Constitution and rights, not about the courts and judicial review. We can have Jordan's faith in the Constitution without having any interest at all in the courts.[27] And we can have the rights Williams celebrates without having judicial review.

Faith in the Thin Constitution. Jordan's faith in the Constitution was whole and total, but it seems unlikely that it was in the whole Constitution. Passion about the Emoluments Clause or about the allocation of two senators for each state no matter what its population would be misplaced, for example. Jordan's eloquence resonated because she implicitly referred to the Constitution understood as the repository of the principles of the Declaration and the Preamble. Eliminating judicial review would not eliminate our ability to appeal to those principles in constitutional discourse outside the courts. Indeed, that was precisely what Representative Jordan was doing.

Rights as Ideals. Williams defends rights talk for more basic reasons. Constitutional rights are important parts of the self-understanding of minority communities, and they are a source of power for those communities. Ideas about rights played a central role in the civil rights movement "not simply because of the occasional legal victories that were garnered, but because of the transformative dimension of African-Americans reimagining themselves as full, rights-bearing citizens with the American political imagination."[28]

Williams argues that invoking the Constitution is an important way to honor those who gave their lives to create even the limited rights she believes now available. But eliminating judicial review does not deprive us of the language of constitutional rights, and so would not make it impossible to continue to honor such heroes.[29]

Others have suggested that the benefits Williams describes come with costs as well. To be able to claim rights may be empowering, but it has an underside. Sociologist Kristin Bumiller studied women who claimed to have been the victims of sex discrimination at work.[30] She found that some were profoundly troubled by the process of claiming their rights, which forced them to see themselves as victims, as people tossed around by the whims of others—their coworkers, but lawyers and judges as well—rather than as active people working their way through the world as they chose.

Williams appeals powerfully to the idealized Constitution. But she recognizes as well that making the idealized Constitution real is quite chancy. African-Americans may be the nominal beneficiaries of constitutional rights, but that does not mean that they enjoy those rights in reality. Even more, constitutional rights are almost inherently ambiguous, and being the nominal beneficiary of an ambiguous right may mean nothing at all. Here the Supreme Court's recent position on affirmative action is instructive. As Williams says, African-Americans struggled to make the notion of racial equality real, and what they have received from recent Supreme Court decisions is the back of the hand—in the name of the very principle for which they fought so hard.

Courts as Educators. In our political system courts play an important role in explaining constitutional values to those in the public who pay attention. Eliminating judicial review would reduce that teaching role. But it would not deprive the public of the education that comes from the Constitution itself.

James Madison initially opposed including a bill of rights in the Constitution. He thought that such provisions would be mere "parchment barriers" against oppression: They would exist on paper but would not in fact limit the government. The Constitution's opponents thought that the absence of a bill of rights was a fatal defect. Madison and others responded by promising to amend the Constitution to add a bill of rights. He agreed that a bill of rights could help the *public* limit government: "The political truths declared in that solemn manner acquire by degrees the character of fundamental maxims of free Government, and as they become incorporated with the national sentiment, counteract the impulses of interest and passion." A bill of rights, Madison thought, could be "a good ground for an appeal to the sense of the community." Or, as another framer put it, a bill of rights would give the public "a plain, strong, and accurate criterion by which the people might at once determine when, and in what instance, their rights were violated."[31]

Madison carried through on his promise after his narrow election to the House of Representatives in 1789. Now he was less skeptical about a bill of rights. He gave two reasons for supporting it. One was that the courts would enforce its limitations. The other was this: "[P]aper barriers . . . have a tendency to impress some degree of respect for them, to establish the public opinion in their favor, and rouse the attention of the whole community."[32] In terms used in chapter 5, Madison thought that a bill of rights would give politicians value-based incentives to comply with its provisions.[33]

Judicial review today does much to educate the attentive public about the Constitution. Some people pay attention to the Supreme Court, and perhaps not as many to the Constitution. At the same time, however, what the courts say about the Constitution is specialized and driven at times by special institutional concerns, as we saw in chapter 2. The lessons people learn about equality from Supreme Court decisions describing two or three "tiers" of "review," and the lessons they learn about free speech from decisions distinguishing among content-based, content-neutral, and viewpoint-based regulations—all staples of Supreme Court opinions—may be more qualified than we should like. The technicality that necessarily goes along with opinion-writing may interfere with the educational force of Supreme Court opinions.

The courts are educators because they engage in a complex interaction with the public and legislators over questions about the Constitution's meaning. The thinness of the Constitution outside the courts leaves so much open for discussion that similar interactions would occur among legislators, and between legislators and their constituents. The courts are surely not the only institutions that educate us about our fundamental rights, and we might get a decent education even if the courts played a much smaller role.

It would certainly take some time to redirect our attention to the Constitution itself, which is why I opened this chapter with a proposal to eliminate judicial review several years in the future. We might find that we did not need the courts' help once we start to think about the Constitution directly—if, that is, the Constitution outside the courts is relatively simple and understandable. Again, the Declaration's principles rather than the Emoluments Clause should provide the model.

Statutory Rights. Eliminating judicial review does not mean doing away with judicially enforceable rights. We can still create statutory rights that can be as inspiring as constitutional ones, and sometimes more so. The Americans With Disabilities Act is a civil rights statute dealing with people whom the Supreme Court never found specially protected by the Constitution.[34] And, as we saw in chapter 3, the Supreme Court has never found social welfare rights in the Constitution. Even so, advocates for the poor strenuously objected to the elimination of entitlements to public assistance during debates over welfare reform in 1996. As I have suggested, their rhetorical position may actually have been weakened by the existence of Supreme Court opinions rejecting constitutional social welfare claims, but those opinions did not deprive them entirely of the rhetoric of rights. We do not have to have a court that will strike down laws— a court with the power of judicial review—to have a vibrant language of fundamental rights available to us. We can support and oppose *legislation* by invoking the Declaration's principles. Law professor Ira Lupu calls such laws "statutes revolving in constitutional orbits."[35]

Professor Mary Ann Glendon has argued that we would be better off if whatever rights we had were based on statutes. As she sees it, the way people in the United States talk about rights "is set apart from rights discourse in other liberal democracies by its starkness and simplicity, its prodigality with the rights label, its legalistic character, its exaggerated absoluteness, its hyperindividualism, its insularity, and its silence with respect to personal, civic, and collective responsibilities."[36] Some of Glendon's examples of impoverished rights talk involve statutory rights, but sometimes she praises statutes. The problem as she sees it is that "the language of rights is the language of no compromise."[37] But politics is the arena of compromise. As legislators develop statutes, even civil rights statutes, they necessarily listen to their opponents and often develop compromises accommodating some of their opponents' concerns—accommodations that courts would be hard-pressed to create.

Constitutional Social Welfare Rights. Freed of concerns about judicial review, we might also be able to develop a more robust understanding of constitutional social welfare rights, which are recognized in many constitutions around the world. Generally, constitutions adopted after 1945 contain guarantees of such rights—to employment, to housing, to a minimally decent standard of living, and the like. Today as nations contemplate constitutional revisions—in Canada and in the European Union, for example—strong voices urge that the new documents should contain a "Social Charter."[38]

Like the Supreme Court, most constitutional scholars in the United States shrink in horror at the idea of constitutional social welfare rights.[39] The argument is simple: Any serious constitutional right must be enforced by the courts, and the courts cannot effectively enforce social welfare rights. What sort of order would it take, for example, for a court to guarantee that everyone had a job or adequate housing? A nation might have a public housing program. If a court held that the program did not satisfy the constitutional requirement of adequate housing for all, how could it prescribe a better program? And, even if we can somehow imagine what a court might say, implementing the court's order would be really expensive. In the end, we would have the courts running everything—raising taxes and deciding how the money should be spent. Some people think we have all too much of that today, but the problem they see would be much worse if we constitutionalized social welfare rights.

One response, naturally, is to say that we can include those rights in a constitution, and then tell courts not to enforce them. The Irish Constitution has a section headed "Directive Principles of Social Policy." These principles include adequate jobs and support of the poor. The section also says that "[t]he application of those principles in the making of laws shall be the care of the [legislature] exclusively, and shall not be cognisable by any Court. . . ."[40] German courts recognize a constitutional right to public assistance, but let legislatures decide how and to what extent to actually provide it.

What would it mean to have a constitution that the courts did not enforce? In 1978 law professor Lawrence Sager wrote an important article with the subtitle "The Legal Status of Underenforced Constitutional Norms."[41] As that indicates, Sager saw the Constitution in the courts' shadow. Underenforced constitutional norms are, simply, ones the courts do not enforce. But, Sager argued, they were just as fully "constitutional" as the ones the courts did enforce.

What does that mean? International human rights documents typically acknowledge that the degree to which any nation can effectively provide social welfare rights depends on the nation's economic development. The Irish phrase "Directive Principles of Social Policy" points us in the right direction. Constitutional social welfare rights direct legislators to implement their provisions.[42] As Sager put it, public officials—legislators and executive officials—had a duty to make their "best efforts" to carry out the Constitution's directives.[43]

A constitutional guarantee of adequate housing, for example, would mean that legislators had to give housing policy a rather high priority in their budget decisions. To take a United States scenario: Suppose Congress decided that it simply had to balance the budget for important reasons of long-term fiscal stability. Recent debates about balancing the budget typically assume that few budget savings will come from the defense budget and nearly all must come from domestic discretionary nondefense spending. If the Constitution guaranteed social welfare rights, legislators might have a constitutional duty to treat the defense budget no differently from the housing and social welfare budget—or at least, to offer strong reasons for treating the two budgets differently.

Note that social welfare rights as directive principles of public policy do not operate to displace everything else from a legislator's consideration. They only—but importantly—tell legislators to take social welfare rights very seriously.

A person sympathetic to the idea of a populist constitutional law might raise some skeptical questions. How would calling social welfare rights *constitutional rights* change the way legislators acted? Don't they take social welfare concerns seriously already? Glendon, the nation's leading scholar of comparative constitutional rights, points out that we cannot tell how much a nation will devote to social welfare rights by looking at its constitution: She notes that Great Britain, with no constitution at all, "devotes proportionately more of its resources to social expenditures than its richer 'neighbor' Denmark, where rights to work, education, and social assistance are constitutionally guaranteed."[44]

The reason that constitutional provisions may not affect outcomes strongly is straightforward. Politicians respond to the incentives they face as they try to get elected and reelected.[45] They care about what voters care about, but only to the extent that the voters are able to communicate their preferences effectively. Some groups can communicate more effectively than others, because they can get together to lobby or raise campaign contributions more easily than others. But nothing inherent in the structure of politics implies that voters who care about social welfare expenditures are at a systematic disadvantage compared to voters who care about defense. So policy will reflect only the relative strength of voters' interest in social welfare and defense.

The sympathetic skeptic might suggest that today's budget policy would be reproduced in a different rhetoric. Legislators told that they had to have very good reasons for insulating the defense budget while looking for cuts in domestic nondefense spending would point out that they had a constitutional obligation to "provide for the common defense," which was surely as important as their constitutional obligation to "promote the general Welfare" (a phrase I use here to carry the implication, not part of today's constitutional law, that there are constitutional social welfare rights).

Chapter 3's discussion of legislative debates as ways of educating the public and constructing the Constitution shows that in this context at least rhetoric may matter. Of course, as Glendon points out, the loose connection between constitutional social welfare rights and actual policy means that we can only speculate about what such rights might mean in the United States. Perhaps, however, a constitutional world in which legislators talk about social welfare rights and national defense as *constitutional* interests is different enough from one in which they are merely matters of social policy. The debates might have a seriousness that would create a rather different sense of what this nation was all about than one in which national defense and social welfare policy are ordinary political concerns.

Finally, populist constitutional law offers a way of thinking about social welfare rights as constitutional rights that makes sense of an important dimension of our national experience. The transformation of American politics since 1980, and the 1994 elections, put in question the New Deal's legacy. Franklin Roosevelt saw the New Deal in constitutional terms, and not merely because the Supreme Court stood in his way. In his 1944 State of the Union address, Roosevelt said that the nation had come to accept what he called "a second Bill of Rights" dealing with economics and social welfare: "[t]he right to a useful and remunerative job . . . , to a decent home . . . , to adequate medical care . . . , [and] to a good education."[46] The second Bill of Rights, along with the first, would, in Roosevelt's view, carry out the project the United States began in the Declaration of Independence. The New Deal was part of that project, and so is part of our constitutional legacy. Populist constitutional law can make that clear in a way that other approaches to constitutional law obscure.

The Current Balance

What should we make of judicial review? Our conclusion must consider *all* issues, not just the ones where the Court happens to be coming out on our side at the moment. And it must not idealize the Court by saying that the good decisions—the ones we like—occur when the Court gets the Constitution right, and the bad ones occur when we happen to have the wrong justices.

At the moment, progressives and liberals are losing more from judicial review than they are getting. The Supreme Court has restricted affirmative action and the people's ability to regulate campaign finance. Women have obtained enough political power that most of their gains have come from legislation rather than constitutional interpretation. If Bickel's argument applies to the case of gays and lesbians, we can expect more political victories for those groups in the near future.

But nothing is certain. Political gains may erode or, in the case of gays and lesbians, may never come to fruition. A political leader interested in populist constitutional law might not emerge, or the ones who do might not be talented enough. This makes a final conclusion difficult. Each of us can see ourselves as the *potential* beneficiary of some constitutional ruling, and our hope for rulings in our favor may blind us to the risk that rulings will go against us—not in the limited sense that the Court will not take our side, but in the broader and more troubling sense that the Court will actively join our adversaries.

Even more, at any moment the Court is likely to be helping some people or groups that can be described roughly as liberal or progressive, and hurting others that are equally liberal or progressive. The people the Court is currently helping are likely to see proposals to abolish judicial review as a threat, dividing the liberal and progressive side. Finding the political support for such proposals is therefore likely to be quite difficult—again, as I suggest in the next section, a task for a talented political leader.

Finally, we should not overlook the fact that we are dealing with a problem that is perfectly symmetrical: If abolishing judicial review hurts some who now benefit from it, retaining judicial review continues to hurt those who are now harmed by it. Specifically, in 1999 that means that maintaining judicial review harms African-Americans.

WHY BOTHER?

I realize that I am swimming upstream in this chapter. Robert Bork's nomination to the Supreme Court failed in large measure because his opponents convinced a large segment of the American people that he wanted to limit judicial review much more sharply than people thought appropriate. Different people disagree about when the courts abuse their power, but we seem to think that an institution pretty much like the one we have is good for us. Arguments against judicial review are in this sense antipopulist, for they try to argue that we should not want what we actually do want.

But perhaps we can account for the fact that we like judicial review in a way that is consistent with a populist anti-judicial review position. The assessment of judicial review in chapter 6 presented the idea's core. Judicial review may serve politicians' interests, not their constituents'. Political leaders often find judicial review a convenient way to hand off hard decisions to someone else. Abolishing judicial review conflicts with those politicians' interests. Just as they have found ways of working around constraints they do not like when imposed by the thick Constitution, so they would develop some other institution to insulate them from political responsibility if they did not have the courts to rely on. Indeed, we might expect that among the first responses to the Supreme Court's announcement that it was going out of the judicial review business would be a flurry of bills designed to instruct the Court to stay in the business.[47] Taking the Constitution away from the courts would be inconsistent with our expressed interests to the extent that the American people have chosen politicians who like judicial review for these strategic reasons.

This argument against abolishing judicial review fails to take account of the important role that political leaders play in shaping the people's constitutional understandings. Political scientist Rogers Smith has offered an instructive analysis of the way in which politicians have helped construct what he calls the civic identities of the American people.[48] According to Smith, the American people have multiple traditions, not just the tradition that I have called the thin Constitution. An important countertradition treats the American identity as nonegalitarian, placing white, Anglo-Saxon male Protestants at the center of the American tradition. And, Smith argues, politicians deploy these competing traditions strategically. Suppose a politician has a program that would hurt lower-class American whites, who make up a majority of the politician's constituency. The politician can package that program with a nativist one, appealing to the sense of worth that constituents derive from the countertradition of hierarchy, and may thereby get elected and advance the program that hurts the constituents materially.

An analogous point might be made about politicians' interest in maintaining judicial review. It is indeed a fact of political life, but not necessarily an admirable one. Consider one facet of Smith's analysis: Not all politicians have found it politically appropriate to invoke the countertradition of hierarchy strategically, and the ones we honor most tend to be the ones who have resisted the temptation to do so. So too, we might think, with political leaders who made abolishing judicial review a part of a political agenda devoted to advancing populist constitutional law. A talented politician might succeed by appealing to the best in us, the tradition linked to the thin Constitution in which we take an active role in constructing our constitutional rights without relying on the courts to save us from ourselves.

This may rehabilitate the thought experiment of abolishing judicial review. As I explain in more detail in chapter 8, I believe that populist constitutional law is valuable because it is an important part of the way we constitute ourselves as the people of the United States. Still, vigorous judicial review is part of our self-constitution. Why should we allow ourselves to be persuaded by the right kind of political leader to give it up?

That question is particularly bothersome because I argued in chapter 6 that vigorous judicial review does not make much difference one way or the other. It has some effects, but basically judicial review is an institution that operates around the margins of our political life. If judicial review does not make much difference, how could abolishing it make much difference either—except by changing our self-understanding, and perhaps not for the better? It might increase our power of self-government at relatively low cost. But, precisely because judicial review is a marginal institution, we would not increase our power of self-government that much. More important, it may contribute to serious thinking about the Constitution outside the courts. Populist constitutional law seeks to distribute constitutional responsibility throughout the population. Thinking about a world without judicial review, toting up the costs and benefits of the institution, may contribute to that goal. A modest conclusion, perhaps, but probably the only one an academic's analysis can provide. What a political leader might do is of course another question.

CONCLUSION: HOW TO DO IT

My wife is Director of the National Prison Project of the American Civil Liberties Union. She disagrees with almost everything I have written in this chapter. Sometimes, late at night, as I drift into sleep, so do I.

In the morning, however, I am more alert. After all, the Supreme Court is never going to say it is going out of the business of judicial review. Judicial review is what makes the justices' job interesting and gets their names in the newspaper. It is, in short, an important component of their power, and people with power rarely give it up willingly.

Of course I am going to cheer for my side if the Court is going to continue to exercise its power to invalidate statutes. I actually do not want my arguments against judicial review to persuade people who share my political predispositions. Unilateral disarmament is rarely a good idea. Even worse is selective disarmament, in the form of proposals to deny courts the power to review some subset of statutes, ordinarily ones that the proposals' proponents think the courts will in fact invalidate. Selective "court-stripping" laws are transparent attempts to achieve particular substantive goals rather than serious efforts to rethink the role of the courts in society.

The only way to make sure that both sides disarm completely is to amend the Constitution. In response to President Franklin Roosevelt's proposal that the Supreme Court's membership be expanded so that it would no longer be able to obstruct New Deal legislation, Senator Burton Wheeler, a Democrat who supported the New Deal, countered by proposing a constitutional amendment: If the Supreme Court held a federal statute unconstitutional, Congress could override it by a two-thirds majority in both houses, as long as an election intervened between the Court decision and the override. More recently Judge Robert Bork has proposed an amendment allowing an override by a simple majority vote.[49] As mentioned earlier, there is a comparative analogue to consider: the Canadian Charter's provision, referred to as the "notwithstanding" or "override" clause, allowing the national parliament or a provincial legislature to declare that a statute shall go into effect notwithstanding provisions in the Charter that might make the statute unconstitutional.[50]

The proposals by Wheeler and Bork retain an important role for the Supreme Court. In doing so they may still lead to problems associated with the judicial overhang, discussed in chapter 3. And they may perpetuate the illusion that the Supreme Court can actually save us from ourselves. Why not go all the way?[51] The Irish Constitution provides a model. As we saw in chapter 3, that constitution describes its social welfare provisions as "directive principles of social policy." It then says that applying those principles "shall be the care of the [parliament] exclusively, and shall not be cognisable by any Court." Consider, then, this proposed amendment to the United States Constitution: "The provisions of this Constitution shall not be cognizable by any court."[52] These days liberals do not like the idea of amending the Constitution. Those who support populist constitutional law, in contrast, have no problems with the idea of amending the Constitution, though we object to particular amendments.[53] The next chapter begins by examining opposition to amending the Constitution, and offers an extended defense of the project of populist constitutional law.

Chapter Eight

POPULIST CONSTITUTIONAL LAW

FEAR OF VOTING

Liberals today seem to have a deep-rooted fear of voting. They are more enthusiastic about judicial review than recent experience justifies, because they are afraid of what the people will do. They ask the courts to review legislation adopted by popular initiative and referendum more aggressively than statutes legislatures adopt. They shudder at the prospect of a constitutional convention at which the people would think about redesigning the structure through which we govern ourselves. And Kathleen Sullivan, a prominent liberal constitutional scholar, has diagnosed the disease of *amendmentitis*—an unjustified desire by the people to amend the Constitution.[1] I conclude this book by examining liberal arguments against constitutional amendments because one could characterize the proposal I have made for creating a vibrant populist constitutional law as suggesting a mechanism for amending the Constitution by simple majority vote. I explain why the project of populist constitutional law deserves to be carried out in arguing that such a characterization would be improper.

Sullivan purports to be against amending the Constitution as such, not against the particular amendments, mostly sponsored by conservative Republicans, that she discusses. She notes that Thomas Jefferson cautioned against "look[ing] at constitutions with sanctimonious reverence," but believes that Jefferson's position "lost out . . . for good reasons." Those reasons are basically procedural.

According to Sullivan, stability is an important constitutional virtue, and curing amendmentitis would enhance public confidence that the constitutional system is stable. This is particularly true of proposals to amend such fundamental guarantees as the First Amendment. We ought not—ever?—amend the Bill of Rights.

In addition, she argues, frequent amendments undermine the important distinction between fundamental law and ordinary politics. "[T]he more you amend the Constitution, the more it seems like ordinary legislation. And the more the Constitution is cluttered up with specific regulatory directives, the less it looks like a fundamental charter of government." In addition, many specific proposals attempt to entrench in the Constitution a "controversial substantive choice." Like Prohibition, a failed constitutional experiment, a balanced budget amendment "would enshrine . . . a particular and highly contestable macro-economic policy . . . in the Constitution."

Further, amendments may introduce incoherence into the Constitution. The incoherence may occur because the new amendment may change the relations among political actors in ways not fully understood when the amendment is adopted. A balanced budget amendment would affect the relative power of president and Congress, but no one can tell now exactly how. Such an amendment would give minorities new power in Congress, which they might use to extract pork barrel concessions. Or the incoherence may occur because the new amendment may have to be integrated with the rest of the Constitution. Eventually someone would have to figure out how an amendment allowing states to ban flag-burning fits together with the First Amendment's general protection of free expression.[2]

Finally, any amendment is going to leave some questions open for later interpretation, which threatens an even more serious problem of unanticipated consequences: How can you know what effects an amendment will have on the government's overall operation if you do not know how some question about the amendment's interpretation is going to be resolved? Amendments would inevitably come to the Supreme Court. The more the amendments purported to resolve issues that remained contentious, the more deeply the Court would be involved in continuing controversy. And, when amendments overrule controversial Supreme Court decisions, they inevitably undermine the "finality" of the Court's decisions, which would reduce "the social benefits of peaceful conflict resolution."

Sullivan agrees that amendments make sense when they respond to "structural biases in ordinary legislation." For example, today's legislators may not have much incentive to worry about the burdens unbalanced budgets place on future generations, and they surely are unsympathetic to the arguments for term limits. But, she argues, these structural arguments play too small a role in today's debates over constitutional amendments, and some amendments—the anti-flag-burning amendment, for example—cannot be defended by such arguments.

More recently Sullivan has joined with others to propose a set of guidelines for adopting constitutional amendments. Aside from their obvious motivation, they are entirely uncontroversial: Amendments "should address matters of more than immediate concern," they should be used "only when there are significant practical or legal obstacles to the achievement of the same objectives by other means," they "should be enacted using procedures designed to ensure full and fair debate," and their supporters "should attempt to think through and articulate the consequences of their proposals."[3] One may say, of course, that these are sensible guidelines for ordinary legislation as well: Enact a statute only after full and fair discussion, enact a statute only if you cannot do what you propose under existing rules, and think about a proposed statute's consequences. So why should we be any more concerned about amending the Constitution than we are about enacting statutes that might have long-term consequences?

Like many liberals, Sullivan and her collaborators try to provide procedural reasons for rejecting proposed amendments they dislike on the merits. I would have thought that the answer to the question, "When should we amend the Constitution?" would have to be, "When amending it would improve things." But that opens up arguments about which constitutional policy is better than alternatives. And contemporary liberals seem to be afraid that they cannot win those arguments. I am hard-pressed to understand why liberals think they should be able to prevail by procedural subterfuges like "guidelines" for amendments if they cannot persuade the people that the policies they prefer are actually good ones.

We have seen arguments like this before.[4] Sullivan takes arguments against amending the Constitution *frequently* to support an argument against amending the Constitution *at all*. She wrote in the fall of 1995, when Congress was *considering* a number of amendments. Notably, not a single one had been adopted by the strong majorities the Constitution requires by the end of 1997. Having failed in Congress, the amendments' supporters did not have the opportunity to struggle to obtain ratifications by thirty-eight state legislatures. To say that we should not adopt six amendments in a year is hardly an argument against adopting one.

The fact that the fever of amendmentitis ran its natural course is itself significant. As Sullivan says, the Constitution is hard to amend. Amendments succeed when large majorities in the country think they offer good solutions to problems people—or their political leaders—find quite serious. Under those circumstances, it is not easy to figure out why an amendment adopted with such support would "embody a specific and controversial social or economic policy." When adopted, the policy could not be all that controversial.[5] Similarly, to say that *some* proposed amendments might have unanticipated consequences is a cautionary point, not an argument against any particular amendment.

Sometimes arguments that a proposal is ambiguous are simply efforts to throw sand in the works. For example, one anti-flag-burning amendment would have said that legislatures "have the power" to ban flag-burning. An occasional critic pointed out that this amendment would not technically overcome the Supreme Court's decisions as its proponents thought: The Court did not say that legislatures lacked power to regulate flag-burning; it said that the First Amendment limited the power legislatures had. But of course everyone knew this argument was phony. The proposed amendment would have overturned the Supreme Court's decisions had it been adopted, whatever a technical lawyer might say.

Other arguments about a proposal's ambiguities are more serious, and proponents should take them seriously. But the proponents have disposed of the arguments once they think about them and address them to their own satisfaction. An important ambiguity about the proposed balanced-budget amendment was whether the courts would be allowed to enforce its provisions (or whether arguable violations would be treated as political questions). In the end proponents redrafted it to make it clear that the courts would have no role in enforcing the amendment. What more could they possibly have done?

Of course an amendment will destabilize existing arrangements. Why bother to adopt it otherwise? And everything has unanticipated consequences. But if an amendment's proponents think that what they are sure to achieve is really important, they may reasonably think as well that uncertainties about what they might lose should not stand in the way of adopting their proposal.

We might think about the problem in this way: The amendments Sullivan worries about all come from the political right. Suppose a newly mobilized populist coalition proposed to amend the Constitution to overturn the Supreme Court's restrictions on campaign finance legislation. All of Sullivan's arguments about amendmentitis would apply: The amendment would undoubtedly have some ambiguities, it would have uncertain effects on the relative power of incumbents and challengers, it would undermine respect for the Supreme Court, it would amend the First Amendment. And, the coalition might reasonably say, so what?

It is not as if the Constitution does not get amended. It does—when the Supreme Court reinterprets the Constitution to satisfy contemporary political desires.[6] I suspect that some people think that a campaign finance amendment is a bad idea *because* they think the Supreme Court should be asked to overrule *Buckley v. Valeo*. There is nothing wrong with asking the Court to do what you want, under the guise of interpreting the Constitution, at least as long as we have judicial review. But it strikes me as a bit peculiar to *prefer* doing that to finding out directly what the people want by seeking to amend the Constitution. Or, if not peculiar, at least rather openly antidemocratic.

Sullivan's procedural arguments against amending the Constitution are explicitly anti-populist. She worries that the people will make the wrong decisions, but she appears to be unwilling to argue openly that the theory of a balanced budget is a bad one, or that it is a good thing that the First Amendment protects flag-burners.

Populist constitutional law deals with the values that ought to animate our public life. It would offer *substantive* arguments against particular proposals to amend the Constitution, and would not be embarrassed to do so.

CONSTITUTING THE PEOPLE

"This country," Abraham Lincoln said in his First Inaugural Address, "with its institutions, belongs to the people who inhabit it."[7] Populist constitutional law takes that to heart. And the Constitution belongs to us collectively, as we act together in political dialogue with each other— whether we act in the streets, in the voting booths, or in legislatures as representatives of others.

What *is* populist constitutional law? Throughout this book I have described it as a law oriented to realizing the principles of the Declaration of Independence and the Constitution's Preamble.[8] More specifically, it is a law committed to the principle of universal human rights justifiable by reason in the service of self-government.

—Universal, because *all* men are created equal. As we will see, honoring the Declaration's principles does not require us to overlook the racism and sexism that characterized the Founding generation. Indeed, acknowledging those flaws deepens the argument for populist constitutional law.

—Human rights, because people are endowed with inalienable rights.

—Justifiable by reason, because the Declaration's authors thought an explanation was required by a decent respect for the opinions of mankind. Similarly, the *Federalist Papers*, written as a political tract but transformed by history into a fundamental constitutional document, begin by noting that the prospect of adopting the Constitution opens the possibility of creating a government "by reflection and choice."[9]

—And in the service of self-government, because governments derive their just powers from the consent of the governed.

We could defend populist constitutional law defined in this way by explaining why the idea of universal human rights is a good one. That would be a philosopher's task rather than a lawyer's.

There is another way of justifying populist constitutional law. The idea of universal human rights resonates powerfully with the historical experience of the people of the United States. Our public policies have been guided by that idea, imperfectly to be sure but consistently through our history.[10] Abraham Lincoln has appeared so often in this book because he worked to restyle the silver frame, the Constitution, around the apple of gold, the Declaration's principles.

Astute observers have understood that the Constitution *was* a populist document, in the sense that the American people were constituted by our adherence to the thin Constitution. As Abraham Lincoln put it at Gettysburg, the United States was "dedicated to the proposition that all men are created equal." But Lincoln's observation was only the most dramatic of many in our history.

"What then is the American, this new man?" wrote Hector St. John Crevecoeur in 1782. The American, according to Crevecoeur, was "a new race of man," a mixture of the peoples who had settled in its territory. A person "becomes an American by being received in the broad lap of our great *Alma Mater.*" This new man "acts upon new principles." For Crevecoeur, the most important new principle was equality of station, arising in part from the material abundance of the land but in part from the principles on which the new world was organized: "From nothing to start into being; from a servant to the rank of a master; from being the slave of some despotic prince, to become a free man, invested with lands, to which every municipal blessing is annexed!" As Crevecoeur saw it, the homogenizing influence of material abundance and principles of equality would eliminate the conflicts Europeans experienced arising from national allegiances and religious diversity: "[T]he Americans become as to religion, what they are as to country, allied to all. In them the name of Englishman, Frenchman, and European is lost, and in like manner, the strict modes of Christianity as practiced in Europe are lost also."[11]

Two generations later Frances Wright, a social reform lecturer from Great Britain, asked the same question—"What is it to be an American?"—and offered the same answer: "They are Americans who have complied with the constitutional regulations of the United States . . . [and] wed the principles of America's declaration to their hearts and render the duties of Americans practically to their lives."[12]

Populist constitutional law takes these observations seriously. It treats constitutional law not as something in the hands of lawyers and judges but in the hands of the people themselves. Constitutional law creates the people of the United States *as a people* by providing a narrative that connects us to everyone who preceded us. As Lincoln put it at a July 4 celebration in 1858, "We find a race of men living in [1776] whom we claim as our ancestors. . . . We have besides these men—descended by blood from our ancestors—among us perhaps half our people who are not descendants at all of these men. . . . [W]hen they look through that old Declaration of Independence they find that these old men say that 'We hold these truths to be self-evident, that all men are created equal,' and then they feel that the moral sentiment taught in that day evidences their relation to those men, that it is the father of all moral principle in them, and that they have a right to claim it as though they were blood of the blood and flesh of the flesh of the men who wrote that Declaration, and so they are."[13]

SOME DIFFICULTIES WITH THE PROJECT

The project for populist constitutional law is to continue and extend the narrative of the thin Constitution. In Frances Wright's terms, we must take the Declaration's principles to our hearts and work to realize them practically in our political lives. Or, as contemporary political theorist Anne Norton writes, a written constitution enables later generations "to become their own authors," but only by "mak[ing] the words their own."[14]

That project must avoid two serious but unfortunately common missteps. We could mistakenly treat the Declaration and the Constitution as the organic seeds of a process that has been working *itself* out over history, almost without regard to what the people of the United States actually choose. That denies that we are dealing with a *project*, that is, a self-creating activity in which the people of the United States daily decide whether to continue to pursue the course we have been pursuing. This expresses the Declaration's commitment to self-government.

The second mistake is to offer a highly celebratory account of the choices we have made. This account offers a story of essentially uninterrupted progress in eliminating practices inconsistent with the Declaration's principles. "Sure," a superficial populist constitutionalist might say, "the United States has an unfortunate history of racism, exemplified by slavery and the apartheid system that replaced it, sexism, and nativism. But all those were mere aberrations. Deep down we knew that they were inconsistent with the Declaration's principles, sometimes forced on us by considerations of political expediency. But when political circumstances were favorable, the people of the United States moved to vindicate the Declaration's principles and eliminate these excrescences."

This celebration is both risky and erroneous. The risk is self-satisfaction, in two forms. We may think that we have gone quite a way toward realizing the Declaration's principles, and need not work hard to "complete" the American project. Or, as we saw in the discussion of the idealized Constitution in chapter 7, we may think that whatever injustices we see around us somehow fall outside the scope of the Declaration's project, and conclude that we need not address them as we continue to honor that project.

Our economy's failure to satisfy the basic needs of many people shows that we have not come close to fulfilling the Declaration's project. Proponents of populist constitutional law must keep that failure, and others, clearly in view. Advocates of the thin Constitution may blur our ability to see continuing injustice if they describe populist constitutional law too forcefully as carrying out the Declaration's project.

A celebratory account is wrong, as well, because it does not take our history seriously enough. A real constitutional narrative must treat racism, sexism, nativism, and all those other "aberrations" as deep commitments of the people of the United States.[15] When Thomas Jefferson wrote that "all men are created equal," he excluded women from large domains of social life even as he acknowledged the equal *moral* standing of women and men. The Constitution compromised with slavery, failing to mention it but protecting it by allowing slaveholders to count three-fifths of the slave population toward representation in the House of Representatives. Our foreign policy in the twentieth century has been imperialistic, and not always defensible even as a flawed effort to guarantee fundamental human rights elsewhere in the world.

Perhaps our national self-understanding should not treat racism, sexism, and nativism as commitments running as deep as our commitment to the Declaration's principles, but it must not treat them as aberrations that everyone knew all along were inconsistent with who we were. Everyone did not know that. Many people were—and remain—entirely comfortable with the privileges that racism, sexism, and nativism confer on them. It demeans our national experience to read those people out of the narrative. Building the underside of United States constitutional history into our narrative gives it a richness and complexity that in the end makes the story more attractive than the purely celebratory account. Acknowledging that Thomas Jefferson owned slaves, and that Martin Luther King Jr. had numerous personal flaws, deepens our appreciation for what they accomplished. As we realize that those who did so much probably did not see their own flaws as we do, we may become appropriately humble as we pursue our projects with a new awareness of the possibility that we too are flawed and have a limited understanding of our circumstances. As Anne Norton puts it, "We lie, and we know we lie. . . . But we begin to overcome ourselves in this duplicity."[16]

Again the analogy on the personal level is helpful. Consider the stories people tell about their families, when they regard the family as a pretty good one on the whole. One superficial narrative might include some stories about the family's black sheep, no longer considered by the family as part of itself. Another superficial narrative might treat such people as lovable rogues, fundamentally good people who had an unfortunate flaw or two. But the best, the deepest, and most satisfying family narrative understands these people as deeply flawed, sometimes even evil, whose flaws are and remain the family's responsibility.

Carrying out the project of populist constitutional law is not easy. Some people have vested interests in sustaining a system that fails to satisfy the populist's demand for universal human rights justified by reason. Even more, populists themselves have such an interest to the extent that we are part of the complex and not uniformly attractive narrative of the American people.

POLITICS AND THE THIN CONSTITUTION

As I have described it, populist constitutional law might seem pretty thin compared to the rich body of constitutional law inside the courts: No three-part tests, no balancing of interests, no distinctions between content-neutral and subject-matter-based regulations of free expression—and no Emoluments Clause.[17] Just the Declaration of Independence and the Preamble.

Thin, perhaps, but still enough to sustain a nation. The very thinness of populist constitutional law may be an advantage. It signals that the Constitution and the courts do not produce results across the entire domain of politics, but also that the Constitution, seen through a populist lens, has some bearing on many political issues. So, for example, populist constitutionalism does not dictate the position we must take on affirmative action. Instead, it sets the terms of discourse. Justice Harry Blackmun's claim that affirmative action programs are justified because, as he put it, "[i]n order to get beyond racism we must first take account of race,"[18] is an expression of populist constitutionalism because it invokes an ultimate universalist hope. But so too is Justice Anthony Kennedy's observation, in support of his challenge to affirmative action programs, that "[t]he moral imperative of racial neutrality is the driving force of the Equal Protection Clause,"[19] and for exactly the same reason.

One advantage of the thin Constitution is that it leaves a wide range open for resolution through principled political discussions—principled because they are oriented toward the Declaration's principles. In this way the thin Constitution may constitute us as a people. But exactly what sort of people?

Supreme Court decisions interpreting the First Amendment express an understanding of who we are. *Cohen v. California* found it unconstitutional for a state to prosecute a person for carrying a jacket with "Fuck the Draft" on its back.[20] *Hustler Magazine v. Falwell* found it unconstitutional for a state to allow Reverend Jerry Falwell to recover damages for emotional distress caused by an outrageously obscene parody describing Falwell's first sexual encounter.[21] These cases show that the Court rejects the proposition that the government has power to regulate expression in order to elevate public discourse. Law professor Robert Post has suggested that the Court's message could properly be modulated so as to allow regulations that might have some modest effect in inducing a greater degree of civility in our public discourse.[22]

Perhaps Post is right. The Court's vision, however, has its own attractions. It sees the people of the United States as a fractious, contentious lot. To that extent it may be compatible with the idea of a thin Constitution that leaves much to political resolution. Yet we might wonder whether the Court's vision constitutes us in a distinctively male, combative way. One advantage of the thin Constitution, however, is that it leaves it to us to constitute ourselves either as fractious or pacific, contentious or civil, rather than relegating that choice to the courts.

Populist constitutional law returns constitutional law to the people, acting through politics. Just as judges can, the people can give wrong answers to important questions. Populist constitutional law offers no guarantees that we will end up with progressive political results. But, of course, neither does elitist constitutional law.

Contemporary constitutional discourse is torn between two poles. Liberals have an impulse to treat all political issues as ultimately constitutional. If an issue is important enough, liberals think, surely the Constitution tells us what to do about it. The criterion of *importance* allows liberals to assert that they reserve a domain for politics. Unfortunately, applying that criterion simply brings out contemporary liberalism's limits. The defense budget is important in a colloquial sense, but it is not *fundamental* in the special constitutional sense that liberals use. But why not? Because liberals either really do not think it that important, or because they believe that courts will not try to regulate the defense budget. For liberals, however, judicial reluctance is a contingent historical fact: They would constitutionalize the defense budget if they could persuade enough judges that controlling the defense budget was really important.

Mark Graber has argued, against liberal constitutional theorists, that their willingness to develop ingenious constitutional arguments supporting a woman's right to choose with respect to abortion must be coupled with their unwillingness to develop constitutional arguments supporting poor people's rights to the material goods essential for minimal well-being.[23] Graber shows that liberal constitutional theory has the *intellectual* resources sufficient for the latter task, but its adherents apparently lack the *political* will to make the effort.

The boundary liberals draw between the Constitution and politics either exposes contemporary liberalism's limits or ultimately dissolves. Liberals leave no domain for a principled, constitutional politics.

Contemporary conservatives have the same problem, although it arises in a different way. If liberals have an impulse to constitutionalize everything, conservatives have an impulse to deconstitutionalize everything.[24] The heart of contemporary conservative constitutional discourse is advocacy of judicial restraint and opposition to judicial activism. True, conservatives leave room for judicial review in the service of the original understandings of the Constitution's provisions. They have rarely done well in explaining to people who do not share their prior political commitments exactly what those understandings were and, more important, how we ought to apply those understandings in the different circumstances of contemporary life.[25]

The central rhetorical move of contemporary conservative constitutional discourse is this: "The Constitution does not say anything about X—abortion, the right to die, or whatever. It therefore leaves it up to our democratically elected legislatures to decide what to do about X."[26] When pushed, conservatives might even give up on restrictive definitions of X, and would go along with saying, "The Constitution does not say anything about affirmative action either." The conservative position leaves no room for a principled politics in either version.

For both liberals and conservatives, then, we have a principled Constitution, where courts rule, and unprincipled politics, where the mere preferences of democratic majorities rule. The only disagreement is where to draw the line (and, to some liberals, whether there is any space left for politics at all).

Populist constitutional law is different. It creates space for a politics oriented by the Declaration's principles by taking constitutional law away from the courts. Such a politics actually can have real bite, but no one can guarantee that it will produce specific results.

CITIZENSHIP, THE THIN CONSTITUTION, AND THE AMERICAN PEOPLE

The Republican party was the moving force behind the Fourteenth Amendment after the Civil War. That Amendment's first sentence was designed to overturn the Supreme Court's *Dred Scott* decision, one of whose holdings was that African-Americans could not be citizens of the United States. To the contrary, the Fourteenth Amendment says: "All persons born . . . in the United States, and subject to the jurisdiction thereof, are citizens of the United States."

The 1996 Republican party platform supported "a constitutional amendment or constitutionally valid legislation declaring that children born in the United States of parents who are not legally present in the United States or who are not long-term residents are not automatically citizens."[27] Is this an example of the amendmentitis disease? More important, is it consistent with the thin Constitution?

Only someone who thinks the amendment a bad idea would agree that the proposal would trivialize the Constitution by entrenching a permanent solution to a transient political controversy. Its proponents think that it addresses a permanent problem that the existing Constitution itself exacerbates. Denying birthright citizenship to children of persons not lawfully present would remove one incentive for people to come to the United States, and would make it somewhat easier, proponents believe, to address the problem of illegal immigration.

Like all constitutional amendments, this one would pick a side in a contemporary political controversy. But it would succeed only if large majorities of the American people supported it. And, of course, if people later decided that birthright citizenship was a good idea, perhaps because circumstances changed, they could enact legislation re-creating birthright citizenship. The results under this amendment, that is, can be revised by ordinary political means.

Nor does the proposed amendment inject incoherence into the Constitution. Birthright citizenship does not seem to interact strongly with other constitutional provisions.[28] And the proposed amendment could readily be drafted to avoid potential problems of interpretation or unintended scope. For example, this might do the job: "Notwithstanding any other provision of this Constitution, Congress shall have the power to determine the conditions under which persons born in the United States to parents not lawfully present in the United States shall become citizens." Or, "No person born in the United States to parents who are not lawfully present in the United States shall be entitled to citizenship except under such conditions as Congress may prescribe."[29] I offer these as simple first tries, written off the top of my head. I am sure that clever lawyers could invent interpretive ambiguities, but I am equally sure that these two off-hand drafts go 90 percent of the way to doing the job.

I doubt that the proposed amendment is pathological in any procedural way. It is, however, anti-constitutional, and supporters of populist constitutional law ought to oppose it.[30]

The *Dred Scott* case and its repudiation in the Fourteenth Amendment show that questions about who the members of a political community are, are among the most difficult ones the United States has faced. Germany gives citizenship to those born of German parents, and makes it quite difficult for nonnatives to become naturalized citizens. Israel's Law of Return allows any Jew to return to Israel and take up Israeli citizenship.[31] The birthright citizenship in the Fourteenth Amendment, and relatively easy naturalization policies, show that the United States is different.

Why *should* a nation restrict citizenship? Because a nation is made up of its citizens. Change the composition of the population and you change the character of the nation. This is entirely understandable for nations like Germany, where the national character is ultimately ethnic. The idea of changing the national character is more problematic for the United

States. For, again, "what is it to be an American?" Our national character is value-driven, but the values, though fundamental, are not extensive: Anyone committed to the Declaration's principles can become an American.

Would it be consistent with the value-basis of United States citizenship to exclude people on the basis of the values they hold? Undoubtedly, admitting people with different values will *change* the United States. The changes might not be as large as those already present in the country might think, however. A substantial number of immigrants demonstrate by the very fact of their movement that they have the value sometimes called "American get up and go," for they have already gotten up and gone. Natives' experiences of life shortly after an influx of immigrants may be unsettling, but after a while the differences the immigrants introduce— including tacos and egg rolls—may well come to seem natural and desirable side effects of cultural diversity.

In addition, we should not overestimate the degree to which U.S. natives share a single set of values. As I have noted repeatedly, the common culture of the United States is a commitment to the principles of the Declaration of Independence. And that commitment has few implications for specific public policies or—by extension—cultural values.

The Supreme Court's decision in *Schneiderman v. United States* (1943) shows how limited those implications are.[32] The government had moved to revoke William Schneiderman's naturalization on the ground that he was not "a person attached to the principles of the Constitution of the United States and well disposed to the good order and happiness of the United States," as the naturalization statute then required, because he was a member of the Communist party. Schneiderman testified that he believed in social ownership of the means of production, and that he "hoped" that could be done "by democratic means," but believed that history showed that "the ruling minority has always used force against the majority." According to the Supreme Court, the fact that Schneiderman wanted such sweeping changes in our economic and political system did not show that he was not attached to the Constitution's principles. The Court noted the argument that you could be attached to the Constitution no matter what changes you wanted, as long as you were willing to use the Constitution's amendment procedures to change it. But its holding was seemingly more limited. The Court applied the test the government proposed and found that Schneiderman had demonstrated sufficient attachment to the Constitution's principles.

In *Schneiderman* the government described the nation's "general political philosophy" that was a condition of naturalization:

[W]hether [Schneiderman] substitutes revolution for evolution, destruction for construction, whether he believes in an ordered society, a government of laws, under which the powers of government are granted by the people but under a grant which itself preserves to the individual and to minorities certain rights or freedoms which even the majority may not take away; whether, in sum, the events which began at least no further back than the Declaration of Independence, followed by the Revolutionary War and the adoption of the Constitution, establish principles with respect to government, the individual, the minority and the majority, by which ordered liberty is replaced by disorganized liberty.

Nationalization of property, a representative "dictatorship of the proletariat," abolishing the Senate and the Supreme Court: None of these were inconsistent with the nation's political philosophy.[33] The *Schneiderman* decision shows that, within the broad framework created by the Constitution to implement the Declaration's principles, the values that constitute the American people are always subject to change as the people change.

Universalism and the Thin Constitution of the American People

Schneiderman demonstrates again how thin populist constitutional law is. That very fact amounts to a response to a commonly voiced objection to the view that people ought to be committed to universal human rights above all else. According to some critics, most notably Harvard political theorist Michael Sandel, the claims of universal human rights contradict the real commitments people have to smaller communities like families, neighborhoods, religions, and nations. As a result, those claims cannot motivate people to support a government dedicated to pursuing universal human rights above all else.[34]

The argument I have developed offers three replies.

Thinness. The claims of universal human rights are thin, and therefore need not displace the claims of smaller communities in many areas. Universal human rights simply may not speak to a large range of practices within families or religious groups. As a result those smaller communities can sustain themselves and provide people with the more local identities that critics like Sandel believe essential.

Principled Politics. The claims for universal human rights leave the details of what those rights are to be worked out in a principled—constitutional—political debate outside the courts. All that populist constitutional law requires is that the debate take those claims quite seriously. An apparent conflict between a community's practices and universal human rights provides the occasion for open political discussion in which neither the claim for the community's practice nor the claim for universal human rights automatically defeats the other.

Consider, for example, members of a religious community who discipline recalcitrant children in a way that looks to outsiders like physical child abuse. Defending against child abuse charges, the members assert that their religious beliefs require such discipline. Populist constitutional law does not dictate the resolution of this case. It requires only that prosecutors and jurors take seriously the claims on both sides—the claim that severe physical abuse of children is a violation of a universal human right defensible by reason, and the claim that the demands placed on people by their god must be honored if they, and we, are to take their religion seriously.[35]

Nationalism But Not Nativism. Perhaps most important, populist constitutional law *does* invite people to be committed to a national community rather than a universal one. It urges that the people *of the United States* continue to constitute ourselves by a commitment to universal human rights. We are citizens of the United States—not citizens of the world at large, or cosmopolitans indifferent to the place we happen to find ourselves in—because of that commitment.

The Republicans' proposed amendment is anti-constitutional because it rejects the narrative of populist constitutional law. The first sentence of the Fourteenth Amendment defines citizenship in terms consistent with the Declaration's project of realizing universal human rights.[36] It tells us who are citizens of the United States. The proposed amendment, in contrast, would tell us who is not a citizen. The amendment would endorse nativism and thereby reject the Declaration's principles, rather than addressing the problematic relation between nativism and the Declaration's principles.[37]

A critic of the idea of populist constitutional law might note a problem with this. I have not yet defended populist constitutional law on the philosophical ground that universal human rights are indeed justified by reason. Rather, I have defended it as offering an attractive narrative of the complex history of the people of the United States: We are who we are because we are committed to the project of realizing the Declaration's principles. But we can start telling a different story about ourselves precisely because we constitute *ourselves*. We can, in short, change who we are, and the proposed amendment might be the first step in the reconstruction of a narrative of the people of the United States.

In taking that step, of course we would have to rethink how we understand the original Constitution, the post–Civil War amendments, and the New Deal and the Great Society programs. It would be a massive task, I believe, because the Declaration's principles provide a story line that is much closer at hand. But perhaps the task is not impossible.

Understanding constitutional law as a populist narrative that can be retold dissolves one puzzle that has run through this book: Why should we today be bound by decisions made a long time ago when, after serious deliberation, we think that those decisions lead us to undesirable policies today? The answer is that we are *not* bound by those decisions, but we have an obligation to take those decisions seriously because they were decisions that we ourselves made, in an important—albeit constructed—sense. We can reject those decisions, but in doing so we embark on a project of reconstruction that can threaten our national identity. The analogy on the individual level is obvious: As a matter of brute fact, anyone can throw aside the deepest commitments he or she made a decade ago, but doing so raises questions about that person's psychological and moral integrity.[38]

A historical narrative connecting us to our past is important because it acknowledges and promotes the fundamental human good of connection between people. We are not monads simply pursuing our individually constituted projects unaffected in principle by anyone else. We are embedded in historically created supra-individual entities—families, neighborhoods, a nation—and we are constrained by them and responsible for them simultaneously. The experience of constraint and responsibility is an important human value.[39]

That alone will not buy us much, however. Having connections to historically embedded communities may be a fundamental human good, which all social orders ought to seek to achieve, or it may be an inescapable aspect of the human condition. Still, one can be connected to many such communities: one's family or one's religious group, for example. Preserving a national identity of the sort we have in the United States is important only if being connected to a historically constructed *political* community is a fundamental human good or aspect of the human condition.

Families and neighborhoods differ from larger political communities. In a family or neighborhood you are responsible for and constrained by people whom you know personally. Larger political communities differ in two ways. Only in them do you have the experience of constraint by and responsibility for people merely because they are people.[40] Perhaps more important, larger political communities are composed of people who are *very* different from you. Your experience of constraint by and responsibility for such people deepens and enriches your own life.[41]

A people can be constituted in many ways. But any one people is historically constituted in only one way. Consider key episodes in our constitutional history: the adoption of the Constitution, the amendments adopted after the Civil War, the New Deal and Great Society programs that responded however imperfectly to Roosevelt's "Second Bill of Rights" speech, the post-1945 orientation of United States foreign policy, again imperfectly, to human rights. These show that it is possible to create an attractive narrative of the constitution of the people of the United States. As Crevecoeur, Wright, and Lincoln understood, the people of the United States are constituted by the Declaration's principles.

We can reconstitute ourselves. But we should not. We ought to take as our project realizing the Declaration's principles because, in the end, those principles are good ones. The nativism expressed in the Republican platform proposal is not, even though it is the contemporary manifestation of another American tradition.

CONCLUSION: PROPOSITION 187 REVISITED

We can end by returning to Proposition 187. Though related to the Republican platform proposal in its political orientation, Proposition 187 is different. It does not propose to make a fundamental change in our understanding of who the people of the United States are. Instead, it is a relatively detailed policy proposal, aimed at regulating illegal immigration by making it less attractive in a number of ways.

I doubt that a proponent of populist constitutional law would *have to* oppose Proposition 187. The issue for such a person is whether Proposition 187 is consistent with the project of realizing the principles of the Declaration and the Preamble. Proposition 187 is in tension with the way in which the Declaration's principles have gradually been realized in our history. It limits the scope of the welfare state's benefits instead of expanding them.

But it does so to serve the general welfare, according to its supporters. Whatever the ultimate scope of the Declaration's principles, the people of the United States do not yet have general responsibility for the well-being of people all over the world. At least for the time being, we can limit the benefits of *our* welfare state to those who are in some meaningful sense part of us. And perhaps membership can be a matter of degree: Perhaps some people are more deeply embedded in our narrative than others. Proposition 187's supporters could say that under today's circumstances, in a world of limited resources, there is nothing wrong—nothing inconsistent with our commitment to the project of realizing the Declaration's principles—in allocating limited resources to maximize the well-being of those who have a larger degree of membership than do children of persons illegally present in the country.

Proposition 187 may set up a tension within the populist constitutional project.[42] What matters to the populist constitutionalist, however, is not primarily how controversy over Proposition 187 is resolved, but the terms in which it is discussed. The populist constitutionalist would oppose it to the extent that its supporters rely explicitly or implicitly on nativist urges. But if its supporters cast their arguments in terms of promoting the general welfare, defend the idea that there are degrees of membership, and confront the tension between that idea and the Declaration's universalist tendencies, the populist constitutionalist ought to take them on in those terms.[43]

Populist constitutional law does not determine the outcomes of political controversies or dictate much about public policy. Instead, it orients us as we think about and discuss where our country ought to go.

Some think that the Supreme Court's elaboration of constitutional law has given us a rich vocabulary of practical political philosophy. It has not. It may have given the Supreme Court and some constitutional lawyers such a vocabulary. The populist constitutionalist believes that the public generally should participate in shaping constitutional law more directly and openly. The Declaration of Independence and the Preamble to the Constitution give all of us that opportunity. As Lincoln said, the Constitution belongs to the people. Perhaps it is time for us to reclaim it from the courts.

NOTES

PROLOGUE

1. 374 U.S. 398 (1963).
2. Goldman v. Weinberger, 475 U.S. 503 (1986).
3. Employment Division v. Smith, 494 U.S. 872 (1990).
4. City of Boerne v. Flores, 117 S.Ct. 2157 (1997).

CHAPTER ONE
AGAINST JUDICIAL SUPREMACY

1. 457 U.S. 202 (1982).
2. League of United Latin American Citizens v. Wilson, 908 F.Supp. 755 (C.D. Cal. 1995) (noting that it had temporarily enjoined relevant provisions of Proposition 187 one week after its effective date).
3. 5 U.S. (1 Cranch) 137 (1803).
4. 358 U.S. 1 (1958).
5. 60 U.S. (17 How.) 393 (1857).
6. Sparks, *Lincoln-Douglas Debates*, pp. 257, 372.
7. Basler, *Collected Works of Abraham Lincoln*, vol. 2, pp. 516, 518.
8. First Inaugural Address, March 4, 1861, 6 Richardson, *Messages and Papers of the Presidents*, vol. 6, p. 9.
9. The Civil War crisis elicited Lincoln's analysis, but he gave reasons that are available in more ordinary situations.
10. U.S.Const., art II, § 2.
11. This is the subject of chapter 5.
12. This is the subject of the next chapter.
13. Immigration & Naturalization Service v. Chadha, 462 U.S. 919 (1983).
14. Young v. American Mini-Theatres, 427 U.S. 50, 70 (1976).
15. Nagel, *Constitutional Cultures*, chap. 7 (chapter entitled "The Formulaic Constitution").
16. Adarand Constructors, Inc. v. Pena, 515 U.S. 200 (1995).
17. Jacobsohn, *Apple of Gold*, p. 3 (quoting Lincoln; emphasis omitted).
18. The distinction is familiar to legal academics from Ronald Dworkin. Dworkin, *Taking Rights Seriously*, pp. 134–35.
19. For a discussion of the relation between religious reasons and secular justifications, see chapter 4.
20. Frederick Douglass, "The Dred Scott Decision," in Foner, *Life and Writings of Frederick Douglass*, vol. 2, p. 419.
21. The otherwise excellent treatment in Paulsen, "Most Dangerous Branch," is flawed because it overlooks the procedural and substantive issues I discuss here. Another recent overview of the issues discussed in this chapter is Gant, "Judicial Supremacy."

22. Special Session Message, July 4, 1861, in Richardson, *Messages and Papers of the Presidents*, vol. 6, p. 25. Lincoln proceeded to defend the suspension as justified within the Constitution. He was willing to provoke a constitutional crisis, that is, but did not believe he had actually done so.

23. Chapter 2 demonstrates some of the difficulties associated with a populist constitutionalism based on a thicker Constitution.

24. *Compare* Adarand Constructors, Inc. v. Pena, 515 U.S. 200, 240 (1995) (Thomas, J., concurring) (citing the Declaration of Independence), *with* Regents of the University of California v. Bakke, 438 U.S. 265, 407 (1978) (Blackmun, J., concurring) ("In order to get beyond racism, we must take account of race").

25. Miller, "President's Power of Interpretation."

26. Worcester v. Georgia, 31 U.S. (6 Pet.) 515 (1832).

27. In fact Georgia acquiesced in the Court's decision, although with some hesitation; eventually the state's governor pardoned Worcester. See White, *Marshall Court and Cultural Change*, pp. 737–39.

28. For additional discussion of this objection, see chapter 2.

29. One could construct an account of judicial review as dialogue, in which the justices serve as discussion leaders of this sort. Chapter 6 assesses such accounts, and concludes that the justices' contributions to the dialogue are smaller than one might think. The notion of judicial supremacy impedes our coming to understand the Court's work in such terms.

30. Easterbrook, "Presidential Review," deals with the issues raised in this section rather more casually than they deserve. He reaches conclusions generally compatible with mine, although without working through some of the complications.

31. Jefferson to Abigail Adams, Sept. 11, 1804, in Bergh, *Writings of Thomas Jefferson*, vol. 11, pp. 311–13.

32. The Supreme Court itself never ruled on the act's constitutionality, but Jefferson did not appear to consider that an important analytic feature of the problem.

33. Veto Message, July 10, 1832, in Richardson, *Messages and Papers of the Presidents*, vol. 2, pp. 576–91.

34. Chapter 5 shows how the political questions doctrine can be reconciled with *both* a theory of judicial supremacy and populist constitutional law.

35. Such a rule is not an inherent part of a constitutional system. We could design ways of ensuring that presidential decisions to pardon or veto on constitutional grounds could be reviewed by the courts. (Barzilai v. Government of Israel [The General Security Service Pardon Case], *Selected Judgments of the Supreme Court of Israel*, vol. 6 [Jerusalem: Supreme Court of Israel, 1986], suggests that that Court would review presidential pardons using a standard like "unreasonableness.") Consider the veto. We could interpret the Constitution to require the president to veto bills *only* on constitutional grounds, or *only* on policy grounds. In the first situation, if the president's veto message asserted either a policy ground or a constitutional interpretation that the Court rejected, the courts could invalidate the veto and the bill would become law. In the second, a veto message asserting a constitutional ground, as Jackson's did, would be ineffective even if it contained policy arguments against the bill as well. (This latter course is not en-

tirely satisfactory. A president whose decision to veto was controlled by constitutional concerns—either entirely or enough to tip the balance against a bill about which the president had policy doubts—might send a veto message expressing only policy concerns.)

Odd as this system sounds to contemporary U.S. ears, the proposition that the president's veto power was limited had some support in the nation's early years. According to one study, from 1789 to 1840 presidents vetoed twenty-one bills, "and only five or six were based upon other than constitutional grounds." Mason, *Veto Power*, p. 129; Mayer, "Jefferson's Conception of the Presidency," pp. 142–43 (describing Jefferson's "understanding—shared generally not only among the founders' generation but also among virtually all the presidents before the twentieth century— . . . that use of the veto should be confined to unconstitutional legislation"). We might take this practice to indicate an understanding that bills ought to be vetoed only on constitutional grounds as a general rule, albeit with some exceptions. But, whether or not there was such an understanding, it surely is possible to design a system in which the president's veto power is limited. And in such a system, judicial review would always be possible.

The Senate has a procedure that might be used more widely than it has been. Under the Senate's rules, a senator can raise a question of constitutionality, which must be submitted to the Senate as a whole for resolution. Policy debate ends when such a motion is made. Senators then may discuss only constitutional questions. If the motion succeeds—that is, if the Senate believes that the proposal is unconstitutional—the underlying legislative proposal is defeated. If the motion fails, the Senate turns back to policy questions. What would happen if this procedure were widely used in both houses of Congress? If Congress enacts the bill, it is subject to judicial review. Suppose the Senate or the House accepts the motion, finding the proposal unconstitutional. It is not hard to see how a constitutional system could still provide judicial review, although we might have to change some details of the Supreme Court's holdings about who can raise constitutional challenges to get to this point. Perhaps a legislator who voted *against* the motion could ask the courts whether the legislative majority's view of the constitution was right. If the courts said the majority was wrong, the effect would be the same as defeating the motion of unconstitutionality: Congress would then go back to discussing only the proposal's policy dimensions.

The French constitutional system does use motions of unconstitutionality. Two points about the French practice deserve note here. First, they almost never succeed, because of the structure of party politics in the French legislature: from 1958 to 1984, ninety-six motions were made, seventy-one were voted on, and only one passed. Second, the use of the motion has grown as the French Constitutional Council has expanded its own reach.

36. Paulsen, "The *Merryman* Power," p. 100. People who are less bothered by presidential "defiance" in refusing to prosecute for violations of laws the courts have found constitutional than by presidential attempts to prosecute for violations of laws the courts have found unconstitutional do not accept the strong theory of judicial supremacy, particularly to the extent that they rely on the thought that the potential targets of prosecution have justifiable reliance interests in thinking they will not be prosecuted after the courts have struck a statute down.

37. Technically, President Jefferson could not have prosecuted people for violating the anti-sedition act, which had expired according to a sunset provision before he took office. The analytic point I make is, however, still available, but harder to state as concisely as the version in the text.

38. Most of the examples that follow involve the president and members of Congress. Chapter 2 shows why the examples are relevant for understanding issues faced by all public officials and ordinary citizens.

39. Courts have in fact upheld denial of publicly funded nonemergency medical care even to aliens legally present in the country.

40. Coker v. Georgia, 433 U.S. 584 (1977).

41. Stanford v. Kentucky, 492 U.S. 361 (1989).

42. There are other ways: Enact a statute purportedly distinguishable and hope that the Court will say: "This case is actually not distinguishable from our precedent, which we hereby overrule." Here the legislator has to hope that the Court will bite the bullet; in the case involving a reenacted statute already held unconstitutional, the Court has no choice.

43. Texas v. Hopwood, 518 U.S. 1033 (1996). The original court of appeals opinion is at 78 F.3d 932 (5th Cir. 1996).

44. After the Supreme Court denied review, attorneys for the Texas plaintiffs asserted that officials and schools that continued to take race into account risked liability for punitive damages. Where there is a reasonable basis for believing that a test case would succeed, and when race is taken into account to provide the basis for such a case, I doubt that punitive damages would actually be available.

45. Minersville School Dist. v. Gobitis, 310 U.S. 586 (1940).

46. West Virginia Board of Education v. Barnette, 319 U.S. 624 (1943). The head-counting is done in the lower court opinion, 47 F. Supp. 251 (S.D. W.Va. 1942).

47. See, e.g., Caminker, "Precedent and Prediction," pp. 22–23 (1994) (describing but not endorsing these concerns).

48. Planned Parenthood of Southeast Pennsylvania v. Casey, 505 U.S. 833 (1992).

49. Texas v. Johnson, 491 U.S. 397 (1989); United States v. Eichman, 496 U.S. 310 (1990). More precisely, the Court held such statutes unconstitutional when they outlawed flag-burning as an expression of opposition to public policy.

50. That majority has been unable to effectuate its preferences because doing so would require amending the Constitution, and the majority may not be the supermajority—represented by two-thirds in both houses of Congress and by majorities in legislatures of three-fourths of the states—that the Constitution requires for a constitutional amendment. Alternatively, the majority may be the requisite supermajority among the people, but finds its desires obstructed by opposition from within the political elites who are members of Congress.

51. Of course, precisely because dismissal is certain, the costs to the defendant will not be that great.

52. Daniel Patrick Moynihan, "What do you do when the Supreme Court is wrong?" *The Public Interest*, 57, 1979, p. 3. There are overtones in this article suggesting that it asserts the more limited proposition discussed earlier, that Con-

gress can enact statutes when it reasonably believes that the Court might overrule the decision with which Congress disagrees.

53. I draw my account of *Merryman* from Paulsen, "The *Merryman* Power," pp. 89–91.

54. Meese, "The Law of the Constitution."

55. Second Inaugural Address, March 4, 1865, in Richardson, *Messages and Papers of the Presidents*, vol. 6, p. 277.

56. City of Boerne v. Flores, 117 S.Ct. 2157, 2171 (1997).

57. One might even argue that the Court was *less* responsible about its exercise of power-maximizing capacity than Congress was. For example, Congress made a deliberate decision that the religious freedom interests it sought to promote were more important than the federalism and law-enforcement interests raised by a number of state prison administrators, in rejecting a proposed modification of RFRA to exempt prison rules from its coverage. Over forty senators thought the federalism and law-enforcement claims were substantial enough to justify a limit on Congress's power-maximizing activity.

58. There is a common intuition that Congress cannot be trusted to protect either individual rights or federalism issues because of its self-interest. That, it is said, would be like setting the fox to guard the chicken coop. But the Court is a fox too. Even if the Court makes good faith efforts solely to enforce the limits the Constitution places on Congress, its interest in maximizing its power will induce it to err on the side of limiting Congress too much. Those who assume that the *Court* will act in good faith to enforce the Constitution seem, in this context, unwilling to assume that *Congress* will act in good faith. Somehow Congress's power-maximizing interests are thought, not simply to operate alongside of, but to displace its good faith; I know of no reason to adopt that assumption with respect to Congress but not with respect to the courts.

59. Alexander and Schauer, "On Extrajudicial Constitutional Interpretation."

60. Oddly, Alexander and Schauer say that their analysis "is neither empirical nor historical." Id. at 1369.

61. One simply restates the issue: "[T]here is little reason to believe that a legislature or an executive is best situated to determine the contours of the constraints on its own power." True enough, but equally true as to the Supreme Court.

62. Payne v. Tennessee, 501 U.S. 808 (1991); Agostini v. Felton, 117 S.Ct. 1997 (1997).

63. Alexander and Schauer's final reason for preferring the Supreme Court to Congress as the single authoritative interpreter is that "constitutions are designed to guard against the excesses of majoritarian forces that influence legislatures and executives more than they influence courts." This is an important assertion, which I question in detail in chapter 6, which argues that "majoritarian forces" influence courts no less than they influence legislatures and executives, though they influence them in a different way and on a somewhat different timetable.

64. Chapter 2 examines in more detail an alternative institutional design that satisfies Alexander and Schauer's requirements for a rule-of-law system.

65. Chapter 5 provides a more extended analysis of interbranch interaction. Some of Alexander and Schauer's discussion gets off on the wrong foot by failing to attend to the difference between the behavior of legal institutions, which is

what their analysis is really about, and the decision-making processes of individuals within those institutions. As long as the institutions ensure reasonably stable legal decisions, it is irrelevant on their analysis whether particular individuals arrive at their own independent judgments about what the Constitution means. Notably, sometimes, perhaps often, a person's independent constitutional analysis will lead him or her to agree with the Court's interpretation. And nearly every Court decision has *some* constituency to support it, which provides a check on wild oscillations in policy.

66. A different set of issues arises when Congress and the president disagree about the Constitution's meaning—for example, when the president refuses to enforce a law enacted over a presidential veto because the president believes it to be unconstitutional. Chapter 5 takes up these issues.

67. There is some reason to believe that some voters voted in favor of Proposition 187 because they had been convinced that it was *un*constitutional. Such voters might believe that Proposition 187 would not have the dire effects its opponents predicted, and they could express their disapproval of illegal immigration without having to worry that their actions would have real consequences. See Sklansky, "Proposition 187," pp. 36–39.

68. For a survey presenting the consensus view, see Reynolds, "Critical Guide." For a critique, see Wills, "To Keep and Bear Arms." The article that opened the issue for law professors is Levinson, "Embarrassing Second Amendment." For an overview of the judicial interpretations, see Herz, "Gun Crazy."

CHAPTER TWO
DOING CONSTITUTIONAL LAW OUTSIDE THE COURTS

1. Under some definitions, conventions can supplement the written Constitution. See, e.g., Wilson, "American Constitutional Conventions." By using the term here, I do not intend to foreclose the possibility that some conventions might displace the written Constitution. I only want to explore the problems associated with a convention that might contradict the written Constitution.

2. See Paulsen, "Is Lloyd Bentsen Unconstitutional?"

3. A point made by then-Professor Breyer in a letter to Senator Robert Byrd, 119 Cong. Rec. S21282 (daily ed. Nov. 28, 1972), quoted in Brest, *Processes of Constitutional Interpretation*, pp. 43–44.

4. Testimony of Dean Willard D. Lorenson, in Hearing on S. 2673 Before the Committee on the Judiciary, U.S. Senate, 93d Congress, 1st Sess., "To Reduce the Compensation of the Office of Attorney General," p. 43.

5. It has been suggested to me that as a matter of psychology this is an unlikely position for someone to take. Particularly when offered an interpretation of the Emoluments Clause that would allow Senator Mitchell's confirmation, a senator who believes that Senator Mitchell is supremely well qualified to serve on the Supreme Court is likely to take up the offer, thereby reducing cognitive dissonance.

6. It is inaccurate because it fails to distinguish between the oath with respect to particular provisions and the oath with respect to the Constitution as a whole.

7. For a discussion, see Levinson, "Presidential Elections."

8. This dodge plays an important role in Paulsen's analysis. See Paulsen, "Is Lloyd Bentsen Unconstitutional?" pp. 916–17.

9. Or, at least, that your policy analysis, particularly its emphasis on the role of investigative journalism, would not be fully available to the Court. This raises questions of why the Supreme Court might refrain from making all-things-considered judgments, which are discussed below.

10. Cf. Ex parte Lévitt, 302 U.S. 633 (1937). Lévitt contended that Hugo Black's appointment to the Supreme Court violated the emoluments clause because Congress had improved the justices' pension plan during Senator Black's term. The Court held that Lévitt lacked standing because he suffered an undifferentiated harm "common to all members of the public." Note that the case might be distinguished from the present one on the ground that receiving a pension will take place so far in the future that the prospect of an improved pension plan could not possibly corrupt a senator.

11. See, e.g., Amendments XX, XXI, XXII.

12. You might want to rethink your own judgment that the provision is silly to the extent that the public cannot be convinced, over the long term, that it is. This is particularly so because the costs are only the marginal difference between appointing someone disqualified by the provision and appointing someone else. You may believe that the nation suffered because Stephen Breyer became a justice rather than George Mitchell, but the amount of suffering may not be great.

13. Hampton, "Democracy and the Rule of Law," in Shapiro, *The Rule of Law*, pp. 36–37, argues that a rule-guided amendment process may "contribute[] to what many see as the remarkable stability of modern democratic states." In its own way, so does Bruce Ackerman's work, as I argue in "Living in a Constitutional Moment." Guidance by rules *may* contribute to stability, but so can other settled practices, of the sort discussed here and in chapter 5.

14. 290 U.S. 398 (1934).

15. Classic debtor relief laws, Hughes argued, completely abrogated the debtor's obligation to repay. Minnesota's statute, in contrast, only temporarily suspended the debtor's obligation, under reasonable conditions. The statute did of course reduce the value of the obligation somewhat, but not enough to amount to a constitutional violation.

16. 462 U.S. 919, 959 (1983).

17. Thomas Jefferson to Samuel Kercheval, July 12, 1816, in Peterson, *Writings of Thomas Jefferson*, p. 1401.

18. My position here rejects Lawrence Lessig's. Lessig asserts that it is "the minimal requirement of fidelity" that "matters that were both contested and constitutionalized . . . continue to be binding." Lessig, "What Drives Derivability," p. 865.

19. Holmes, "Precommitment and the paradox of democracy," in Elster and Slagstad, *Constitutionalism and Democracy*, p. 216.

20. Hardin, "Why A Constitution." Warren, "Deliberative Democracy," makes a similar argument.

21. The class of direct taxes includes at least taxes imposed on land, and may have a broader scope.

22. Again, Holmes makes the point, although here somewhat obliquely: "[A] group can use its scarce resources more effectively if it dodges an irksome issue. By refraining from opening a can of worms, discussion leaders can prevent its lively contents from absorbing 100% of everyone's attention—at least for the time being." Holmes, "Gag rules or the politics of omission," in Elster and Slagstad, *Constitutionalism and Democracy*, pp. 19–20. I stress Holmes's final qualification.

23. Elster, "Introduction," in id., p. 9.

24. Plainly one would need some supplementary procedural mechanism to enforce the rule that only one fundamental would be reconsidered within some specified period.

25. The apparent triviality of the Emoluments Clause is precisely what makes it a good vehicle for exploring the issues that I think most difficult in constitutional law. In the present context, for example, the Clause seems so loosely connected to other constitutional provisions—though not of course unrelated to them—that it does not seem patently unreasonable to consider changing the Constitution to eliminate the Emoluments Clause and doing nothing else.

26. Rudolph v. Alabama, 375 U.S. 889 (1963).

27. Law professors Bruce Ackerman and Akhil Reed Amar have developed elaborate arguments about the possibility of constitutional amendments outside the framework created by Article V. Ackerman, *We the People: Foundations*; Amar, "Philadelphia Revisited." Each requires some formal processes before such an amendment would be legally valid, to guard against instability. In my view such formalisms are unnecessary because the complex decision procedures that pervade our political system are an adequate substitute.

28. The current litany is "text, structure, and history," but nothing turns on the precise formulation. In addition, nothing turns on the level of generality at which one specifies "structure" and "history." The now-familiar "level of generality" problem functions to license a decision-maker to make an all-things-considered judgment by manipulating the level of generality, but it does not in itself justify such manipulations.

29. Schauer, "Formalism."

30. My argument here is related to, but somewhat different from, the standard arguments for act-utilitarianism against rule-utilitarianism, and for the proposition that act-utilitarianism is extensionally equivalent to rule-utilitarianism when the rules are appropriately specified.

31. 466 U.S. 429 (1984).

32. A particularly poignant problem can arise for a judge in a case like *Palmore*. The appellate judge may say to herself, "I would award custody to the father here if I made an all-things-considered judgment. And, indeed, that's what the family court judge did. But I can improve the system's overall performance by articulating a rule barring consideration of private biases. To do so, I will have to reverse the family court's custody decision, knowing that I am directing that custody be awarded to the 'wrong' parent."

33. This shows why a common criticism of formalism, that it leads decision-makers to make mistakes that they would not make if they made all-things-considered judgments, is itself mistaken.

34. 480 U.S. 321 (1987).

35. I note, only to put aside, an additional problem this example introduces: whether the Supreme Court's interpretations of the Constitution should be treated the same as the Constitution itself, discussed in chapter 1. Here I assume only that the Supreme Court's decision in *Hicks* is within the range of permissible conscientious analyses of the Fourth Amendment's requirements.

36. Whether legislators and police officers actually will do so is the subject of chapters 3 and 4.

37. For present purposes, conscientiousness requires only that the decision-maker have available and be willing to produce in an appropriate arena reasons justifying his or her actions. It does not require that the decision-maker actually produce them on the occasion of acting.

38. United States v. Johnson, 333 U.S. 10, 14 (1948).

39. Black, *Structure and Relationship*, pp. 69 ("Whose action is the court annulling? Whom is the Court second-guessing?"), 78 ("The only constitutional judgments made on this investigative technique, before the case came under the judicial hand, were made by investigators and prosecutors").

40. I note that police officers may well think that the Fourth Amendment is a hypertechnical constitutional requirement, and that the comparison between police officers and senators is invidious and erroneous; so may others.

41. U.S. Term Limits, Inc. v. Thornton, 514 U.S. 779 (1995).

42. The classic discussion of such arguments is Schauer, "Slippery Slopes."

43. This is what Schauer calls the problem of limited comprehension, id., pp. 373–76. People in the future may not understand the complexity of the all-things-considered judgment you made today, and may erroneously believe that their judgments are entirely compatible with yours.

44. Michael Stokes Paulsen has suggested that Republicans refrained from nominating Orrin Hatch to replace retiring Justice Lewis F. Powell because of a perceived Emoluments Clause problem. If so, they would have faced the problem discussed here if Senator Mitchell had been nominated and a salary rescission enacted.

45. Paulsen, "Is Lloyd Bentsen Unconstitutional?" pp. 914–15.

46. Elster, *Sour Grapes*, p. 43.

47. Ibid., p. 53.

48. See, e.g., Jacobsohn, *Apple of Gold*; Levinson, *Constitutional Faith*.

49. Again I defer a full discussion of the reason to value preserving a national identity until chapter 8.

50. A condition inserted to deal with the conservation-of-political energy argument.

51. As the Emoluments Clause example suggests, particular issues might be so hypertechnical that even the most able leader would find it impossible to use them in this transformative way.

52. Waldron, "Kant's Legal Positivism," p. 1539.

CHAPTER THREE
THE QUESTION OF CAPABILITY

1. Mikva, "How Well Does Congress Support and Defend the Constitution?" Judge Mikva wrote this article while he was a judge.

2. What they do say, ordinarily, is that although the Supreme Court has rejected *one* of our positions, it will still accept another one that we are going to present to it as soon as we can.

3. A.L.A. Schechter Poultry Corp. v. United States, 295 U.S. 495 (1935).

4. Letter to Congressman Hill, July 6, 1935, in Roosevelt, *Public Papers and Addresses*, vol. 4, pp. 297–98.

5. Carter v. Carter Coal Co., 298 U.S. 238 (1936).

6. Thayer, "Origin and Scope."

7. For a discussion of Thayer's argument in its historical setting, see Tushnet, "Thayer's Target." I should note that I find the argument I made provocative and not entirely wrong, but in the end overstated.

8. There are a number of studies of constitutional interpretation in nonjudicial settings, including a course book, Fisher and Devins, *Political Dynamics of Constitutional Law*. See also Fisher, *Constitutional Dialogues*; Andrews, *Coordinate Magistrates*.

9. For a more formal analysis, see Tushnet, "Policy Distortion and Democratic Debilitation."

10. Board of Airport Commissioners v. Jews for Jesus, 482 U.S. 569 (1987).

11. Texas v. Johnson, 491 U.S. 397 (1989).

12. For a discussion of the legislative response, see Tiefer, "The Flag-Burning Controversy."

13. The dean of the University of Chicago's Law School, for example, said: "I cannot say—and I do not think anyone can fairly say—that the Flag Protection Act is necessarily constitutional or necessarily unconstitutional under existing law. There are at least reasonable grounds to believe, however, that the proposed legislation might be upheld by the Supreme Court." Hearings on the United States Supreme Court Decision in *Texas v. Johnson*, p. 200.

14. United States v. Eichman, 486 U.S. 310 (1990).

15. There is a cynical view, which I do not share, that the Flag Protection Act's sponsors supported it to delay final resolution of the flag-burning controversy as the courts considered the new statute's constitutionality. By that time, according to the cynical view, public outrage over the Court's initial decision would have subsided, and there would be no need to consider whether to amend the Constitution to override the Court's decision. Supporters of the cynical view support their position by pointing to legislators who voted in favor of the flag-protection statute but against a constitutional amendment. The cynical view does not take into account the possibility that a person might sincerely think that it would be best to have a constitutional anti-flag-burning statute, next best to have no anti-flag-burning statute, and worst to amend the Constitution. I think this is precisely the ranking of values of at least some of the legislators who voted for the statute and against the proposed amendment.

16. For a discussion of the amendment process and populist constitutional law, see chapter 8.

17. For a specification of the problem of policy distortion that is more complex than necessary here, see Tushnet, "Policy Distortion and Democratic Debilitation."

18. Formalist doctrines, some of which we examined in chapter 2, are an example.

19. Dandridge v. Williams, 397 U.S. 471 (1970).

20. Of course the answer may well be that it does, because of the limited funds available for the plan.

21. Easterbrook, "Presidential Review," pp. 916–17.

22. Fisher, "Constitutional Interpretation by Members of Congress," pp. 727–31, offers a brief account of the resources available to Congress in the mid-1980s, and argues that they were substantial.

23. I believe that historical inquiry into constitutional interpretation in Congress, and elsewhere, is likely to disclose large variations in quality, which would support my judgment that whatever incapacities Judge Mikva identifies are the product of particular historical circumstances and not, or at least not entirely, the result of structural features of our constitutional system.

24. It is worth remembering that in the republic's early years ordinary jurors drawn from the general public were thought capable of interpreting the Constitution as they considered constitutional defenses in criminal cases.

25. Black, *New Birth of Freedom*, p. 125.

26. Hearings on the Nomination of Robert H. Bork, pp. 428–34.

27. Schenck v. United States, 249 U.S. 47 (1919).

28. Dennis v. United States, 341 U.S. 494, 510 (1951) (opinion of Vinson, C. J., joined by Reed, Burton, and Minton, J. J.) (endorsing formulation in lower court opinion by Learned Hand).

29. 381 U.S. 479 (1965).

30. Rostow, "Democratic Character," p. 208.

31. Whittington's case studies, most drawn from the nineteenth century, show that members of Congress can conduct serious constitutional discussions while simultaneously using extremely harsh and personalized rhetoric. Whittington, *Constitutional Construction*. This suggests that we ought to be skeptical about the argument that today's politics are so driven by desires to get ten-second sound bites on the evening news makes it unlikely that today's politicians could conduct serious constitutional discussions.

32. RFRA raised two other questions. The Court's opinion in the peyote case might be read to suggest that the courts simply could not sensibly apply the "compelling state interest" test that RFRA directed them to apply. For myself, I find this the most troubling aspect of RFRA: Congress had told the courts to do what the courts themselves said they lacked the ability to do. But that was not the reason the Court found RFRA unconstitutional. The Court's reason was based on federalism. Chapter 5 describes arguments—not uncontroversial, but not frivolous either—that members of Congress have the right incentives to protect the interests of states as general law-makers. If those arguments are right, RFRA

shows that members of Congress have the right incentives to deal with two of the three constitutional issues raised by RFRA.

33. The distinction between the long run and the short term is not the same as the distinction between constitutional matters and ordinary policy. Similar incentive difficulties arise in connection with funding Social Security, for example. Yet, if we think that ordinary politics will find a way to deal with such issues, it is not clear why we should think that ordinary politics would be unable to deal with constitutional issues as well.

34. We encountered the problem in a slightly different guise in the discussion of character-building in chapter 2.

35. Ackerman, *We the People: Foundations*.

36. I do not believe that this is the best understanding of Ackerman's argument, but I do believe that it is the most common one. For my views on Ackerman's project, see Tushnet, "Living in a Constitutional Moment?"

37. Garvey, "Black and White Images."

38. Yeazell, "Intervention and the Idea of Litigation."

39. 489 U.S. 189 (1989).

40. Chapter 7 considers whether it is worth the cost to populist constitutional law to keep the courts available to correct these mistakes.

CHAPTER FOUR
THE CONSTITUTIONAL LAW OF RELIGION OUTSIDE THE COURTS

1. Armstrong Williams, "Two Wrongs Don't Make a Right for Thomas," *Charleston Post and Courier*, Aug. 17, 1995, p. A-13.

2. One survey challenges the widely made claim that Americans have an extraordinarily high rate of church attendance. Hadaway, Marler, and Chaves, "What the Polls Don't Show," finds that church attendance rates in the United States are not dramatically different from those in Western European countries.

3. Some of Carter's examples are far more ambiguous than he appears to believe. For example, Carter writes, "When Hillary Rodham Clinton was seen wearing a cross around her neck at some of the public events surrounding her husband's inauguration, . . . many observers were aghast, and one television commentator asked whether it was appropriate for the First Lady to display so openly a religious symbol." Carter, *Culture of Disbelief*, pp. 4–5. Carter takes the reaction of some unspecified number of observers to be more important than the fact that Mrs. Clinton wore the cross. For a critique of the "marginalization" thesis, see Blumoff, "New Religionists' Newest Social Gospel."

4. I offer an interpretation of Rawls in this chapter that I think is sensible and consistent with his writing, but I do not contend that his critics have badly misread him. Rawls's presentation is complex and open to alternative readings. In addition, my reading simplifies Rawls's position, though I believe without distorting it. There is of course an enormous interpretive literature on Rawls, which I do not review here.

5. This fact also illustrates a point made in passing earlier, that people can use Supreme Court opinions as sources of insight into the Constitution's meaning even if they do not take the Court's decisions as authoritative or supreme.

6. Audi and Wolterstorff, *Religion in the Public Square.*

7. In early 1998 the Alabama Supreme Court directed that this lawsuit be dismissed as well.

8. Stone v. Graham, 449 U.S. 39 (1980).

9. Even if we thought Judge Moore's actions inconsistent with the Supreme Court's decision, we would of course then have to consider questions raised in chapter 1: For example, is this an appropriate occasion for defying the Supreme Court, given the chance that Judge Moore's defiance will ultimately fail?

10. For a similar conclusion, see Perry, *Religion in Politics*, pp. 34–36 ("government [may] not make [certain] political choices . . . unless a plausible secular rationale supports the choice without help from a parallel religious argument").

11. Harris v. McCrae, 448 U.S. 297 (1980).

12. Adarand Constructors, Inc. v. Pena, 515 U.S. 200, 240 (1995) (Thomas, J., concurring).

13. For a sympathetic and in my view unpersuasive presentation of the claim that creation science is a science, see Johnson, "Book Review."

14. In saying that the theory of evolution and the theory of creation fall into different domains, I do not mean to suggest that either domain has priority over the other—that science is better than or more real than religion, for example.

15. There are other ways of explaining these cases. A common one, for example, is that the practices amount to an impermissible government endorsement of religion. That interpretation leads to more difficult questions—from what point of view do we determine that something endorses religion, for example—than the one I offer here.

16. My approach eliminates a great deal of the complexity in the discussion of these issues by the theorists I discuss. That complexity results from the theorists' attempt to prescribe principles that, I argue, are too broad; the excessive breadth requires that the principles be repeatedly qualified by introducing fine distinctions that my approach makes irrelevant.

17. The fact that religious contention has diminished to the point that it does not directly threaten stability becomes irrelevant as well once the principle of nonestablishment becomes part of a free-standing liberal political theory.

18. Perry, *Religion in Politics*, pp. 54–55, argues that Rawls's restriction of his arguments to questions about the basic structure is only a preliminary to a broader application of those arguments. Rawls does say that his *method* seems to him likely to yield appropriate conclusions when it is applied to less fundamental political issues, and he thinks that the conclusions may sometimes mirror the results he arrives at in dealing with the basic structure. But these are only hopes at most, and it seems to me wrong to attribute to Rawls conclusions that, as I argue here, are implausible. Greenawalt, "Some Problems With Public Reason," pp. 1306–8, similarly questions Rawls's "uneasy division" between basic structure and other political issues, primarily on the ground that at least some apparently ordinary political issues are closely linked to issues about the basic structure. Greenawalt uses the example of the connection between research using fetal tissue, an ordinary political issue, and abortion, an issue that Rawls treats as implicating the basic structure. For a discussion of the limited scope of Rawls's argument, see Griffin, "Good Catholics," pp. 312–14.

19. For an explicit statement regarding the revisability of views, see Rawls, "Idea of Public Reason," pp. 782–83 n. 46.

20. Audi and Wolterstorff, *Religion in the Public Square*, pp. 14, 21.

21. Ibid., p. 19.

22. Greenawalt, *Religious Convictions and Political Choice*; Audi, "Separation of Church and State."

23. Rawls, "Idea of Public Reason," pp. 783–84.

24. Audi, "Separation of Church and State," p. 280.

25. Audi, "Place of Religious Argument," pp. 685–86, describes expressive, communicative, persuasive, evidential, and heuristic roles of religious arguments.

26. For a restatement, see Bernardin, "The Consistent Ethic."

27. Rawls, "Idea of Public Reason," p. 769 n. 57, describes witnessing as a mode of dissent aimed at changing an unjust law, and connects his analysis of witnessing to his analysis of the circumstances under which civil disobedience is justified.

28. See Audi and Wolterstorff, *Religion in the Public Square*, pp. 34–35 (asserting that a "mixed voice produced by combined religious and secular motivation" is "consonant with civic virtue" and can "yield harmony" and "produce a more powerful voice").

29. Minow's comments are contained in Symposium, "Political Liberalism: Religion & Public Reason," Religion & Values in Public Life, vol. 3, no. 4 (Summer 1995), p. 4.

30. Gutmann and Thompson, "Moral Conflict and Political Consensus," p. 76.

31. As stated, though, it seems unlikely to describe a person who is passionate about the views he or she holds at present, and it may overestimate the ability of a person with the traits Gutmann and Thompson enumerate to be steadfast in his or her provisional but at present firmly held commitment to particular views.

32. For a succinct presentation of these latter points, see Galston, "Liberal Virtues."

33. Gutmann and Thompson, "Moral Conflict and Political Consensus," pp. 64–65, 76.

34. Lincoln, *Speeches and Writings*, vol. 2, p. 686. See Wolgast, "Demands of Public Reason," p. 1947 ("There are times when dividing the community is a necessary and inevitable risk connected to making a change in political directions and when, if the debate could proceed without dividing the community, it would be both less true as debate and less effective as a wind for change").

35. Walzer, "Communitarian Critique," pp. 11–12.

36. Rutherford, "Islamic Group," suggests that this may be the path taken by some fundamentalist Islamic groups in the Middle East, although his analysis may have been overtaken by events.

37. Carter, *Culture of Disbelief*, p. 23.

38. Carter, "Religiously Devout Judge," p. 942.

39. Audi, "Separation of Church and State," pp. 275 (discussing what churches should do), 279 (discussing citizens).

40. Ibid., p. 279 (emphasis added).

41. Ibid., p. 284.

42. I do not engage in an extended analysis of the question of coercion because I conclude that the thin Constitution generates an even less restrictive notion of proper political behavior than Audi's.

43. Audi and Wolterstorff, *Religion in the Public Square*, pp. 49–51.

44. Ibid., p. 282.

45. Ibid., p. 283. See also Wolgast, "Demands of Public Reason," pp. 1943–44.

46. Audi, "Place of Religious Argument," p. 695, calls this "*leveraging* by reasons." For a similar characterization, see Greenawalt, *Religious Convictions and Political Choice*, p. 221. Rawls, "Idea of Public Reason," pp. 768–69, calls it an argument by "conjecture."

47. Audi, "Separation of Church and State," p. 282. Audi, "Religious Commitment and Secular Reason," pp. 73–74, suggests that because the advocate would be making "a *merely* persuasive, not an evidential appeal to a reason," she might be "distanc[ing]" herself from the reason "in such a way that the appeals might well be consistent with my overall position on the use of reasons."

48. For a cogent explanation of how the conversation might continue, which assumes that both parties "are working with a conception of God" and therefore in my view does not avoid the difficulty I have identified, see Cook, "God Talk." In an interview Carter responded to the objection that "the moment 'God's will' is invoked as the basis for a position in a conversation, further discussion is made pointless," by observing that the objection rested on a "stereotype" that "people who are deeply moved by their religion are not amenable to reason," and referred to the Catholic natural law tradition. Carter, "Conversation." But, I would think, to the extent that a person is amenable to reason, the invocation of God's will is irrelevant, as indeed the natural law tradition demonstrates. Carter's position seems to me to resemble Audi's, in addressing only the views of deeply religious adherents of mainstream religions.

49. See also Audi and Wolterstorff, *Religion in the Public Square*, pp. 135 ("I take it to be largely a matter of practical wisdom what reasons to bring to public political debate, though I note that using religious reasons may be highly divisive"), 164 (contribution by Wolterstorff, describing desirability of offering reasons other than religious ones as "a requirement of strategy, not a requirement embodied in the ethic of the citizen in a liberal democracy").

50. See Audi and Wolterstorff, *Religion in the Public Square*, p. 141.

51. This position, however, gives the religious believer an incentive to overstate the intensity of his or her views.

52. A useful discussion of the issues addressed in these paragraphs is Blumoff, "Holocaust and Public Discourse."

53. We would have to distinguish between such rhetoric working in the short run, with respect to a particular political issue like abortion, and working in the long run, with respect to maintaining the place of religion in public life generally. Sometimes a religious person might decide that using religious language would not advance the immediate goal (and might even be an obstacle), but would advance the long-range prospects for religion in public life.

54. Blumoff, "Holocaust and Public Discourse," p. 614.

55. Wolgast, "Demands of Public Reason," p. 1948.

56. See Audi and Wolterstorff, *Religion in the Public Square*, pp. 78–79 (contribution by Wolterstorff).

57. Greenawalt's rhetorical tone suggests to me a rather more skeptical attitude toward the use of such arguments than his explicit argument supports, perhaps because he thinks that publicly accessible reasons run out sooner for ordinary citizens than he thinks they should. Put another way, he may think that ordinary citizens are not working hard enough to develop publicly accessible reasons that are in fact available to them.

58. Perry, *Religion in Politics*, pp. 102–3.

59. Greenawalt, *Religious Convictions and Political Choice*, p. 233.

60. Waldron, "Religious Contributions in Public Deliberation," p. 830.

61. Ibid., p. 232 (legislators "are also leaders of public political opinion").

62. Ibid., p. 234.

63. Ibid.

64. See Perry, *Religion in Politics*, pp. 50–52, for a similar criticism.

65. This conclusion, I must note, is roughly the same as Greenawalt's: There is no substantial difference between the constraints that political theory places on a legislator and those that it places on a citizen. I have been discussing the problem, if it is one, of a legislator who follows constituent views. Greenawalt also discusses the legislator whose religious views differ from those of her constituency. Greenawalt, *Religious Convictions and Political Choice*, pp. 237–38. He concludes that such a legislator "should be very hesitant to override contrary constituent judgments." Again, though I agree, I doubt that any religion-specific theory is needed to generate that recommendation; the general desire for reelection should be sufficient. (This is particularly true in light of Greenawalt's elaboration that a legislator who cares very deeply about what she believes to be a truly fundamental issue can properly override her hesitation, id., p. 238; this seems to me to describe a legislator who does not care about the electoral consequences of her actions. In both branches, then, the only analytic work that needs to be done is done by consideration of the relation between the legislator's actions and her electoral prospects.)

66. Greenawalt, "Use of Religious Convictions," p. 543.

67. Bowers v. Hardwick, 478 U.S. 186, 196 (1986) (Burger, C. J., concurring).

68. David Richards suggests that liberal political theory would withdraw issues from the public domain whenever secular reasons run out. Richards, "Book Review," p. 1194. But that purportedly neutral resolution is actually a partisan choice among contending positions.

69. Waldron, "Religious Contributions in Public Deliberation," pp. 831–33, agrees. Griffin, "Good Catholic," pp. 316–17, describes Rawls's "hope" that a judge will be able to resolve cases within the overlapping consensus.

70. Sunstein, *Legal Reasoning and Political Conflict*.

71. City of Boerne v. Flores, 117 S.Ct. 2157, 2172 (Stevens, J., concurring).

72. Precisely for this reason, I am skeptical about whether RFRA would in fact have been interpreted to confer benefits quite as widely as its proponents suggested.

CHAPTER FIVE
THE INCENTIVE-COMPATIBLE CONSTITUTION

1. The combination that works best will depend on the characteristics of the market. For example, if the demand for cars varies so much that the dealer can't tell how much effort it takes to sell a car in any period, the bonus system will be better. If the demand is relatively stable, the commission system ensures that the sales staff doesn't expend too much effort in trying to milk out the sale that will guarantee the bonus.

2. The technical definition of incentive-compatibility is somewhat different from the more informal description I offer here, but not in ways that affect the basic argument.

3. Paying bonuses is not a perfect solution. Consider what happens when the sales staff get together and agree that everyone of them will slack off. Someone still gets the bonus even though fewer cars are sold than could be.

4. The phenomenon of self-enforcement is common. See Laudan, *Science and Relativism*, p. 155 ("We have loads of other social institutions where the reward structure encourages participants to perform in ways which conduce to the ends of the institution. . . . [I]n science, we have set up rewards and punishments which have the practical effect of keeping scientists more or less on the cognitive straight and narrow").

5. One obvious move is to allocate some rights to judicial enforcement and some to self-enforcement. I discuss this possibility later in this chapter.

6. Madison himself rarely wrote about judicial review. *The Federalist Papers* occasionally assume that courts would refuse to enforce unconstitutional laws, and the framers generally seem to have made the same assumption. Oversimplifying, their views accepted judicial review in three increasingly powerful forms: Courts would refuse to comply with unconstitutional laws affecting their own operation; courts would refuse to lend their assistance when other branches sought aid in enforcing unconstitutional laws; and courts would award damages for actions taken pursuant to unconstitutional laws.

7. *The Federalist* no. 10.

8. *The Federalist* no. 51.

9. Treanor, "Fame, the Founding, and the Power to Declare War."

10. See generally Fiorina, *Divided Government*, pp. 85–110.

11. Wechsler, "Political Safeguards."

12. For discussions of federalism explicitly invoking the idea of self-enforcement, see Bednar and Eskridge, "Steadying the Court's 'Unsteady Path,' " pp. 1476–79 ("Self-Enforcing Political Structures"); Weingast, "Economic Role," p. 4 ("the *autonomy* of each government is institutionalized in a manner that makes federalism's restrictions self-enforcing").

13. Madison's arguments were made in *The Federalist*, nos. 45 and 46.

14. For an extensive discussion of the role of parties, see Kramer, "Understanding Federalism."

15. Garcia v. San Antonio Metropolitan Transit Auth., 469 U.S. 528 (1985).

16. United States v. Lopez, 514 U.S. 549 (1995).

17. Printz v. United States, 117 S.Ct. 2365 (1997).

18. Acknowledging this, the Court said that it would not try to balance the impairment of state interests against the national interests; it seems clear to me that had it done so, the balance would have favored the statute.

19. Madison was arguing that the Constitution ought not *bar* the people from giving that confidence to Congress, but the point is symmetrical: In allowing the people to give Congress their confidence, the Constitution also allows them to give it to the states.

20. The extensive literature, which demonstrates the depth of the disagreements over assessing the facts, is cited in Merritt, "Commerce!" p. 692 n. 71.

21. Alexander Hamilton thought that term limits for the president were a bad idea (*The Federalist* no. 72). His very first argument was that term limits would lead to "a diminution of the inducements to good behavior," and he echoed Madison's concerns by pointing out how important it was "to make their interest coincide with their duty." Presidents would behave better if they had "a hope of *obtaining*, by *meriting*, a continuance" in office. They would be more likely to pursue projects that took a long time to pay off. Hamilton noticed the last-period problem too: "An avaricious man, who might happen to fill the office, looking forward to the time when he must at all events yield up the emoluments he enjoyed, would feel a propensity, not easy to be resisted by such a man, to make the best use of the opportunity he enjoyed while it lasted." And term limits would "depriv[e] the community of the advantage of the experience gained by the chief magistrate in the exercise of his office." Finally, we should recall Madison's argument that we can design our representative bodies to increase the likelihood that our representatives will try to advance the public good rather than concentrate exclusively on what is necessary to get reelected.

22. California state assemblywoman Delaine Eastin, quoted in Price, "The Guillotine Comes to California," p. 126.

23. For a critique of term limits on expertise grounds, see Muir, *Legislature*.

24. An important recent analysis is Elhauge, "Are Term Limits Undemocratic?" which concludes that they are not undemocratic because they make it easier for constituents to assure that their representatives' views remain consistent with the constituents' views: Without term limits, constituents may sacrifice ideological consistency and reelect representatives with whom they disagree because representatives with seniority may produce legislation that provides pork-barrel benefits to the district.

25. Another example is the critical analysis of the Seventeenth Amendment's provision for direct election of senators, in Bybee, "Ulysses at the Mast."

26. Chief Justice Rehnquist's opinion for the Court does contain passages that can be read to make the argument that Judge Nixon did get a trial within the meaning of the Constitution. But the Court's formal holding was that the courts should not address the merits of Judge Nixon's claim.

27. 506 U.S. 224 (1993).

28. Ibid., p. 254 (Souter, J., concurring in the judgment). Justice Souter's phrasing itself raises the question: Would he refuse judicial intervention if the Senate acted a little bit beyond its constitutional authority, but not "so far beyond" it?

29. Ibid., p. 238 (Stevens, J., concurring).

30. As the court of appeals put it in the Walter Nixon case, "If the Senate should ever be ready to abdicate its responsibilities to schoolchildren, . . . the republic will have sunk to depths from which no court could rescue it." Nixon v. United States, 938 F.2d. 239, 246 (D.C. Cir. 1991).

31. For a recent study concluding that "the House has rarely, if ever, and the Senate has never, successfully committed a serious or extreme abuse of its impeachment authority," see Gerhardt, *Federal Impeachment Process*.

32. 506 U.S., p. 253 (Souter, J., concurring in the judgment).

33. Rakove, *Original Meanings*, p. 150, quoting *The Federalist* no. 46.

34. Henkin, "Is There a 'Political Questions' Doctrine?" p. 599.

35. Gerhardt, *Federal Impeachment Process*, pp. 13–14.

36. For a recent overview of the scholarly literature, see Stromseth, "Understanding Constitutional War Powers Today."

37. Mayer and Abramson, *Strange Justice*, pp. 251, 337.

38. Carter, *Confirmation Mess*, defends a value-based view. For a defense of the purely political view from a conservative point of view, written before the Bork nomination, see Rees, "Questions for Supreme Court Nominees."

39. Whittington's analysis of the unsuccessful effort in 1805 to remove Justice Samuel Chase from his position supports this conclusion. Whittington, *Constitutional Construction*, chap. 2.

40. Nagel, *Constitutional Cultures*, pp. 121–55.

41. United States v. O'Brien, 391 U.S. 367, 376–77 (1968), quoted in Nagel, *Constitutional Cultures*, p. 127.

42. Recall the discussion of formalism in chapter 2.

43. For a version of that statement, see Black, *Constitutional Faith*, p. 45.

44. Quoted in Tushnet, *Making Constitutional Law*, p. 137.

45. On the advantages of constitutional obscurity, see Foley, *The Silence of Constitutions*, pp. 79–80.

46. 117 S.Ct. 1636 (1997).

47. This example does not illustrate a pure incentive-compatible constitutional solution because it tries to identify the rule the courts should invoke in response to the president's constitutional arguments.

48. I put aside, as largely uninteresting, the proposition that the president can disregard a law in circumstances of true national emergency. In such circumstances, one might say, all constitutional bets are off anyway. For a discussion of an early dispute in which this proposition played a role, see Currie, *Constitution in Congress*, pp. 164–66.

49. Chapter 1's discussion of a president's power to disregard judicial interpretations presented a theory of judicial supremacy according to which a president would act improperly in disregarding a judicial interpretation. I argued against that theory there; the argument here is against a parallel theory of congressional supremacy.

50. For this to be a true line-item veto, the president would have to inform Congress of his decision, then abide by a two-thirds vote in both houses directing the expenditure.

51. For a review of the episode and the arguments, by proponents of the view that a line-item veto was constitutional, see Sidak and Smith, "Why Did President Bush Repudiate the 'Inherent' Line-Item Veto?"

52. In the end the lawsuit was rendered moot by a modification of the statutory provision the administration objected to.

53. Professor Neal Devins provides the best general accounts of these political interactions that recognizes the constitutional significance of political interactions. See, e.g., Devins, "Reagan Redux"; Devins, "Political Will and the Unitary Executive." See also Tiefer, "Constitutionality of Independent Officers."

54. For a brief summary of executive practices, see Easterbrook, "Presidential Review," pp. 913–14.

55. As in earlier examples, here the availability of the courts affects the political calculations that make aspects of the Constitution self-enforcing. The president reduces the political risks that nonenforcement creates by telling Congress that ultimately the courts will resolve the constitutional question.

56. If the president thinks that there is a 70 percent chance of getting what he wants from the courts (call his most desired position 100, which corresponds to a position of zero for Congress), he will accept any offer from Congress giving him more than 70. If Congress thinks that there is an 80 percent chance that the president will win, it will offer something less than 80. The bargaining range is 70 to 80.

57. For a discussion, see Fallon, "Foreword: Implementing the Constitution."

58. Speiser v. Randall, 357 U.S. 513, 526 (1957).

59. Chapter 6 offers such an empirical assessment.

60. 469 U.S., p. 565 n.8 (Powell, J., dissenting).

61. More completely, the claim is that adding judicial review as another layer of enforcement would actually reduce the degree to which the entire system protects the values of federalism, because judicial review would introduce more errors than it would correct: The courts will strike down more statutes than they should, while upholding some they should not.

62. Planned Parenthood of Southeastern Pennsylvania v. Casey, 505 U.S. 833 (1992).

63. By early 1998, almost six years after the Court's decision, only eleven states had effective regulations in force of the one type clearly barred before *Casey* and permitted after it, a waiting period between seeking and obtaining an abortion (Idaho, Indiana, Kansas, Louisiana, Mississippi, Nebraska, North Dakota, Ohio, Pennsylvania, South Dakota, and Utah. South Carolina had a one-hour waiting period). Barring public funding for abortions was nearly universal, but the constitutionality of doing so had been affirmed by the Supreme Court for many years before 1992.

64. Sunstein, "Against Positive Rights," pp. 226–27.

65. The underenforcement may occur for good institutional reasons like formalism.

66. I discuss amending the Constitution again in chapter 8.

67. Lutz, "Toward a Theory of Constitutional Amendment."

68. Gerhardt, *Federal Impeachment Process*, p. 137.

69. Chapter 8 discusses the nature of that historical commitment.

CHAPTER SIX
ASSESSING JUDICIAL REVIEW

1. (1988).

2. Buckley v. Valeo, 424 U.S. 1 (1976); Colorado Republican Federal Campaign Committee v. Federal Election Commission, 518 U.S. 604 (1996); First National Bank of Boston v. Bellotti, 435 U.S. 765 (1978).

3. My argument takes as its audience liberal supporters of judicial review, largely because they have been the most prominent defenders of judicial review in recent decades. The conclusion I offer, that judicial review makes rather little difference, is equally applicable to conservative defenders—or critics—of judicial review.

4. I consider only cases in which free speech claims prevailed because only those cases show who benefits from judicial review.

5. Capitol Square Review & Advisory Board v. Pinette, 515 U.S. 753 (1995); McIntyre v. Ohio Elections Commission, 514 U.S. 334 (1995); City of Ladue v. Gilleo, 512 U.S. 43 (1994); Texas v. Johnson, 491 U.S. 397 (1989).

6. City of Cincinnati v. Discovery Network, Inc., 507 U.S. 410 (1993); Buckley v. Valeo, 424 U.S. 1 (1976).

7. The best recent discussion, on which I draw, is Schauer, "Political Incidence of the Free Speech Principle."

8. Balkin, "Some Realism About Pluralism," p. 384.

9. A peculiarity of this argument deserves note. Why should we expect legislatures to enact laws consistent with populist constitutional law if people with economic power tend to have political power as well? As many observers have noted, for example, the campaign finance "reforms" proposed by legislators tend to protect incumbents against challengers. Still, sometimes political miracles happen. A confluence of unusual political circumstances may produce populist legislation. Or the people may bypass legislators and enact campaign finance reforms through the initiative and referendum process. It seems peculiar for the courts to step in when these unusual events occur and tell the people that we have to live with the ordinary regime in which economic power structures the political marketplace and the marketplace of ideas as well.

10. As we will see, not all who call themselves liberals today are reluctant to use the government's power in this way.

11. Balkin, "Some Realism About Pluralism"; Balkin, "Ideological Drift."

12. It strikes me as a bit ironic, and more than a bit cynical, that the most vigorous defenders of free speech against liberal political correctness include people who, a few decades ago, demonstrated precious little affection for free speech principles. Consider what James Jackson Kilpatrick or William F. Buckley had to say about free speech when civil rights or antiwar protestors were claiming that *their* rights were being violated.

13. See, e.g., Sunstein, *Democracy and the Problem of Free Speech*.

14. Adarand Constructors Inc. v. Pena, 515 U.S. 200 (1995); Miller v. Johnson, 515 U.S. 900 (1995).

15. Missouri v. Jenkins, 515 U.S. 70 (1995); Board of Education v. Dowell, 498 U.S. 237 (1991).

16. Batson v. Kentucky, 476 U.S. 79 (1986), overruling Swain v. Alabama, 380 U.S. 202 (1965); Powers v. Ohio, 499 U.S. 400 (1991); Georgia v. McCollum, 505 U.S. 42 (1992); Purkett v. Elem, 514 U.S. 765 (1995).

17. I have altered Dunne's imputation of an Irish accent to Mr. Dooley. Dunne, *Mr. Dooley at His Best*, p. 77. The Supreme Court decisions are known as The Insular Cases, the principal one of which is Downes v. Bidwell, 182 U.S. 244 (1901).

18. Dahl, "Decision-Making in a Democracy."

19. Shapiro, *Courts*.

20. Notably, by the time that happened many people had come to think that de facto segregation was at least as important, and that *Brown* was a failure because it did not address that problem.

21. Rosenberg, *Hollow Hope*.

22. Investing in legal strategies may be unwise if other aspects of cultural change are more important than legal victories in producing ideological or material change. That is, if a progressive movement has a choice between investing its resources in a legal strategy and investing in some other strategy, such as community mobilization through its churches (a major factor in the civil rights movement), it may make sense to avoid investing in a legal strategy even though the strategy would result in victories in court. Social movements rarely are faced with such discrete choices about investing resources, however; things tend to be much more catch-as-catch-can, driven by personalities and chance opportunities rather than by deliberate reflection.

23. Balkin, "Agreements With Hell."

24. As historian David Garrow has shown, the real story is somewhat more complicated. Anti-choice political forces had begun to mobilize in response to *political* pro-choice lobbying before *Roe v. Wade*, and the pro-choice political agenda had shifted from efforts to reform restrictive abortion laws to efforts to make abortion available essentially on demand. Garrow, *Liberty and Sexuality*.

25. This interpretation of the abortion litigation is consistent with the astute analysis in Fung, "Making Rights Real," which argues as well that state-level reforms would not have produced the degree of abortion access that *Roe* did.

26. In chapter 7 I discuss and criticize the hope that we can design judicial review so that we get only decisions we like, or restrict its domain so that on balance we get more than we lose from review in the areas where we have it, and do not give up much.

27. To the relatively small extent that people make decisions about where to allocate their limited resources, the cautions serve to improve the accuracy of the calculation of the possible benefit of investing in legal action rather than in something else—street demonstrations, public opinion campaigns, or whatever.

28. MacKinnon, "*Roe v. Wade*."

29. Ginsburg, "Some Thoughts on Autonomy and Equality"; Sunstein, "Neutrality in Constitutional Law." For a counterargument, see Allen, "Proposed Equal Protection Fix"; Kamm, *Creation and Abortion*, p. 98.

30. These group rights have two characteristics: Recognizing them as rights is quite controversial, and their recognition has been quite recent. These characteristics actually support the broader version of the argument that rights are ideologically troublesome because they are almost necessarily individualistic, because rights-claims really do have a strong individualist spin in the modern world.

31. 381 U.S. 479 (1965).

32. Moore v. City of East Cleveland, 431 U.S. 494 (1977).

33. Duckworth v. Arkansas, 314 U.S. 390, 400 (1941) (Jackson, J., concurring).

34. We might design a populist institution to deal with these petty aberrations, for example, by creating Ombudsmen with the power to set aside aberrational regulations after receiving citizen complaints. The Ombudsmen could be elected, or appointed by elected officials for a term of years and required to make regular reports, to ensure their control by popular majorities.

35. Bell, *"Brown v. Board of Education."*

36. Rosenberg, *Hollow Hope*; Klarman, *"Brown."*

37. Greenberg, *Crusaders in the Courts*, p. 286.

38. Rosenberg, *Hollow Hope*, found relatively little evidence in African-American newspapers of attention to *Brown*. He concluded from this evidence that African-Americans were not mobilized by *Brown*. It is not clear to me, however, that Rosenberg's evidence supports his conclusion. A significant number of African-American newspapers were relatively conservative on race relations issues. In addition, newspaper accounts may not capture the views of the activists who pushed the civil rights movement forward. Notably, Rosenberg reports that, at least in retrospect, most activists give *Brown* a large role in their account of the civil rights movement.

39. See, e.g., Garrow, "Hopelessly Hollow History."

40. Garrow, *Liberty and Sexuality*, is the basic source one must consult.

41. Casey v. Planned Parenthood of Southeast Pennsylvania, 505 U.S. 833 (1992).

42. Berman, *America's Right Turn*, pp. 40, 43, 58–59.

43. Edsall, with Edsall, *Chain Reaction*, p. 9.

44. The account that follows is roughly consistent with what political scientists call an attitudinal model of Supreme Court behavior. See generally Segal and Spaeth, *Supreme Court and Attitudinal Change*. However, it uses a more finely grained classification of attitudes than Segal and Spaeth do. Their interest in developing a scientific model of Supreme Court behavior, which seems to me the product of their field's disciplinary requirements, appears to demand too large a number of instances to analyze than would be available to someone offering an account like mine. Their analysis uses the cruder classifications of *liberal* and *conservative*.

45. Jeffries, *Justice Lewis F. Powell*, p. 347.

46. Harris v. McRae, 448 U.S. 448 (1976). The pattern is even clearer after the Court's decision in Webster v. Reproductive Health Services, 492 U.S. 490 (1989), and Casey v. Planned Parenthood of Southeastern Pennsylvania, 505 U.S. 833 (1992).

47. United States v. Virginia, 578 U.S. 515 (1996). The Supreme Court has been reasonably active in support of women's claims, but most of them have been *statutory* claims, once again showing that women, like African-Americans, have become significant participants in ordinary politics.

48. Graber, "Nonmajoritarian Difficulty."

49. Bickel, *Supreme Court and the Idea of Progress*, p. 100. Bickel used the phrase *remembering the future*, id., p. 102, but my restatement does not change the thrust of Bickel's point.

50. 517 U.S. 620 (1996).

51. Bowers v. Hardwick, 478 U.S. 186 (1986).

52. Chapter 7 examines another way of answering this question.

53. For a recent discussion, see Silverstein, *Judicious Choices*.

CHAPTER SEVEN
AGAINST JUDICIAL REVIEW

1. Texas v. Johnson, 491 U.S. 397, 420–21 (1989) (Kennedy, J., concurring).

2. McConnell, "Originalism."

3. 347 U.S. 497 (1954).

4. One can gin up a theory that the adoption of the Fourteenth Amendment, referring only to states, actually modified the Fifth Amendment and the national government's power. Something like that was the Court's theory in *Bolling*, which asserted that "it would be unthinkable" for the Constitution to bar segregation in the states but allow it in the District of Columbia. Whatever might be said about such a theory, it clearly is not a theory of original understanding.

5. Planned Parenthood of Southeastern Pennsylvania v. Casey, 505 U.S. 833 (1992).

6. Scalia, "Originalism," p. 862.

7. Lucas v. South Carolina Coastal Commission, 505 U.S. 1003, 1028 n.15 (1992).

8. Justice Scalia argued that by the time the Fourteenth Amendment, the one applicable in *Lucas*, was adopted, existing practices were consistent with *no* coherent theory of takings. Justice Scalia thought his approach justified because it was coherent and compatible with the Fifth Amendment's language, though not compelled by it.

9. I believe that I have already written that book. Tushnet, *Red, White, and Blue*.

10. Ely, *Democracy and Distrust*.

11. United States v. Carolene Products, 304 U.S. 144, 152–53 n. 4 (1938).

12. Minorities cannot engage in beneficial deals when no one will deal with them. Why, however, would the pro-environment or pro-logging group, each just short of enough votes to get its program enacted, refuse to deal with a group that could give it another 10 percent of the votes and put it over the top? There are two possibilities. The minority group could be something like the Ku Klux Klan in contemporary politics: If they endorse you, you actually lose votes. We can call this a *pariah* group. They can offer 10 percent of the votes, but 15 percent on the

pro-logging side will defect to the other side if the loggers strike a deal with the pariah group. Alliances with pariah groups can produce net losses to the coalition.

Pariah groups might not be able to cut a deal for another reason. The environmentalists have to say, "We'll take your votes on the environmental issue and in exchange we will vote for your program of aid to distressed cities." But if the environmentalists are *really* prejudiced, they will never be willing to make that deal. Here *prejudice* means that people are willing to give up things they might be able to achieve simply to ensure that the people they are prejudiced against do not get what *they* want. This can happen, and it almost certainly describes a fair amount of the politics of race in the early twentieth-century United States. I think we can reasonably wonder how significant prejudice of this sort is today. The role of African-Americans in the Democratic party coalition suggests that it is no longer true of the minority most important to the development of our constitutional history.

13. Ely, *Democracy and Distrust*, p. 181.

14. The Indian Supreme Court did pose some resistance to some aspects of Indira Gandhi's emergency regime, but general political resistance was far more important in ending that regime.

15. Schenck v. United States, 249 U.S. 47 (1919); Abrams v. United States, 250 U.S. 616 (1919); Dennis v. United States, 341 U.S. 494 (1951); Yates v. United States, 354 U.S. 298 (1957).

16. For a discussion of the Johnson administration's response to political protests, see Finman and Macaulay, "Freedom to Dissent."

17. Letting them decide statutory cases while they wait for the really important constitutional ones will therefore not work: They need to keep their *constitutional* muscles toned up.

18. The Netherlands Supreme Court does invalidate legislation when it finds it to conflict with international law that is, in the jargon, directly enforceable in Dutch courts.

19. Kreimer, "Exploring the Dark Matter."

20. The Supreme Court or Congress would have to tinker with the statutes regulating Supreme Court jurisdiction, or more likely with the way they are interpreted, to ensure that this sort of *ultra vires* review was possible.

21. Several problems in implementing the approach I describe could probably be dealt with by revising congressional procedures. The most obvious problem is this: Suppose that in 2005 the Court gives a statute enacted in 1999 a restrictive interpretation in light of constitutional values. When enacted the statute had the support of both Congress and the president, but by 2005 the new president opposes the statute, and would veto any revision designed to implement the 1999 statute despite the Court's constitutional misgivings. Under these circumstances the Court's interpretation sticks even though a majority in Congress supports the statute's policy. It is less clear, however, that the people of the nation do, given that the president they elected opposes it. A variant of this problem would occur if supporters of the 1999 policy had a majority in Congress, but the minority in opposition had enough power to block the statute's reenactment. This is a problem because Congress may not operate in a completely majoritarian way. It might

be addressed by placing proposals that respond to restrictive Supreme Court interpretations on some sort of fast track.

22. South Dakota v. Opperman, 428 U.S. 364 (1976).

23. Whren v. United States, 517 U.S. 806 (1996).

24. They might also raise a practical concern: An *ultra vires* rule would give departments an incentive to write their regulations to let every officer do everything. The response is that well-formulated *ultra vires* rules can ensure that higher police officials think through carefully what they want to tell their officers.

25. The existence of judicial review may also induce lower-court judges to think in constitutional terms and overlook the possibility of regulating police conduct through an *ultra vires* doctrine. It would have been difficult, though not impossible, for the Supreme Court to use such a doctrine in the undercover officers case, but it should not have been hard for the District of Columbia Court of Appeals to see the possibility of doing so.

26. Jordan is quoted in Levinson, *Constitutional Faith*, p. 15; Williams, *Alchemy of Race and Rights*, p. 163.

27. For examples of substantive constitutional discussion outside the courts, see chapters 2 and 4.

28. Crenshaw et al., *Critical Race Theory*, pp. xxiii–xiv.

29. A stronger claim would be that constitutional rights were the scaffolding of the world we live in, which can now be taken down. But, as Williams says, the imperfect realization of nominal rights, and the possibility that others we cannot now imagine would benefit from creating new rights as African-Americans did, suggests that this stronger claim is unsupportable.

30. Bumiller, *Civil Rights Society*.

31. Rutland, *Papers of James Madison*, vol. 11, pp. 298–99; Rakove, *Original Meanings*, p. 323.

32. James Madison, Amendments to the Constitution (June 8, 1789), in Hobson, *Papers of James Madison*, pp. 197, 204–5.

33. Writing in 1941, free speech scholar Zechariah Chafee echoed Madison's points. To Chafee, the bill of rights "fix[ed] a certain point to halt the government abruptly with a 'Thus far and no farther'; but long before that point is reached they urge upon every official . . . a constant regard for certain declared fundamental policies of American life." Chafee, *Free Speech*, p. 7.

34. The Supreme Court did find a zoning restriction on housing for the mentally retarded unconstitutional in City of Cleburne v. Cleburne Living Center, 473 U.S. 432 (1985), but only on the ground that the city had no acceptable reason at all for restricting the home's location. See also Heller v. Doe, 509 U.S. 312 (1993) (rejecting a constitutional challenge to statutes creating different standards for involuntary commitment of the mentally retarded and mentally ill). Further, early efforts to protect the disabled did occur in the shadow of judicial review, at a time when it seemed possible that the courts would hold disability to be a category requiring special constitutional protection. By the late 1980s, however, it was clear that the courts would not do so. Civil rights laws protecting the disabled were enacted then anyway.

35. Lupu, "Statutes Revolving in Constitutional Law Orbits." See also Shane, "Voting Rights." Lupu and Shane deal with statutory development and interpreta-

tion in the shadow of a judicially enforceable Constitution, a somewhat different context than the one I have developed.

36. Glendon, *Rights Talk*, p. x.

37. Ibid., p. 9. For a similar view, see Burt, *Constitution in Conflict*.

38. Constitutional guarantees of social welfare rights have a complicated background. Post-1945 constitutions were written for nations that had strong socialist political movements, which would not accept a new constitution that lacked social welfare rights. The Catholic Church, an important influence on many more conservative parties, responded in the late nineteenth century to the simultaneous emergence of socialist parties and what Catholic leaders saw as the excesses of unbridled capitalism with a set of social teachings that supported the inclusion of social welfare rights in these new constitutions.

39. For a version of the argument, see Sunstein, "Constitutionalism, Prosperity, Democracy."

40. Constitution of Ireland, art. 45.

41. Sager, "Fair Measure."

42. They might also direct courts to take them into account in construing statutes.

43. Ibid., p. 1227. Sager continued, this "should alter discourse among and about officials," but unfortunately legal scholarship did not pick up that observation.

44. Glendon, "Rights in Twentieth Century Constitutions."

45. Chapter 5 deals extensively with the constitutional implications of politicians' incentives.

46. Address to Congress on the State of the Union (Jan. 11, 1944), in Roosevelt, *Public Papers and Addresses*, vol. 13, p. 32.

47. Debate over such bills might be productive. In particular, we might get some interesting discussions of what we cared about if some bills sought to authorize judicial review of *some* statutes but not others. And, in any event, a statute authorizing judicial review could be repealed by a new majority if experience proved that the practice was undesirable.

48. Smith, *Civic Ideals*.

49. Bork, *Slouching Toward Gomorrah*, p. 117.

50. Canadian Charter of Rights and Freedoms, § 33. Legislatures can override provisions dealing with fundamental freedoms such as free expression, and equality rights. They cannot override guarantees of voting rights. The override is effective for no more than five years, which means that it cannot be renewed until there has been a parliamentary election in which the override might be a political issue.

51. The Canadian Charter technically does go all the way, because legislatures can invoke the override even before a court decision holding a statute unconstitutional. Its commitment to majority rule is not as transparent as would be the case if a constitution simply eliminated judicial review. The notwithstanding clause got caught up in the controversy over the status of Quebec, and something like a convention against using the override appears to have emerged.

52. *Cognizable* here means *the basis for holding a statute unconstitutional*, to ensure that courts can rely on constitutional provisions in interpreting statutes and in determining whether an official's actions were authorized by law.

53. Another possible course, suggested by the analysis in chapter 2, is to ignore the Supreme Court's constitutional interpretations. Here as there, the role played by astute political leadership in the analysis should be clear.

CHAPTER EIGHT
POPULIST CONSTITUTIONAL LAW

1. Eule, "Judicial Review"; Levinson, "A Constitutional Convention," p. 27 (describing and criticizing the fear); Sullivan, "Constitutional Amendmentitis."

2. Michelman, "Saving Old Glory," argued that an anti-flag-burning constitutional amendment was preferable to an anti-flag-burning statute that the Supreme Court would uphold as consistent with the First Amendment. The Supreme Court's decision would integrate the statute into First Amendment law, thereby making general First Amendment law more tolerant of speech restrictions. The proposed amendment, in contrast, could be treated as an exception that did not have to fit together with the rest of the Constitution. Some constitutional amendments have that detached quality. Others, however, have been taken to state general principles that affect the interpretation of the rest of the Constitution. The best example is the Eleventh Amendment, which by its terms simply protects states from suits in federal court by citizens of other states but which has been taken to express a far broader degree of state immunity from suit.

3. Citizens for the Constitution, " 'Great and Extraordinary Occasions.' "

4. See chapter 2.

5. The Prohibition experience may cut against Sullivan: When a large majority decided that a policy adopted by another large majority was a bad idea, the people repealed the policy without too much difficulty.

6. See Levinson, "Accounting for Constitutional Change."

7. First Inaugural Address, March 4, 1861, in Richardson, *Messages and Papers of the Presidents*, vol. 9, p. 10.

8. Maier, *American Scripture*, pp. 197–208, describes the historical process by which the Declaration of Independence came to be understood as offering a program or project for the American people rather than merely what it purports to be, a political declaration of independence.

9. Alexander Hamilton, *The Federalist* no. 1.

10. Recall here my observation in chapter 1 that I would not be committed to democracy if it produced permanent or severe evils. The same can be said about a decision to continue in defining the project of self-government as realizing the Declaration's principles: If those principles produced permanent or severe evil, one should not attempt to realize them.

11. Crevecoeur, *Letters from an American Farmer*, pp. 54–56, 79, 62.

12. Address by Frances Wright in Cincinnati, Ohio, printed in *The Beacon*, Mar. 17, 1838, quoted in Sollors, *Beyond Ethnicity*, p. 152.

13. Speech at Chicago, July 10, 1858, in Basler, *Collected Works of Abraham Lincoln*, vol. 2, pp. 499–500.

14. Norton, *Republic of Signs*, p. 137.

15. For a political scientist's discussion of the competing American political traditions, see Smith, *Civic Ideals*.

16. Norton, *Republic of Signs*, p. 132.

17. The discussion of a populist approach to the religion clauses of the First Amendment in chapter 4 also illustrated the thinness of populist constitutional law.

18. Regents of the University of California v. Bakke, 438 U.S. 265, 407 (1978).

19. City of Richmond v. J.A. Croson Co., 488 U.S. 469, 518 (1988).

20. 403 U.S. 15 (1971).

21. 485 U.S. 46 (1988).

22. Post, "Constitutional Concept of Public Discourse."

23. Graber, "Clintonification of American Law."

24. As we saw in chapter 7, describing contemporary conservative constitutional views is complicated by conservatives' willingness to accept aggressive judicial review when it produces results they like in areas such as affirmative action.

25. This book is not the place to rehearse the well-known difficulties with a jurisprudence of original understanding. For my discussion, see Tushnet, *Red, White, and Blue*, pp. 23–45.

26. For a dramatically contrary illustration, see Justice Scalia's opinion for the Court in Printz v. United States, 117 S.Ct. 2365 (1997), which held unconstitutional a provision in the Brady Handgun Violence Prevention Act. Justice Scalia's opinion stated early on, "Because there is no constitutional text speaking to this precise question, the answer . . . must be sought in historical understanding and practice, in the structure of the Constitution, and in the jurisprudence of this Court." Had the case raised a question about abortion rights, the sentence would surely have ended, "we have nothing further to say about the claim."

27. See Robert Shogan, "Abortion Foes Shred Dole's Tolerance Clause; GOP: Draft Platform Would Also Deny Citizenship to Children Born in United States to Illegal Immigrants," Los Angeles *Times*, Aug. 6, 1996, p. A1. The reference to constitutionally valid legislation suggests that such children may not be "subject to the jurisdiction" of the United States in a constitutionally relevant sense. The phrase was inserted in the Amendment to deal with the citizenship status of ambassadors' children. Yale professors Peter Schuck and Rogers Smith have argued that the clause can fairly be read to allow Congress or the courts to reject the principle of birthright citizenship. Schuck and Smith, *Citizenship Without Consent*, pp. 75–86, 116–17. Their reasons include "theoretical ambivalence on the part of the Fourteenth Amendment's framers concerning the basis for citizenship; the inconsistencies that have always pervaded American citizenship law; the contemporary irrelevance of many of the reasons that led courts to perpetuate the medieval ascriptive principle in the past; and the existence of policy considerations today that increase the practical and theoretical attractiveness of [their alternative proposal]." They argue that "[i]t is appropriate for the judiciary to adopt this reinterpretation because it is chiefly the judiciary that created the rival common-law understanding of political membership and defended it as authoritative. . . . [A] judicial reinterpretation is possible where, as here, its original reading of ambiguous language reflected policies and principles at variance with most contemporary views of American constitutional theory and with current national policy objectives."

28. Indeed, it coheres well with the Constitution's requirement that the president be "a natural born Citizen." As Post observes, "at the very heart of the constitutional order, in the Office of the President, the Constitution abandons its brave experiment of forging a new society based upon principles of voluntary commitment." Post, "Constitution's Worst Provision," p. 193.

29. One pending proposal seems to me not as well drafted. It would provide: "All persons born in the United States . . . of mothers who are citizens or legal residents of the United States . . . are citizens of the United States. . . ." This restricts congressional power unnecessarily, and would cause real trouble as the technology of reproduction advances to the point where some persons may not be "born . . . of mothers" at all.

30. For a discussion, see Neuman, *Strangers to the Constitution*, pp. 165–87.

31. Israeli lawyers and judges have sometimes debated the criteria for deciding who is a Jew, but they have not yet questioned the principle underlying the Law of Return, that Israeli citizenship is available to all Jews. Non-Jews—Muslims and Christians—can be and are citizens of Israel, but the Law of Return ties Israeli citizenship to religion in a distinctive way.

32. 320 U.S. 118 (1943).

33. In light of the discussion in chapter 7, the Court's observations about judicial review may be of interest:

It is true that this Court has played a large part in the unfolding of the constitutional plan (sometimes too much so in the opinion of some observers), but we would be arrogant indeed if we presumed that a government of laws, with protection for minority groups, would be impossible without it. Like other agencies of government, this Court at various times in its existence has not escaped the shafts of critics whose sincerity and attachment to the Constitution is beyond question—critics who have accused it of assuming functions of judicial review not intended to be conferred upon it, or of abusing those functions to thwart the popular will, and who have advocated various remedies taking a wide range.

34. Sandel, *Democracy's Discontent*.

35. The problem here does not involve a conflict between constitutional principles. As we saw in the discussion of the *DeShaney* case in chapter 3, the Constitution does not protect the children's physical integrity. And the problem would be the same if the parents made purely secular arguments about the best way to raise children.

36. "Consistent with," but not a complete realization of universal human rights. The Fourteenth Amendment expanded citizenship, but citizenship remains an important legal and constitutional category, as it would not be in a regime in which rights were truly universal.

37. In saying that the proposed amendment is anti-constitutional, a supporter of populist constitutional law would not be committing himself or herself to a position on what courts ought to do if the amendment is adopted. Although the idea that a constitutional amendment could be *un*constitutional strikes most U.S. constitutionalists as peculiar, it is not unknown elsewhere. The German Basic Law makes some of its provisions unamendable. The Indian Supreme Court held un-

constitutional some constitutional amendments adopted in a formally correct way during a declared state of emergency. And two provisions in the United States at least purport to be unamendable: a bar to amending the Constitution before 1808 to ban the interstate slave trade and, of more contemporary relevance, a bar on depriving any state of its equal representation in the Senate without its consent.

38. For a complex view that appears to me similar to mine with respect to the question of transformability, see Michelman, "Always Under Law?"

39. This is the truth in modern communitarian thinking, however overstated are the conclusions that some communitarians draw from that truth.

40. Some religious communities may support similar experiences, depending on the content of the religious beliefs that constitute them.

41. See Waldron, "Legislation, Authority, and Voting."

42. See Bosniak, "Opposing Prop. 187."

43. For example, the idea of degrees of membership may have some intuitive appeal, but it may not ultimately be defensible: We would not want to say that second-generation citizens are somehow not quite as much members as tenth-generation citizens are. The populist constitutionalist who opposes Proposition 187 might point out the anomaly that naturalized citizens have to take a test to show that they understand our constitutional principles, while people born in this country do not. This suggests that our operative philosophy does not recognize degrees of membership.

BIBLIOGRAPHY

Ackerman, Bruce. *We the People: Foundations.* Cambridge: Harvard University Press, 1991.

Alexander, Larry, and Frederick Schauer. "On Extrajudicial Constitutional Interpretation," 110 *Harv. L.Rev.* 1359 (1997).

Allen, Anita. "The Proposed Equal Protection Fix for Abortion Law: Reflections on Citizenship, Gender and the Constitution," 18 *Harv. J.L. & Pub. Policy* 419 (1995).

Amar, Akhil. "Philadelphia Revisited: Amending the Constitution Outside Article V," 55 *U. Chi. L. Rev.* 1043 (1988).

Andrews, William G. *Coordinate Magistrates: Constitutional Law by Congress and President.* New York: Van Nostrand Reinhold Co., 1969.

Audi, Robert. "The Place of Religious Argument in a Free and Democratic Society," 30 *San Diego L.Rev.* 677 (1993).

———. "Religious Commitment and Secular Reason: A Reply to Professor Weithman," 20 *Phil. & Pub. Aff.* 66 (1991).

———. "The Separation of Church and State and the Obligations of Citizenship," 18 *Phil. & Pub. Aff.* 259 (1989).

———, and Nicholas Wolterstorff. *Religion in the Public Square: The Place of Religious Convictions in Political Debate.* Lanham, MD: Rowman & Littlefield, 1997.

Balkin, J. M. "Agreements With Hell and Other Objects of Our Faith," 65 *Fordham L.Rev.* 1703 (1997).

———. "Ideological Drift and the Struggle Over Meaning," 25 *Conn. L.Rev.* 869 (1993).

———. "Some Realism About Pluralism: Legal Realist Approaches to the First Amendment," 1990 *Duke L.J.* 375.

Basler, Roy, ed. *Collected Works of Abraham Lincoln.* New Brunswick: Rutgers University Press, 1953.

Bednar, Jenna, and William N. Eskridge, Jr. "Steadying the Court's 'Unsteady Path': A Theory of Judicial Enforcement of Federalism," 68 *S.Cal. L.Rev.* 1447 (1995).

Bell, Derrick. "*Brown v. Board of Education* and the Interest-Convergence Dilemma," 93 *Harv. L.Rev.* 518 (1980).

Benjamin, Gerald, and Michael Malbin, ed. *Limiting Legislative Terms.* Washington: CQ Press, 1992.

Bergh, Albert E., ed. *Writings of Thomas Jefferson.* Washington: Thomas Jefferson Memorial Association, 1905.

Berman, William C. *America's Right Turn: From Nixon to Bush.* Baltimore: Johns Hopkins University Press, 1994.

Bernardin, Joseph. "The Consistent Ethic: What Sort of Framework?" in *Abortion and Catholicism: The American Debate*, ed. Patricia Beattie Jung and Thomas Shannon, 260. New York: Crossroad, 1988.

Bickel, Alexander M. *The Supreme Court and the Idea of Progress*. New Haven: Yale University Press, 1978.

Black, Charles. *A New Birth of Freedom: Human Rights, Named and Unnamed*. New York: Grosset/Putnam, 1997.

———. *Structure and Relationship in Constitutional Law*. Baton Rouge: Louisiana State University Press, 1969.

Black, Hugo. *A Constitutional Faith*. New York: Alfred A. Knopf, 1968.

Blumoff, Theodore Y. "The Holocaust and Public Discourse," 11 *J.L. & Religion* 591 (1994–95).

———. "The New Religionists' Newest Social Gospel: On the Rhetoric and Reality of Religions' 'Marginalization' in Public Life," 51 *U. Miami L.Rev.* 1 (1996).

Bork, Robert. *Slouching Toward Gomorrah : Modern Liberalism and American Decline*. New York: ReganBooks, 1996.

Bosniak, Linda S. "Opposing Prop. 187: Undocumented Immigrants and the National Imagination," 28 *Conn. L.Rev.* 555 (1996).

Brest, Paul. "The Conscientious Legislator's Guide to Constitutional Interpretation," 27 *Stan. L.Rev.* 585 (1975).

———. *Processes of Constitutional Decisionmaking*. Boston: Little Brown, 1st ed. 1975.

Bumiller, Kristin. *The Civil Rights Society: The Social Construction of Victims*. Baltimore: Johns Hopkins University Press, 1988.

Burt, Robert. *The Constitution in Conflict*. Cambridge: Harvard University Press, 1992.

Bybee, Jay S. "Ulysses at the Mast: Democracy, Federalism, and the Sirens' Song of the Seventeenth Amendment," 91 *Nw. U.L.Rev.* 500 (1997).

Caminker, Evan H. "Precedent and Prediction: The Forward-Looking Aspects of Inferior Court Decisionmaking," 73 *Tex. L.Rev.* 1 (1994).

Carter, Stephen. *The Confirmation Mess*. New York: BasicBooks, 1994.

———. "A Conversation with Stephen Carter," *Religion & Values in Public Life*, vol. 2, no. 1 (Fall 1993), p. 2.

———. *The Culture of Disbelief: How American Law and Politics Trivialize Religious Devotion*. New York: BasicBooks, 1993.

———. "The Religiously Devout Judge," 64 *Notre Dame L.Rev.* 932 (1989).

Chafee, Zechariah. *Free Speech in the United States*. Cambridge: Harvard University Press, 1941.

Chapman, John W., and Ian Shapiro, eds. *Nomos XXXV: Democratic Community*. New York: New York University Press, 1993.

Citizens for the Constitution. " 'Great and Extraordinary Occasions': Developing Standards for Constitutional Change" (Washington, 1997).

Cook, Anthony. "God Talk in the Secular World," 6 *Yale J.L. & Human.* 435 (1994).

Crenshaw, Kimberle, Neil Gotanda, Gary Peller, and Kendall Thomas, eds. *Critical Race Theory: The Key Writings That Formed the Movement*. New York: The New Press, 1995.

Crevecoeur, J. Hector St. John. *Letters from an American Farmer.* Reprint ed. Garden City, N.Y.: Dolphin Books (1963).

Currie, David. *The Constitution in Congress: The Federalist Period, 1789–1801.* Chicago: University of Chicago Press, 1997.

Dahl, Robert A. "Decision-Making in a Democracy: The Supreme Court as a National Policy-Maker," 6 *J.Pub. L.* 279 (1957).

Devins, Neal. "Political Will and the Unitary Executive: What Makes an Independent Agency Independent?" 15 *Cardozo L.Rev.* 273 (1993).

———. "Reagan Redux: Civil Rights Under Bush," 68 *Notre Dame L.Rev.* 955 (1993).

Dunne, Finley Peter. *Mr. Dooley at His Best,* ed. Elmer Ellis. Hamden, Conn.: Archon Books, 1969.

Dworkin, Ronald. *Taking Rights Seriously.* Cambridge: Harvard University Press, 1977.

Easterbrook, Frank. "Presidential Review," 40 *Case Western Res. L.Rev.* 905 (1989–90).

Edsall, Thomas Byrne, with Mary D. Edsall, *Chain Reaction: The Impact of Race, Rights, and Taxes on American Politics.* New York: W. W. Norton, 1991.

Elhauge, Einar. "Are Term Limits Undemocratic?" 64 *U.Chi. L.Rev.* 83 (1997).

Elster, Jon. *Sour Grapes: Studies in the Subversion of Rationality.* Cambridge: Cambridge University Press, 1983.

———, and Rune Slagstad, eds. *Constitutionalism and Democracy.* Cambridge: Cambridge University Press, 1988.

Ely, John Hart. *Democracy and Distrust.* Cambridge: Harvard University Press, 1980.

Etzioni, Amitai, ed. *Rights and the Common Good: The Communitarian Perspective.* New York: St. Martin's Press, 1995.

Eule, Julian. "Judicial Review of Direct Democracy," 99 *Yale L.J.* 1503 (1990).

Fallon, Richard H. Jr. "Foreword: Implementing the Constitution," 111 *Harv. L.Rev.* 54 (1997).

Fehrenbacher, Don E., ed. *Abraham Lincoln: Speeches and Writings.* Library of America, New York: Viking Press, 1969.

Finman, Ted, and Stewart Macaulay. "Freedom to Dissent: The Vietnam Protests and the Words of Public Officials," 1966 *Wis. L. Rev.* 632 .

Fiorina, Morris. *Divided Government* (2d ed.). Boston: Allyn & Bacon, 1996.

Fisher, Louis. *Constitutional Dialogues: Interpretation as a Political Process.* Princeton: Princeton University Press, 1988.

———. "Constitutional Interpretation by Members of Congress," 63 *N.Car. L.Rev.* 707 (1985).

———, and Neal Devins. *Political Dynamics of Constitutional Law* (2d ed.). St. Paul: West Publishing Co., 1996.

Foley, Michael. *The Silence of Constitutions.* London: Routledge, 1989.

Foner, Philip S., ed. *Life and Writings of Frederick Douglass.* New York: International Publishers, 1950–55.

Forbath, William. "Why Is This Rights Talk Different from All Other Rights Talk? Demoting the Court and Reimagining the Constitution," 46 *Stan. L.Rev.* 1771 (1994).

Fung, Archon. "Making Rights Real: *Roe*'s Impact on Abortion Access," 21 *Politics & Society* 465 (1993).

Galston, William. "Liberal Virtues," 82 *Am. Pol. Sci. Rev.* 1277 (1988).

Gant, Scott E. "Judicial Supremacy and Nonjudicial Interpretation of the Constitution," 24 *Hastings Const. L.Q.* 359 (1997).

Garfield, Jay, and Patricia Hennessy, eds. *Abortion: Moral and Legal Perspectives.* Amherst: University of Massachusetts Press, 1985.

Garrow, David J. "Hopelessly Hollow History: Revisionist Devaluing of *Brown v. Board of Education*," 80 *Va. L.Rev.* 151 (1994).

———. *Liberty and Sexuality: The Right to Privacy and the Making of* Roe v. Wade. New York: Macmillan Publishing Co., 1994.

Garvey, John H. "Black and White Images," 56 *L. & Contemp. Prob.* no. 4 (Autumn 1993), p. 190.

Gerhardt, Michael J. *The Federal Impeachment Process: A Constitutional and Historical Analysis.* Princeton: Princeton University Press, 1996.

Ginsburg, Ruth Bader. "Some Thoughts on Autonomy and Equality in Relation to *Roe v. Wade*," 63 *N.C.L. Rev.* 375 (1985).

Glendon, Mary Ann. "Rights in Twentieth Century Constitutions," in *Rights and the Common Good: The Communitarian Perspective.* Ed. Amitai Etzioni. New York: St. Martin's Press, 1995.

———. *Rights Talk: The Impoverishment of Political Discourse.* New York: Free Press, 1991.

Graber, Mark. "The Clintonification of American Law: Abortion, Welfare, and Liberal Constitutional Theory," 58 *Ohio St. L.J.* 731 (1997).

———. "The Nonmajoritarian Difficulty: Legislative Deference to the Judiciary," 7 *Studies in Am. Pol. Develop.* 35 (1993).

Greenawalt, Kent. *Religious Convictions and Political Choice.* New York: Oxford University Press, 1988.

———. "Some Problems With Public Reason in John Rawls's *Political Liberalism*," 28 *Loyola (L.A.) L.Rev.* 1303 (1995).

———. "The Use of Religious Convictions by Legislators and Judges," 36 *J. Church & State* 541 (1994).

Greenberg, Jack. *Crusaders in the Courts: How a Dedicated Band of Lawyers Fought for the Civil Rights Revolution.* New York: BasicBooks, 1994.

Griffin, Leslie. "Good Catholics Should Be Rawlsian Liberals," 5 *S. Cal. Interdisciplinary L.J.* 297 (1997).

Grofman, Bernard, and Donald Wittman, eds. *The Federalist Papers and the New Institutionalism.* New York: Agathon Press, 1989.

Gutmann, Amy, and Dennis Thompson. "Moral Conflict and Political Consensus," 101 *Ethics* 64 (1990).

Hadaway, C. Kirk, Penny Long Marler, and Mark Chaves. "What the Polls Don't Show: A Closer Look at U.S. Church Attendance," 58 *Am. Sociological Rev.* 741 (1993).

Hampton, Jean. "Democracy and the Rule of Law," in *The Rule of Law*, ed. Ian Shapiro, 36. New York: New York University Press, 1994.

Hardin, Russell. "Why A Constitution?" in *The Federalist Papers and the New Institutionalism*, ed. Bernard Grofman and Donald Wittman, 116. New York: Agathon Press, 1989.

Hartog, Hendrik. "The Constitution of Aspiration and 'The Rights That Belong to Us All,' " 74 *J. Amer. Hist.* 353 (1987).

Hearings on the Nomination of Robert H. Bork to be Associate Justice of the Supreme Court of the United States, Committee on the Judiciary, United States Senate, 100th Cong., 1st Sess. (1987).

Hearings on S. 2673, "To Reduce the Compensation of the Office of Attorney General," Committee on the Judiciary, United States Senate, 93d Congress, 1st Sess. (1973).

Hearings on the United States Supreme Court Decision in Texas v. Johnson, Committee on the Judiciary, United States Senate, 101st Cong., 1st Sess. (1989).

Henkin, Louis. "Is There a 'Political Questions' Doctrine?" 85 *Yale L.J.* 597 (1976).

Herz, Andrew. "Gun Crazy: Constitutional False Consciousness and Dereliction of Dialogic Responsibility," 75 *B.U. L.Rev.* 57 (1995).

Hobson, Charles F. et al., ed. *Papers of James Madison.* Chicago: University of Chicago Press, 1979.

Holmes, Stephen. "Precommitment and the paradox of democracy," in *Constitutionalism and Democracy,* ed. Jon Elster and Rune Slagstad, 216. Cambridge: Cambridge University Press, 1988.

Jacobsohn, Gary. *Apple of Gold: Constitutionalism in Israel and the United States.* Princeton: Princeton University Press, 1993.

Jefferson, Thomas. *Writings,* ed. Merrill D. Peterson. Library of America, New York: Viking Press, 1984.

Jeffries, John Jr. *Justice Lewis F. Powell, Jr.: A Biography.* New York: Charles Scribner's Sons, 1994.

Johnson, Philip. "Book Review," 7 *Const. Comm.* 427 (1990).

Jung, Patricia Beattie, and Thomas Shannon, ed. *Abortion and Catholicism: The American Debate.* New York: Crossroad, 1988.

Kamm, Frances Myrna. *Creation and Abortion: A Study in Moral Philosophy.* New York: Oxford University Press, 1992.

Klarman, Michael. "*Brown*, Racial Change, and the Civil Rights Movement," 80 *Va. L.Rev.* 7 (1994).

Kramer, Larry. "Understanding Federalism," 45 *Vand. L.Rev.* 1485 (1994).

Kreimer, Seth. "Exploring the Dark Matter of Judicial Review: A Constitutional Census of the 1990s," 5 *Wm. & Mary Bill of Rts. J.* 427 (1997).

Laudan, Larry. *Science and Relativism: Some Key Controversies in the Philosophy of Science.* Chicago: University of Chicago Press, 1990.

Lessig, Lawrence. "What Drives Derivability: Responses to *Responding to Imperfection*," 74 *Tex. L.Rev.* 839 (1996).

Levinson, Sanford. "Accounting for Constitutional Change (Or, How Many Times Has the United States Constitution Been Amended? (A) <26; (B) 26; (C) > 26; (D) All of the Above)," 8 *Const. Comm.* 409 (1991).

———. "A Constitutional Convention: Does the Left Fear Popular Sovereignty?" *Dissent*, Winter 1996, 27.

Levinson, Sanford. *Constitutional Faith*. Princeton: Princeton University Press, 1988.

———. "The Embarrassing Second Amendment," 99 *Yale L.J.* 639 (1989).

———. "Presidential Elections and Constitutional Stupidities," 12 *Const. Comm.* 183 (1995).

———, ed. *Responding to Imperfection: Toward a Theory of Constitutional Amendment*. Princeton: Princeton University Press, 1995.

Lincoln, Abraham. *Speeches and Writings*, ed. Don E. Fehrenbacher. Library of America, New York: Viking Press, 1969.

Lupu, Ira C. "Statutes Revolving in Constitutional Law Orbits," 79 *Va. L.Rev.* 1 (1993).

Lutz, Donald. "Toward a Theory of Constitutional Amendment," in *Responding to Imperfection: Toward a Theory of Constitutional Amendment*, ed. Sanford Levinson. Princeton: Princeton University Press, 1995.

MacKinnon, Catherine. "*Roe v. Wade*: A Study in Male Ideology," in *Abortion: Moral and Legal Perspectives*, ed. Jay Garfield and Patricia Hennessy. Amherst: University of Massachusetts Press, 1985.

Maier, Pauline. *American Scripture: Making the Declaration of Independence*. New York: Knopf, 1997.

Mason, Edward C. *The Veto Power*, ed. Albert Bushnell Hart. Boston: Ginn & Co., 1891.

Mayer, David N. "Jefferson's Conception of the Presidency," 26 *Perspectives on Political Science* 140 (1997).

Mayer, Jane, and Jill Abramson. *Strange Justice: The Selling of Clarence Thomas* Boston: Houghton Mifflin Co., 1994.

McConnell, Michael. "Originalism and the Desegregation Decision," 81 *Va. L.Rev.* 947 (1995).

Meese, Edwin, III. "The Law of the Constitution," 61 *Tulane L.Rev.* 979 (1987).

Merritt, Deborah Jones. "Commerce!" 94 *Mich. L.Rev.* 674 (1995).

Michelman, Frank. "Always Under Law?" 12 *Const. Comm.* 227 (1995).

———. "Saving Old Glory: On Constitutional Iconography," 42 *Stan. L.Rev.* 1337 (1990).

Mikva, Abner. "How Well Does Congress Support and Defend the Constitution?" 61 *N.Car. L.Rev.* 587 (1983).

Miller, Geoffrey P. "The President's Power of Interpretation: Implications of a Unified Theory of Constitutional Law," 56 *Law & Contemp. Prob.* no. 4 (1993), p. 35.

Moore, Wayne D. *Constitutional Rights and Powers of the People*. Princeton: Princeton University Press, 1996.

Moynihan, Daniel Patrick. "What do you do when the Supreme Court is wrong?" *The Public Interest*, 57, 1979, p. 3.

Muir, William K. *Legislature: California's School for Politics*. Chicago: University of Chicago Press, 1982.

Nagel, Robert. *Constitutional Cultures: The Mentality and Consequences of Judicial Review*. Berkeley: University of California Press, 1989.

Neuman, Gerald. *Strangers to the Constitution: Immigrants, Borders, and Fundamental Law*. Princeton: Princeton University Press, 1996.

Norton, Anne. *Republic of Signs: Liberal Theory and American Popular Culture.* Chicago: University of Chicago Press, 1993.

Parker, Richard. *"Here, the People Rule": A Constitutional Populist Manifesto.* Cambridge: Harvard University Press, 1994.

Paulsen, Michael Stokes. " Is Lloyd Bentsen Unconstitutional?" 46 *Stan. L.Rev.* 907 (1994).

———. "The *Merryman* Power and the Dilemma of Autonomous Executive Branch Interpretation," 15 *Cardozo L.Rev.* 81 (1993).

———. "The Most Dangerous Branch: Executive Power to Say What the Law Is," 83 *Geo. L.J.* 217 (1994).

Perry, Michael John. *Religion in Politics: Constitutional and Moral Perspectives.* New York: Oxford University Press, 1997.

Post, Robert. "The Constitutional Concept of Public Discourse: Outrageous Opinion, Democratic Deliberation and *Hustler Magazine v. Falwell*," 103 *Harv. L.Rev.* 601 (1990).

———. "What Is the Constitution's Worst Provision?" 12 *Const. Comm.* 191 (1995).

Price, Charles M. "The Guillotine Comes to California: Term Limit Politics in the Golden State," in *Limiting Legislative Terms,* ed. Gerald Benjamin and Michael Malbin. Washington: CQ Press, 1992.

Rakove, Jack N. *Original Meanings: Politics and Ideas in the Making of the Constitution.* New York: Alfred A. Knopf, 1996.

Rawls, John. "The Idea of Public Reason Revisited," 64 *U.Chi. L.Rev.* 765 (1997).

———. *Political Liberalism.* New York: Columbia University Press, 1992.

Rees, Grover III. "Questions for Supreme Court Nominees at Confirmation Hearings: Excluding the Constitution," 17 *Ga. L.Rev.* 913 (1983).

Reynolds, Glenn Harlan. "A Critical Guide to the Second Amendment," 62 *Tenn. L.Rev.* 461 (1995).

Richards, David A. J. "Book Review," 23 *Ga. L.Rev.* 1189 (1989).

Richardson, James D. *Messages and Papers of the Presidents.* Washington: Government Printing Office, 1896–99.

Roosevelt, Franklin D. *Public Papers and Addresses.* New York: Macmillan and Random House, 1938–50.

Rosen, Jeffrey. "Note: Was the Flag-Burning Amendment Unconstitutional?" 100 *Yale L.J.* 1073 (1991).

Rosenberg, Gerald. *The Hollow Hope: Can Courts Bring about Social Change?* Chicago: University of Chicago Press, 1991.

Rostow, Eugene V. "The Democratic Character of Judicial Review," 66 *Harv. L. Rev.* 193 (1952).

Rutherford, Bruce K. "Can an Islamic Group Aid Democratization?" in *Nomos XXXV: Democratic Community,* ed. John W. Chapman and Ian Shapiro. New York: New York University Press, 1993.

Rutland, Robert et al., eds. *Papers of James Madison.* Chicago: University of Chicago Press, 1962–91.

Sager, Lawrence. "Fair Measure: The Legal Status of Underenforced Constitutional Norms," 91 *Harv. L.Rev.* 1212 (1978).

Sajó, András. *Western Rights? Post-Communist Application.* Boston: Kluwer International, 1996.

Sandel, Michael. *Democracy's Discontent.* Cambridge: Harvard University Press, 1996.

Scalia, Antonin. "Originalism: The Lesser Evil," 57 *U.Cinn. L.Rev.* 849 (1989).

Schauer, Frederick. "Formalism," 97 *Yale L.J.* 509 (1988).

———. "The Political Incidence of the Free Speech Principle," 64 *U.Colo. L.Rev.* 935 (1993).

———. "Slippery Slopes," 99 *Harv. L.Rev.* 361 (1985).

Schuck, Peter H., and Rogers M. Smith. *Citizenship Without Consent: Illegal Aliens in the American Polity.* New Haven: Yale University Press, 1985.

Segal, Jeffrey A., and Harold J. Spaeth. *The Supreme Court and the Attitudinal Model.* New York: Cambridge University Press, 1993.

Shane, Peter M. "Voting Rights and the 'Statutory Constitution,' " 56 *L. & Contemp. Prob.* no. 4 (1993), p. 243.

Shapiro, Ian, ed. *The Rule of Law.* New York: New York University Press, 1994.

Shapiro, Martin. *Courts: A Comparative and Political Analysis.* Chicago: University of Chicago Press, 1981.

Sidak, J. Gregory, and Thomas A. Smith, "Why Did President Bush Repudiate the 'Inherent' Line-Item Veto?" 9 *J.L. & Politics* 39 (1992).

Silverstein, Mark. *Judicious Choices: The New Politics of Supreme Court Confirmations.* New York: W. W. Norton, 1994.

Sklansky, David. "Proposition 187 and the Ghost of James Bradley Thayer," 17 *Chicano-Latino L.Rev.* 24 (1995).

Smith, Rogers. *Civic Ideals: Conflicting Visions of Citizenship in U.S. History.* New Haven: Yale University Press, 1997.

Sollors, Werner. *Beyond Ethnicity: Consent and Descent in American Culture.* New York: Oxford University Press, 1986.

Sparks, Edwin Erle, ed. *The Lincoln-Douglas Debates of 1858.* Springfield, Il.: Illinois State Historical Society, 1908.

Stromseth, Jane. "Understanding Constitutional War Powers Today: Why Methodology Matters (Book Review)," 106 *Yale L.J.* 845 (1996).

Sullivan, Kathleen. "Constitutional Amendmentitis," *The American Prospect,* Fall 1995, p. 20.

Sunstein, Cass. "Against Positive Rights," in *Western Rights? Post-Communist Application,* ed. András Sajó. Boston: Kluwer International, 1996.

———. "Constitutionalism, Prosperity, Democracy: Transition in Eastern Europe," 2 *Constitutional Political Economy* 371 (1991).

———. *Democracy and the Problem of Free Speech.* New York: Free Press, 1993.

———. *Legal Reasoning and Political Conflict.* New York: Oxford University Press, 1996.

———. 'Neutrality in Constitutional Law (with Special Reference to Pornography, Abortion, and Surrogacy)," 92 *Colum. L.Rev.* 1 (1992).

Symposium, "Political Liberalism: Religion & Public Reason," *Religion & Values in Public Life,* vol. 3, no. 4 (Summer 1995).

Thayer, James Bradley. "The Origin and Scope of the American Doctrine of Constitutional Law," 7 *Harv. L.Rev.* 129 (1893).

Tiefer, Charles. "The Constitutionality of Independent Officers as Checks on Abuses of Executive Power," 63 *B.U. L.Rev.* 59 (1983).

———. "The Flag-Burning Controversy of 1989–1900: Congress' Valid Role in Constitutional Dialogue," 29 *Harv. J. on Legislation* 357 (1992).

Treanor, William Michael. "Fame, the Founding, and the Power to Declare War," 82 *Corn. L.Rev.* 695 (1997).

Tushnet, Mark. "Living in a Constitutional Moment: *Lopez* and Constitutional Theory," 46 *Case Western Reserve L.Rev.* 845 (1996).

———. *Making Constitutional Law: Thurgood Marshall and the Supreme Court, 1961–1991.* New York: Oxford University Press, 1997.

———. *Red, White, and Blue: A Critical Analysis of Constitutional Law.* Cambridge: Harvard University Press, 1988.

———. "Policy Distortion and Democratic Debilitation: Comparative Illumination of the Countermajoritarian Difficulty," 94 *Mich. L.Rev.* 245 (1995).

———. "Thayer's Target: Judicial Review or Democracy?" 88 *Nw. L.Rev.* 9 (1993).

Waldron, Jeremy. "Kant's Legal Positivism," 109 *Harv. L.Rev.* 1535 (1996).

———. "Legislation, Authority, and Voting," 84 *Geo. L.J.* 2185 (1996).

———. "Religious Contributions in Public Deliberation," 30 *San Diego L.Rev.* 817 (1993).

Walzer, Michael. "The Communitarian Critique of Liberalism," 18 *Political Theory* 6 (1990).

Warren, Mark. "Deliberative Democracy and Authority," 90 *Am. Pol. Sci. Rev.* 46 (1996).

Wechsler, Herbert. "The Political Safeguards of Federalism," 54 *Colum. L.Rev.* 543 (1954).

Weingast, Barry. "The Economic Role of Political Institutions," 11 *J.L., Econ., & Organization* 1 (1995).

White, G. Edward. *The Marshall Court and Cultural Change, 1815–35.* New York: Macmillan Co., 1988.

Whittington, Keith. *Constitutional Construction: Divided Powers and Constitutional Meaning.* Cambridge: Harvard University Press, 1999.

Williams, Patricia. *The Alchemy of Race and Rights.* Cambridge: Harvard University Press, 1991.

Wills, Garry. "To Keep and Bear Arms," *New York Rev. of Books,* Sept. 21, 1995, p. 62.

Wilson, James G. "American Constitutional Conventions: The Judicially Unenforceable Rules That Combine With Judicial Doctrine and Public Opinion to Regulate Political Behavior," 40 *Buff. L.Rev.* 645 (1992).

Wolgast, Elizabeth. "The Demands of Public Reason," 94 *Colum. L.Rev.* 1936 (1994).

Yeazell, Stephen. "Intervention and the Idea of Litigation: A Commentary on the Los Angeles School Case," 25 *UCLA L. Rev.* 244 (1977).

INDEX